The Major Novels of Susan Glaspell

Florida A&M University, Tallahassee
Florida Atlantic University, Boca Raton
Florida Gulf Coast University, Ft. Myers
Florida International University, Miami
Florida State University, Tallahassee
University of Central Florida, Orlando
University of Florida, Gainesville
University of North Florida, Jacksonville
University of South Florida, Tampa
University of West Florida, Pensacola

# The Major Novels
# of Susan Glaspell

Martha C. Carpentier

University Press of Florida

Gainesville · Tallahassee · Tampa · Boca Raton · Pensacola · Orlando · Miami · Jacksonville · Ft. Myers

Copyright 2001 by Martha C. Carpentier
Printed in the United States of America on acid-free paper

06  05  04  03  02  01   6  5  4  3  2  1

Library of Congress Cataloging-in-Publication Data
Carpentier, Martha Celeste.
The major novels of Susan Glaspell / Martha C. Carpentier.
p. cm.
Includes bibliographical references and index.
ISBN 0-8130-2122-7 (cloth: alk. paper)
1. Glaspell, Susan, 1876–1948—Fictional works. 2. Women and literature—
United States—History—20th century. I. Title.
PS3513.L35 Z63 2001
813'.52—dc21   00-54517

The University Press of Florida is the scholarly publishing agency for the State
University System of Florida, comprising Florida A&M University, Florida Atlantic
University, Florida Gulf Coast University, Florida International University, Florida
State University, University of Central Florida, University of Florida, University of
North Florida, University of South Florida, and University of West Florida.

University Press of Florida
15 Northwest 15th Street
Gainesville, FL 32611–2079
http://www.upf.com

For my mother.

# Contents

# Figures

# Acknowledgments

I would like to acknowledge the University Research Council of Seton Hall University for two summer stipends that helped support my work on the initial stages of this book. I would also like to thank Lee Zimmerman for permission to reprint my article "Susan Glaspell's Fiction: Fidelity as American Romance," originally published in *Twentieth Century Literature*, Vol. 40, No. 1. Many thanks to W. Thomas MacCary for invaluable help with Greek translation. Without the unfailingly generous encouragement of Veronica Makowsky this book would never have been completed, and without the steadfast belief of my editor at the University Press of Florida, Susan Fernandez, it might still be residing in a desk drawer. I also want to thank my intrepid copyeditor and inspiration in so many ways, my mother, Sallie Blake. Finally, I would like to thank my husband, Donald Sherblom, whose patience and understanding supported me throughout both child and book bearing.

mother-daughter relationship, as well as her innovative use of a female semiotic. A brief review of the critical reception of Glaspell's work over the years shows how her construction of such a female aesthetic, particularly in her novels, has become so neglected.

Susan Glaspell (1876–1948) was born in Davenport, Iowa. She graduated from Drake University in 1899, then worked as a reporter on the *Des Moines Daily News* until 1902, when she returned home to focus on her creative writing. She published many stories in journals such as *Harper's*, *The Black Cat*, and *Ladies Home Journal*. In 1912 she collected these stories into a volume titled *Lifted Masks* (reissued in 1993). Her first apprentice novel, *Glory of the Conquered*, was published in 1909 and her second, *The Visioning*, in 1911. Her third novel and first major literary achievement, *Fidelity*, was published in 1915.

In 1913 Glaspell married George Cram Cook, an idealistic, bohemian fellow Iowan. They moved to New York and summered in Provincetown, where they were both instrumental in creating the Provincetown Players and establishing the group in Greenwich Village. Glaspell spent the early 1920s writing plays for the Provincetown theater, and she did not return to the novel form until 1928 with *Brook Evans*, but she always considered herself primarily a writer of fiction. "I began writing plays because my husband forced me to," she recalled later, and after she and Cook left Greenwich Village, she confided in a letter to her mother that "the theater has always made it hard for me to write and now I will have a better chance for my own writing" (Noe 33, 49). Although her play *Alison's House* won the Pulitzer Prize in 1931 and she served briefly as midwest director for the Federal Theatre Project in Chicago during 1934, Glaspell settled in Provincetown after Cook's death in 1924 and returned to her preferred genre, producing five novels: *Fugitive's Return* (1929), *Ambrose Holt and Family* (1931), *The Morning Is Near Us* (1939), *Norma Ashe* (1942), and *Judd Rankin's Daughter* (1945). This solid body of work should have ensured her place in the annals of American fiction, but Susan Glaspell is a classic case study in gender-biased marginalization.

Glaspell was a well-known and critically acclaimed novelist from the 1920s until World War II. *Brook Evans*, *Fugitive's Return*, and *The Morning Is Near Us* all made best-seller lists (Ozieblo 205, 235, 265). Many of her novels were favorably reviewed in the *New York Times*. *Fidelity* was praised by the *Times* reviewer for its convincing realism; however, it was seen to be a romantic tale, "the story of love caught in the mesh of law," so the reviewer found the second half of the novel, in which the theme of love is abandoned, flawed. Although the *Times* reviewer of *Fugitive's Re-*

*turn* found the novel "uneven," he praised Glaspell as "so much of an individual one knows in advance that a novel from her pen will not be an ordinary book." John Chamberlain praised *Brook Evans* in a 1928 *Times* review as "a masterpiece on a small scale."[1] Chamberlain was more attuned to Glaspell's particular style than any other critic. In 1931 he aptly described *Ambrose Holt and Family* as a "tragi-comedy of idealism" and noted Glaspell's "delicately pervasive humor," which "acts as a perpetual stringent" cutting through sentimentality. Later readers, oblivious to Glaspell's tongue-in-cheek mockery, have often misread her work as sentimental. In both reviews Chamberlain discussed Glaspell's idealism in her life and work and praised her courage and integrity as a writer.

Even though *The Morning Is Near Us* was a Literary Guild's Book of the Month choice for April 1940, sold more than 100,000 copies, and led to a lucrative movie rights contract for Glaspell, it was not reviewed in the *New York Times*, nor were any subsequent novels (Ozieblo 265). And after substantial treatment in Arthur Hobson Quinn's 1936 *American Fiction*, she was never again considered in any other critical study of the American novel. What happened to demote Susan Glaspell from the widely respected novelist who vied with Ernest Hemingway on the best-seller lists in 1929 to a has-been whose publisher felt justified in donating the metal plates of her books to the war effort in 1941? According to Paul Lauter's influential work on the shaping of the American literary canon, beginning in the 1920s and culminating in the late 1940s, three forces contributed to the exclusion of women's writing from the canon: "the professionalization of the teaching of literature, the development of an aesthetic theory that privileged certain texts, and the historiographic organization of the body of literature into conventional 'periods' and 'themes'" (27).

The second of these forces particularly affected the marginalization of Glaspell's fiction. Increasing nationalism between the wars contributed to the need to create an American literary tradition that was seen to embody the values of masculine culture and to be distinct from the British tradition. The "grand encounters with nature of Melville" and the "deeper possibilities for corruption [of] Twain and even James" were seen as universal fictions, whereas tags such as "sentimental" and "regional" came to brand women's writing as provincial and inferior (Lauter 34). Judith Fetterly agrees with Lauter, finding "resistance" to reading the work of nineteenth-century American women writers usually presented as an aesthetic judgment against its sentimentality, whereas their work is actually concerned with social injustice and is predominantly realistic, as is

Glaspell's (25). "Sentimental," a label often applied to Glaspell's fiction, is, according to Fetterley, a dismissive "code word for female subject and woman's point of view and particularly for the expression of women's feelings" (25).

Arthur E. Waterman's 1966 contribution on Glaspell to the Twayne's United States Author series exemplifies such critical attitudes toward Glaspell's novels, some of which persist to this day. It represents the sole discussion of her oeuvre until the early 1980s and shows how easily derogatory tags such as "sentimental" and "regional" branded women's fiction as second-rate. Under the heading "Final Estimate," he pronounces authoritative judgment, based upon a weak a priori argument in which he confuses cause and effect: "Like her plays, her novels received widespread reviews on their first appearance, but, outside of brief mention in several surveys of American fiction, there has been no comprehensive examination of her fiction. This situation is not unexpected: for, when everything else has been said, we must agree that Susan Glaspell is a minor writer" (120). One can only reply, with Virginia Woolf, "How much thinking those old gentlemen used to save one! How the borders of ignorance shrank back at their approach! Cats do not go to heaven. Women cannot write the plays of Shakespeare" (*Room* 48).

It was Waterman who first proclaimed the inferiority of Glaspell's fiction as compared to her drama, declaring, "There is no question . . . that Susan Glaspell's importance to our literature derives primarily from her dramatic achievement" (119). This judgment still persists, appearing in the commentaries of contemporary feminist critics, even though it was founded on blatantly gender-biased views. Waterman devalued Glaspell's prose because he perceived that her journalism and fiction were written for a regional female audience or, as he put it, "the feminine reader looking for amusement and some escape from her everyday life to brighten her world" (20). Because Glaspell published her early short stories in the "ladies' magazines," Waterman portrayed her as having to conform to a "dictatorial audience . . . who demanded then—and still demand—escapist fiction which was idealistic and romantic" (20). In a statement typical of his similarly contemptuous attitude toward her novels, he writes: "She shares with many other female authors certain feminine traits: an insistence on romance, an inability to create successful male characters, a tendency to sentimentality, and a vague desire on the part of the heroine for independence" (42).

The few stories Waterman deigned to approve were all "published between 1916 and 1919, showing the beneficent influence of her plays," and he praised "Jury of Her Peers" as Glaspell's finest story because "it was based on the one-act play *Trifles*, which she wrote for the Provincetown Players" (24, 29). Waterman privileged Glaspell's drama because he saw it as addressed to and influenced by a cosmopolitan, bohemian, male-dominated environment. According to him, "the tutelage of Cook and [Floyd] Dell" freed Glaspell from her "medieval-romantic" thinking, and in Greenwich Village, "inspired by the climate of revolt in the bohemian world she inhabited, she became an experimental playwright who was as radical in drama as she was conservative in fiction" (preface, 35).

Glaspell's drama is still judged to be superior because it is formally experimental; that is, it is seen to conform to the standards of European high modernism which, as Shari Benstock and other feminist scholars of modernism have argued, was a masculinist aesthetic that denigrated the differences of women's writing. This aesthetic privileged formal innovation with all the "arcane mysteries of a highly symbolic and allusive artform" over American realism and naturalism with their social and familial themes (Lauter 35). Thus Waterman bewailed Glaspell's return to fiction after her Greenwich Village period as a return to the regional style that, in his remarkably subjective definition, so marred her early writing: "In her work we find all the defects of regional writing: conservativism, unabashed sentiment, an overwhelmingly middle-class point of view, and reverence for tradition for its own sake" (118). Fetterley concludes that "since the vast majority of regionalists were women, the definition of this genre as inherently minor functions to contain the work of American women in a separate category and to accord it secondary status" (20). Waterman's branding of Glaspell as "a writer of regional novels who adopted a ready-made tradition" easily devolved into the death knell of "minor" that he rang over the bulk of her life's work.

The profusion of critical appraisals of "Trifles" and "Jury of Her Peers," the attention given her plays and her ten-year stint as a playwright, and the neglect of her much longer commitment to the novel in even the most recent studies of her work unwittingly perpetuate this spurious division between Glaspell's drama and her fiction. While Marcia Noe's 1983 biographical monograph, *Susan Glaspell: Voice from the Heartland*, is essential reading for anyone studying Glaspell, she, too, devalues the fiction and elevates the drama according to the criteria Waterman established, implying that the "deficiencies in her fiction" resulted from her "desire for commercial success," even though she quotes Glaspell as saying, "One can't be thinking of making a popular hit or of landing a commercial success if expressing the thing one believes and wishes to give form to"

(82–84). Nearly two decades of feminist critical reevaluation have culminated in two major studies: Linda Ben-Zvi's collection, *Susan Glaspell: Essays on Her Theater and Fiction,* and Veronica Makowsky's *Susan Glaspell's Century of American Women.* Fourteen of the sixteen essays included in Ben-Zvi's collection discuss Glaspell's drama, and even Makowsky, the only scholar to attempt a comprehensive feminist review of Glaspell's entire oeuvre, agrees that Glaspell's goal in her fiction was "enough money for a living, not experimentation" and that "the radical plays she wrote for the Provincetown Players" were her "greatest work" (24). Barbara Ozieblo's impeccably researched biography of Glaspell continues the trend, devoting seven of its ten chapters to her marriage with Cook and her playwriting career, a mere decade of her life.

In fact, Glaspell's novels are just as radical as her drama in their portrayal of women's lives, from the naïve, impetuous idealism of youth, to the compromises of marriage, to the problems of aging with its physical changes and fear of lost sexuality. Just like her plays, they speak deeply of feminist issues that are still vital today, such as women's need for free sexual expression in a patriarchal culture that binds them in oppressive pure/fallen, spirit/body, passive/active binarisms; their loving yet fraught relationships with their mothers; their rage against and idealization of their fathers; their need for female friendship; their pain and pleasure in mothering; the solitude of their childlessness.

Nor are the novels formally conservative, as if written by an entirely different author from the radical playwright and one of far less integrity. None of the qualities Waterman attributes to regionalism can be found in Glaspell's novels. Similar to many modernists, Glaspell lived in voluntary exile from her native state of Iowa, traveling often to Europe, Chicago, and New York and settling finally in Provincetown. Her novels are not limited to the Midwest in their setting, which may be New York, Chicago, Boston, Cape Cod, or Greece, but they do often chart a return to the locus of Glaspell's childhood in order to explore a paradoxical longing for, and separation from, a maternal landscape. Her central characters are usually passionate rebels against the conservatism of society, and she consistently portrays the middle class critically, particularly for the restrictions it places on women. Often poor and working-class women provide a moral corrective and an ideal for middle-class women, whose spoiled existences as pretty objects have denied them real life and feeling. Glaspell's major themes—woman's problematic relationship to community, the conflict between her desire for autonomy and individuality, and her need for inclusion in a family or community that denies her those qualities—are common to both her drama and her fiction.

American regionalism in the early twentieth century was, in fact, not conservative but "gave expression to the as yet unvoiced and radical, thus introducing new aspects of American life—the immigrant experience, the black experience, the experience of women—and pointing the path toward social criticism and naturalism" (Ruland and Bradbury 193). Glaspell's exposure to socialism in the Monist Society, an intellectual discussion group she attended with Dell and Cook in Davenport, Iowa, during the early years of the twentieth century, brought class consciousness to her fiction and strengthened her critique of bourgeois values (Makowsky 18–19). In her novels Glaspell was primarily a realist, and Noe is quite right to link her with "'the revolt from the village,' a literary phenomenon to which Sherwood Anderson, Carl Van Vechten, Willa Cather, Glenway Wescott, Edith Wharton, Zona Gale, and Sinclair Lewis would contribute during the early decades of the twentieth century" (30). For instance, the parallels in theme and characterization between Glaspell's 1915 *Fidelity* and Lewis's 1920 *Main Street* are remarkable and point to Glaspell's strong influence on that text. Both focus on women who are oppressed by marriage and small-town mediocrity and conventionality, and in both texts middle-class female protagonists are inspired to rebel by working-class outsiders (Annie in *Fidelity* and Miles Bjornstam in *Main Street*). Indeed, Ozieblo describes Glaspell's mentoring of Lewis (60), and Lewis pays tribute to Glaspell in *Main Street*, when one of its more unconventional characters wants to outrage the town by getting the fledgling theater group to stage Glaspell and Cook's play, *Suppressed Desires*.

In a letter written sometime between 1925 and 1931, Glaspell qualifies her admiration for Virginia Woolf: "I admire Virginia Woolf so much that I wonder why I don't like her more. She makes the inner things real, she does illumine, and she makes relationships realities as well as people. But . . . in *Mrs. Dalloway*, you can about as well read in one part of the book as in another. If one could have what she has, or something of it, and have also story, that simple downright human interest" (Noe 55). While this statement indicates her commitment to realistic narrative, it should not be interpreted as a total rejection of modernist technique. Rather, it reflects the integration Glaspell sought between realism, "that simple downright human interest," and modernism, making "the inner things real." Makowsky believes that by the late 1920s and throughout the 1930s, Glaspell's novels integrate what she regarded as good fictional technique from nineteenth-century women's writing with the aspects of modernism that were meaningful to her. Unlike nineteenth-century novels, whose field of action is largely external and recounted by an omniscient narrator ordering reality according to a moral vision, modernist novels take place largely within the internal, subjective realms of emotion, unconscious impulses, memories, fantasies, and dreams, and thus they undermine socially prescribed moralities. Although Glaspell's roots lay in nineteenth-century American realism, her experience writing expressionistic drama expanded her skills as a writer in whatever genre she chose.

Neither *The Visioning* nor *The Glory of the Conquered* shows the mature craft that begins to be evident in *Fidelity*, written in the midst of her Provincetown years (the reason for my exclusion of the two earlier works from the present study). Thereafter Glaspell was able to meld her inheritance of fictional realism with the expressionistic playwriting techniques she had learned—techniques such as scenes that begin in medias res, extensive dialogue with little exposition, and chronological reversals and flashbacks to create the interplay of past and present so necessary to her concern with psychological self-exploration. While remaining basically within a realistic third-person narrative, in novels such as *Brook Evans* and *Fugitive's Return* Glaspell stretches that form until it becomes as supple as Woolf's stream-of-consciousness, enabling her to portray the internal subjective reality that is the template of most modernist fiction.

Just as Glaspell's place alongside Eugene O'Neill in the canon of modernist dramatists has been established by Linda Ben-Zvi and others, so, too, her novels must be read as modernist texts to be fully appreciated. Glaspell shared certain modernist ideologies, notably the Lawrencian view that the fullest achievement of self, particularly through sexuality, is far more important than social or moral order. Another modernist trend Glaspell shared was a preoccupation with ancient myth and ritual. In 1923 T. S. Eliot praised *Ulysses* for the "continuous parallel between contemporaneity and antiquity" Joyce established by portraying Leopold Bloom as a modern Odysseus. Eliot advocated that other artists follow Joyce's lead, as he himself did in *The Waste Land*, using a subtext of ancient myth as a new way to structure writing. "Instead of narrative method," Eliot portentously announced, "we may now use the mythical method. It is, I seriously believe, a step toward making the modern world possible for art" (177).

In 1922 Glaspell joined her husband on a quixotic two-year sojourn in Greece that ended with his death in 1924. Steeped in ancient Greek myth and literature through Cook's passion as well as her own reading, Glaspell participated vitally in this central aspect of the modernist credo. Two of the novels following her return from Greece, *Fugitive's Return* and *The Morning Is Near Us*, are masterworks in the mythic method, ingeniously paralleling a subtext of classical allusion with contemporary life. But since she has been for so long dismissed as a regionalist, the transformative effect of Greece upon Glaspell's work has never been realized. Because I see the trip to Greece as a watershed experience for Glaspell, I have included a chapter on her biography of Cook, *The Road to the Temple* (1927), which focuses largely on their time in Greece. Autobiography, biography, and historical narratives share a permeable intertextuality with fictional narratives of the same era. All are constructs, and this odd text, even more interpretive and subjective than most biographies, provides an illuminating transition to the novels that follow it.

Glaspell was not solely a modernist, however, just as she was not solely a realist. Her art as a novelist, covering a period of four decades, was not static, and its trajectory parallels the general movements in American fiction of those decades. Glaspell's early novels, such as *Fidelity*, come out of nineteenth-century realist traditions. After her playwriting period with the Provincetown Players (1912–22), novels such as *Brook Evans* and *Fugitive's Return* gain in psychological and artistic complexity because they reflect the ferment of the modernist period—its burgeoning feminism, its preoccupation with psychoanalysis and mythology, and its experimental expressionistic techniques. In *Ambrose Holt and Family*, Glaspell attempted a more playful novel, at times wittily satiric, at times more conventional in style. *The Morning Is Near Us* balances modernist mythic and psychoanalytic themes with a realist concern for national identity typical of the era between the wars, providing a fascinating transitional text between Glaspell's middle and late periods as a novelist. Her later novels, *Norma Ashe* and *Judd Rankin's Daughter*, conclude with a naturalistic focus on social class and historical events that reflects the social realism of the Great Depression and war years.

A novel written by a woman starting an exciting new life in Greenwich Village in 1913 is going to be very different from a novel written near the end of that long and eventful life in 1945. Glaspell's novels reflect her personal growth as well as the decades of social and artistic change in which she participated. Their quality is uneven, and the same theoretical model cannot be applied to all of them. I have therefore employed a variety of critical approaches, each chosen to best explicate the strengths of each novel as I see them. My primary interest is not in placing these novels within the American tradition, which has been initiated quite ably by Makowsky in *Susan Glaspell's Century of American Women*. Nevertheless, since *Fidelity* expresses a modernist woman writer's attempt to break free of nineteenth-century gender constraints and American fictional paradigms, I have used a largely cultural and generic critical approach in the first chapter. Because of my own critical background in British modernism as well as the need to free Glaspell's novels of the "regional" stigma that has unjustly condemned them, I focus more intensely on the novels following her playwriting career with the Provincetown Players and her years in Greece. *Brook Evans, Fugitive's Return,* and, perhaps to a lesser extent, *The Morning Is Near Us* are Glaspell's most modernist novels, and they can support the dense psychoanalytic and myth-critical readings I give them because they partake intensely of these aspects of the international modernist movement. Glaspell's struggle to come to terms with the deaths of her husband in 1924 and her mother in 1929 may also have contributed to the extraordinary psychological depth of these novels. I believe they are her most powerful and successful novels, both in their content and in their narrative style. Other critics will no doubt disagree, and Glaspell's body of work is certainly rich enough to encompass a spirited debate. My intention is not to offer the last word on these novels, but rather one of the first.

The naturalistic focus on social class and historical change in Glaspell's late novels necessitates a return to a more cultural, less psychoanalytic, critical approach in the last chapters. However, despite the differences among Glaspell's novels, there are lifelong themes that preoccupied her and that unite all of them, such as the difficulty of balancing self and society, the circumscription of gender, and, most particularly, her consistent exploration of the triadic daughter-mother-father relation. All of Glaspell's novels chart, to a greater or lesser degree, a female protagonist's journey of self-discovery through the archaeology of a buried past, and a psychic return to mother that empowers her to move forward with her life.

Like other female modernists, Glaspell subverts the hegemony of masculinist values that dominated the formation of modernism because the myth she recounts is not oedipal but pre-oedipal. Instead of the Joycean son seeking union with the father or the "hollow man" seeking eternal values in a seemingly godless, sterile terrain, Glaspell's novels tell of the daughter's journey to selfhood through (re)connection with a female community, with mother earth, and with the pre-oedipal past wherein the mother reigns supreme. *Brook Evans, Fugitive's Return,* and *The Morning Is Near Us* all unfold a daughter's rediscovery of the forbidden, fertile maternal body, and with the recovery of maternal sexuality comes reconnection with her own vitality and bodily jouissance.[2] A feminist psychoanalytic critical methodology is therefore necessary to explicate these novels, and I use the object-relations theories of Nancy Chodorow, Dorothy Dinnerstein, and Jane Flax.

These three novels also contain some of Glaspell's most moving expressions of the female semiotic so praised by Kolodny and Showalter. The women in Glaspell's novels, no less than in "Jury of Her Peers," are silenced by patriarchy. Because women's sexuality and language are bound and silenced in the patriarchal world Glaspell portrays, the women speak, and Glaspell often writes, in ways other than rational discourse: through silence, gesture, rhythm. Their system of signification is a form of nonverbal speaking through the body—eyes, gesture, physical objects—in order to communicate covertly and find strength in that female communion. Gardens and graveyards, edenic loci and archaic ruins, all signify the mother's body, while the daughter's discovery of maternal artifacts such as needlework and clothing answers her longing for maternal presence. Female friends and, in *Brook Evans* and *Ambrose Holt and Family*, feminized men help the protagonist escape the grip of patriarchal symbolic order and reenter the repressed maternal semiotic or, to use the Nietzschean dichotomy Glaspell exploits in *Fugitive's Return*, to exchange Apollonian rationality for Dionysian ecstasy.

Because Glaspell's feminism focuses intensely on female ways of knowing and speaking as well as on the daughter's familial and cultural gendering, American and French feminist theories are both useful in opening the way to a deeper appreciation of her novels. Therefore, in addition to the American object-relationists, I rely on French theorists of the semiotic and l'écriture feminine, Julia Kristeva and Hélène Cixous. These feminists correct Freudian phallocentrism by stressing the importance of the pre-oedipal relation, whether directly or, in the case of the French, through their critique of Jacques Lacan. A significant difference between these two groups of feminist scholars lies in the French application of a revisionary psychoanalysis to linguistic theory rather than, with the Americans, to behavioral or social praxis. The French analysis of female language as a covert subversion of patriarchal power is essential to an appreciation of Glaspell's style. For her, as for Cixous, writing is "an act which will not only 'realize' the decensored relation of woman to her sexuality, . . . it will give her back her goods, her pleasures, her organs, her immense bodily territories which have been kept under seal" (Cixous, "Laugh," 250). Once the seal has been broken and the silenced voice of maternal sexuality uncoded, the protagonist in each of these novels, most of which span three generations, can in turn hand on a female heritage to her own child that is unbound and uncircumscribed. Glaspell's female characters—

Ruth, Naomi, Brook, Irma, Stamula, Lydia, Norma, and others—"break out of the snare of silence," to use Cixous's words, by speaking the body (251). And in her best fiction, Susan Glaspell *writes* the body. Thus these remarkable novels speak vitally to readers today, both in their focus on female sexuality and regeneration and in their narrative form.

The myth narrates a confrontation of the American
individual, the pure American divorced from specific
social circumstances, with the promise offered by the idea of
America. This promise is the deeply romantic one that in this
new land, untrammeled by history and social accident, a person
will be able to achieve complete self-definition.

—*Nina Baym*

# 1

## *Fidelity* (1915) as American Romance

Written during the early years of Glaspell's Greenwich Village period,
*Fidelity* reflects an integration of American fictional tradition with the
expressionism and feminist themes Glaspell was exploring in her drama.
Glaspell adds some tellingly ironic twists to what would at first seem a
conventional plot of a young woman confronting small-town small-
mindedness. Ruth Holland, denied a college education because of her
father's gender bias, turns to love with a married man, Stuart Williams, as
an outlet for her thwarted energies and elopes with him. Years later Ruth
returns to town to her father's deathbed and confronts the pain, bitterness,
and destruction her transgression caused her family. She does not, however, consider the world and her family's suffering well lost for love, for
her unsanctioned liaison with Stuart has become as trite and meaningless
as any traditional marriage. A unique friendship with a farmer's wife helps
Ruth decide to leave Stuart and head for the unknown in the big city
where, the text implies, she will fulfill all the ideals of the 1920s New
Woman.

Linda Ben-Zvi's summary of the subversive role of women in Glaspell's
drama is equally applicable to *Fidelity* and to all of the novels under consideration here: "Repeatedly in her plays her personae—all of whom are
women—break with the confining forms of society, almost always presented as male-dominated, and reach forward to some new awareness,

breaking in the process the traditions of society" ("Imagery" 24). Furthermore, all of the modernist formal innovations of Glaspell's drama that Ben-Zvi discusses can be identified in this novel and in her later novels as well. As Ben-Zvi points out, "Nothing in a Glaspell play is linear. Plots do not have clearly defined beginnings, middles, and ends; they self-consciously move out from some familiar pattern, calling attention as they go to the fact that the expected convention will be violated, the anticipated order will be sundered" ("Contributions" 152). This describes exactly how *Fidelity* is structured. It moves outward from the familiar pattern of adulterous love and violates the expected romantic conventions of that stereotype. None of Glaspell's novels, from *Fidelity* on, proceeds as a straightforward chronological narrative. Events are reordered through flashbacks for two reasons: beginning in medias res and then backtracking makes them highly dramatic, and one of Glaspell's major themes is that life is a process of maturing in which the past always resonates in the present.

"Even more innovative is Glaspell's manipulation of point of view," Ben-Zvi notes about her drama. Through this technique she is able to "force the audience to share the world of her women" (154). Glaspell gave *Fidelity* psychological complexity by shifting the narrative focus in order to present Ruth's character and action from multiple viewpoints. By telling the same story through the eyes of both sexes she disarms her readers, preventing them from immediately rejecting the radicalism of her female protagonist by evoking her through sympathetic male narrators.

Readers do not meet Ruth until the fifth chapter. Chapters 1–4 center around Dr. Deane Franklin, a childhood friend who believed in her defiance, helped her escape with her lover, and continues to defend her actions. Indeed, Deane's story parallels Ruth's throughout, since her return to town eleven years after her exile and soon after his marriage to a beautiful but superficial young woman pushes him to face the same conservative, oppressive forces in his own life that she has confronted in hers. Later in the novel her younger brother, Ted, becomes the focus of the narrative and performs a similar function. An impetuous young character who has strong feelings but does not verbalize them very well, he follows his heart, which is loyal to Ruth's cause, in a direct, simplistic way that is refreshing at the conclusion of a deeply analytic novel. These men defend the excluded Ruth more aggressively than she can defend herself, for they exist within the social circle. Ultimately Deane loses his social status when his medical practice dwindles and his wife leaves him as a result of his adherence to Ruth's principles, but he still maintains that the meaning Ruth brought to his life was worth the price: "It was because of you—through you—that I came to think about things. That's good for our lives, isn't it? . . . Because of you I've questioned things, felt protest" (313).

In chapter 5, direct access to Ruth's consciousness is even further delayed when she is described physically through the eyes of an anonymous man on the two-day train ride as she returns home. He, too, portrays her sympathetically, trying in his imagination to "construct a life for her," but he is unable to pin her down (35). As most scholars of Glaspell's drama have noted, this is a technique she often employs, centering her plays around an absent or dead woman "against whom male characters react, upon whom they impose shape . . . a kind of palimpsest upon which to inscribe their own identities, desires, and language" (Ben-Zvi, "Contributions" 157).

The novel, however, allows Glaspell to explore gender differences in greater complexity than she could in her plays which, due to the demands of the dramatic form for condensation and confrontation, pit women against men more simplistically. When *Fidelity* opens Ruth is the absent woman, the icon upon whom Deane has founded his ideals. Yet in the middle chapters of the novel, Ruth appears and is real. Deane is forced to confront woman as reality, both Ruth and his petulant wife, not as the idealized romantic heroines he has half created. In Deane, Glaspell presents a male character who follows the lead of a female character, rejecting society's rigidity and then abandoning romantic gender ideals for the reality of human needs and individuality. Men and women are not as starkly opposed in Glaspell's novels as they are in plays such as *Trifles*. Although male characters are usually minor, Glaspell is always concerned to show how they are as imprisoned in gender as women, albeit in a position of greater power.

Like Paul Lauter, Nina Baym traces the exclusion of women's fiction from the American canon to the 1940s, when "a group of Americanists . . . found in [nineteenth-century] nonrealism or romanticism the essential American quality they had been seeking," with romanticism defined as a particularly masculine attempt to assert individuality against oppressive social forces (71). According to Baym, influential critics of the 1950s and 1960s continued evolving this "myth of America" as the defining motif of American fiction in which the individual, divorced from society, seeks self-definition in the wilds of a new, unsettled land (71). This quest myth reflects gender because society, with its "unmitigatedly destructive pressure on individuality," is "depicted in unmistakably feminine terms" that "validate the notion of woman as threat" (72–73). Glaspell wrote

*Fidelity* very consciously from within the nineteenth-century American romantic tradition of psychological quest that pits the individual against society. Yet she also wryly deconstructs the myth at the same time, showing how it restricts women's lives—both women who defend and women who rebel against the established order.

In *Fidelity*, most women play the role Baym describes: guardians and enforcers of social conformity. But not all women play it, and Glaspell's novel focuses on the deeply divisive conflict patriarchy imposes upon women, between those who play the game by the rules and one, Ruth, who defies them. In the judgment of Mrs. Lawrence, Ruth's best-friend's mother,

> Ruth Holland is a human being who selfishly—basely—took her own happiness, leaving misery for others. She outraged society as completely as a woman could outrage it. She was a thief, really,—stealing from the thing that was protecting her, taking all the privileges of a thing she was traitor to. . . . society is nothing more than life as we have arranged it. It is an institution. One living within it must keep the rules of that institution. One who defies it—deceives it—must be shut out from it. So much we are forced to do in self-defense. (179)

The novel thus seeks to explain why women are sometimes the harshest critics of women and why mothers often clip the wings of their daughters' autonomy. "There was something in humankind—it was strongest in womankind—made them, no matter how daring for themselves, cautious for others. And perhaps that, all crusted round with things formal and lifeless, was the living thing at the heart of the world's conservatism" (294).

Glaspell would seem to agree here with the depiction of women as social conformists according to the American myth Baym describes; however, she penetrates deeper to the "living thing" at the center of such conservatism. If women's identity and survival are dependent upon their socially sanctioned roles as wife and mother, the rebellious woman poses a far greater threat to other women than she does to men, and they must close ranks against her in self-defense. To Mrs. Lawrence, Ruth outraged the institution of marriage. She gives the clearest explanation as to why Ruth's act is such a threat to other women: marriage is the only protection and privilege they have in patriarchal society. Mrs. Lawrence declares that women must be selfless; their function must be to sacrifice individual expression to the survival of all within a culture that pits the "pure" woman against the "fallen," the mother against the whore.

All the other townswomen similarly ostracize Ruth—her sister-in-law, Harriett; her best friend, Edith Lawrence; Deane's wife, Amy—and Glaspell makes it clear they are protecting their own self-interest in a patriarchal world that turns women against one another in a competitive relation because their survival depends upon marriage. Quixotically, Deane wants his wife to befriend Ruth, to "bring Amy within—within that feeling of his about Ruth," and he imagines that "she would understand that the very thing bringing them their happiness was the thing which in Ruth put her apart from her friends" (141–43). The "very thing" that should bring Amy and Ruth together is their mutual experience of romantic love, but of course that "very thing" sets women against each other. Glaspell shows that a culture that glorifies romantic love teaches bourgeois women that their sole role is to be adored by men: "Until now [Amy] had nothing but adulation from love. A pretty, petted girl she has formed that idea of pretty women in youth that it was for men to give love and women to graciously accept it" (216–17). Inevitably, Amy interprets Deane's friendship for Ruth as a threat to her power over him and rejects sharing any such feeling about Ruth under the guise of her socially appointed role as moral guardian (149–50).

Thus *Fidelity* illustrates Glaspell's characteristic deconstruction of romantic myths surrounding love and marriage. The novel provides a radical critique of a bourgeois society that upholds marriage as the goal of woman's existence and shows that romantic love is not and cannot be enough to fulfill anyone, man or woman. Indeed, the novel dissects several failed marriages wrecked by romantic idealism. Stuart Williams, the man with whom Ruth has her affair, married his wife, Marion, for her physical beauty just as Deane did his, never expecting to come up against a strong will that could defy him, while Marion expected her husband to live up to a chivalrous code of chastity and cannot forgive him for a sexual fling.

Glaspell shows the moral sanctity of the "pure" woman as inextricably linked to her repression of her sexuality and therefore of male sexuality as well. Cold and unforgiving, Marion Williams has punished her husband for the earlier affair by withdrawing sexually and emotionally ever since. Just like Deane's wife, Amy, Marion is unable to love because she clings to the superficial power granted by her role as chaste wife: "She finally found control in that thought of her power over him used to make him suffer" (224). Stuart pleads, "Haven't you any humanity? Don't you ever feel?" "I do not desecrate my feelings," Marion replies, "I don't degrade my humanity" (57). These men are victimized, not by women but by the ideals of moral and sexual purity they project onto women, which women, perforce, uphold. Glaspell portrays a culture in which both sexes are severely circumscribed by conformity to gender and socially prescribed morality. She certainly shares with D. H. Lawrence the conviction that blindly clinging to society's dictates allows people to hide from their fear of discovering the self.[1]

Ruth's love affair with Stuart Williams begins with the words "Our dance" and is described in the language of sappy magazine romances: "With a smothered passionate little sob she had swayed toward him, and then she was in his arms and he was kissing her wet eyes, that tender mouth, the slim throbbing throat" (68). Glaspell's wry sense of humor in her novels has been overlooked by all save the *New York Times* critic John Chamberlain, for what is so often labeled sentimental is in fact parodic. Here Ruth is acting out the melodrama of the adolescent girl who sacrifices all for love. The second half of the novel shows the shallowness of romantic illusions for both men and women, and the language Glaspell employs there is simple and direct without the overblown clichés. Here Glaspell has chosen the language most fitting to her subject matter. She is satirizing romantic love, as she did in her 1918 play *Women's Honor*, where a woman named "The Silly One" utters such banalities as "Darling! I cannot let you die for me! . . . Love is so beautiful. So ennobling!" (131–32).

Ruth takes a stand for the life of "feelings," of being "real," as opposed to the superficiality of social conventions that rule her town (a theme typical of the "revolt from the village" writers). However, this is not a stand for "true love" or even sexual passion, as her lover Stuart is a barely realized character who fades after chapter 7 and is not seen again until chapter 31, where their relationship is shown to have dwindled to a loveless, habitual commitment that stifles both of them. Rather, the novel centers around Ruth's act of rebellion against an oppressive society, not on the love story that initiates that act, but on unfolding and debating its consequences years later. Ruth's escape from societal conformity is portrayed as a flight into the wilderness, illustrating Glaspell's reworking of the American myth discussed earlier:

> There in the Southwest, where they slept out of doors, she had come to know the night. . . . she had many times stepped from a cramping little house full of petty questions she did not know how to deal with, from a hard little routine that threatened their love out to the vast, still night of that Colorado valley and always something had risen in herself which gave her power. (161–62)

That Ruth is driven by a commitment to freedom and to self, and not to romantic love, is clearly established at the beginning of the novel when, through flashback, Glaspell describes what led up to Ruth's escape. Middle-class life at the turn of the century is shown to be especially superficial and limited for women, who are protected from working by servants and whose lives are expected to revolve around socializing. Ruth and her best friend, Edith, "were daughters of two of the town's most important families; they were two of the town's most attractive girls. That fixed their place in a round of things not deepening, not individualizing. It was pleasant, rather characterless living on a limited little part of the surface of life" (38–39). In addition, Ruth's desire for college is thwarted by her father, who believes "women should marry and settle down and have families." Thus it is obvious that this young woman, who yearns for something beyond dresses and teas, is going to rebel: "Her energies having been shut off from the way they had wanted to go, she was all the more zestful for new things from life. There was much in her that her life did not engage" (40–42).

Illicit love represents Ruth's only way to grasp at the American myth of "self-definition" and to escape the suffocating life of the small town. Her options are the dichotomous choices that frame a woman's life when she can define herself only in terms of her relationship to men. Glaspell emphasizes Ruth's position at a crossroad that offers only the two roles of "pure" or "fallen" to women, by staging her elopement with Stuart on the very night of her best-friend's marriage:

> She had a confused sense of Edith as barricaded by her trousseau. She sat behind a great pile of white things; she had had them all out of her chest for showing to some of her mother's friends. . . . Ruth stood there fingering a wonderfully soft chemise. It had come to her that she was not provided with things like these. What would Edith think of her, going away without the things it seemed one should have? It seemed to mark the setting of her apart from Edith. (111)

The barricade of Edith's trousseau is beautifully symbolic. It not only sets Ruth apart from her friend but also keeps wider experience from women's lives, as well as holding together within its walls a female community of shared ideals. By insisting on her individuality, Ruth has sacrificed all the anchors of her gender and identity: all family, all contact with other women, and even childbearing.[2]

Clearly Glaspell finds the American myth that pits the individual against society to be hollow, especially for women. Individuality has little meaning in isolation. The glory of a romantic gesture, as of sexual passion, wears away and needs to be embraced into the continuity of communal life. But the price women pay for sexual freedom is the loss of female companionship and female community. For Glaspell, this is a serious loss. She shows how painful it is to have to choose between self and community when, after returning home, Ruth passes houses where

> children were running from yard to yard; here a woman was standing in her own yard calling to a woman in the house adjoining. She passed a porch where four women were sitting sewing; another where two women were playing with a baby. There were so many meeting places for their lives; they were not shut in with their own feeling. That feeling which they as individuals knew reached out into common experiences, into a life in common growing out of individual things. Passing these houses, she wanted to share in that life in common. (207)

Ruth's exclusion from the community cuts her off from the ebb and flow of life, from birth and death. After her return to the town, seeing that her sister-in-law is pregnant "brought it home hard that she was not one of them any more. . . . Her longing for a baby, longing which circumstances made her sternly deny herself . . . [made her] want to pour all that out to Harriett, want to talk with her of those deep, common things" (159–60). In accepting her Faustian bargain, that in exchange for freedom and individuality she must relinquish womanhood, Ruth has participated in her own punishment by denying herself children.

Initially, Ruth glories in the sacrificial role she has chosen, but Glaspell's ultimate purpose is more subtle. While this naïve heroine thinks she has made a claim for selfhood, selflessness is the result of her choice, no less than it would have been had she chosen chastity. Her defiance has brought martyrdom, and by glorying in the pain and humiliation that romantic love incurs, she has actually conformed to the self-sacrificing ideal prescribed for her gender. The novel goes on to show not only that romantic love is an illusion but that female martyrdom is an illusion, too, based on denial of life, love, community, and continuity. The point of the novel is that as long as woman defines herself solely in terms of her relations to men, her individuality is restricted. Ruth later struggles with conflicting feelings about herself, both accepting that she has caused others to suffer and therefore deserves to suffer herself (the internalized voice of society's judgment upon her) and angrily asserting her right to individuality and her sense that "what she had felt, and her fidelity to that feeling . . . should not have blighted like this" (234).

*Fidelity* reaches this impasse when Glaspell challenges all the assumptions of the novel's world with the introduction of Annie Morris, a woman who offers Ruth a third way that breaks through the seemingly irreconcilable dichotomies that frame her life. Annie is contrasted with Harriett, who has meekly conformed to her husband's and to society's dictates that, as a fallen woman, Ruth is not fit to meet any of her nieces and nephews. Harriett visits Ruth but finds herself "still holding back . . . seeming powerless and hating herself for being powerless." Her timidity embitters Ruth: "Harriett needn't be so afraid!—she wasn't going to contaminate her" (253–57). Into this uncomfortable situation comes Annie, a woman with a "red, rough hand," who "gave the impression of life, work, having squeezed her too hard" (258). She asks Ruth to come visit her, to "come out and play with my baby" (260). Glaspell emphasizes the significance of Annie's invitation by Ruth's emotional reaction, as Ruth twice exclaims, "She wants me to play with her baby!" Annie's offer symbolizes the whole shared world of womanhood, especially motherhood, from which the whore is conventionally excluded. Into this world Annie welcomes Ruth, effectively bridging and defying the patriarchal dichotomies of both gender and class.

Only Veronica Makowsky has recognized the relevance of this character as an outsider who "acts as a catalyst" in Ruth's life (55). Annie Morris is a "pinched, shabby, eager little woman" selling vegetables from a farm buggy, whom Ruth, alone among the middle-class girls, had befriended when they were in high school. Annie had been "poor . . . not in Ruth's crowd," in other words, lower class. In addition, "she was what they called awfully bright in her classes" (201). Both points are important because Annie is the primary instrument of Glaspell's attack upon the bourgeois idealization of woman that sequesters her from work and intellectual life. Just as Ruth had once reached out from within the circle of her class and privilege to the outsider, now Annie returns the gesture and embraces Ruth, giving her new hope that "somewhere outside the things she had known were people among whom she could find friends" (202).

Glaspell further develops her critique of the patriarchal pure/fallen binarism imposed upon women by paralleling Ruth (fallen) with Stuart's wife, Marion (pure). Glaspell shows that, ironically, these supposed opposites are actually two sides of the same coin. Ruth has chosen love, Marion society, but both women are similarly stunted. The fallen woman defies society because of her fidelity to sexuality; the pure woman represses her sexuality because of her fidelity to social mores. Both cut off a different aspect of the self, leading to isolation and powerlessness. In a surprising twist, Ruth's younger brother, Ted, decides to confront Marion. Typical of youthful idealism as it is portrayed throughout the novel, he wants to play the hero who makes his sister's hard life end happily in marriage, by urging Marion to divorce her husband. The effect he has on Marion is radical because, just like the novel's two other major female characters, Ruth and Annie, she has been utterly isolated, unable to share her thoughts with anyone and thus unable to explore them. As Ted says, "Nobody has talked to you about it. Everybody has been afraid to, and so you've just been let alone with it" (343). His intervention causes Marion to think deeply and uncover the real reason her marriage had failed (356). The passage is written in language suggestive of female masturbation because for the first time she is reconnecting with her sexuality: .

> There was a curious emotional satisfaction in thus disobeying herself by rushing into the denied places of self-examination. She was stirred by what she was doing. Her long holding back from this very thing was part of that same instinct for restraint, what she had been pleased to think of as fastidiousness, that had always held her back in love. It was alien to her to let herself go; she had an instinct that held her away from certain things—from the things themselves and from free thinking about them. What she was doing now charged her with excitement. (356)

Also like Ruth, Marion is further liberated by a relationship with a working-class woman, her maid, Lily, whom she nurses following a miscarriage or, as Deane hints, a botched abortion (371). As Annie teaches Ruth, so Lily shows Marion that women's salvation is through community, not competition, through compassion, not judgment.

In chapters 23 and 24, the climax of the novel, Ruth spends five days with Annie, where she is "not set apart from others" but has "the simple feeling of being just one with others" (261). Not only has Annie taken her into the community of female friendship, but she provides Ruth with the model of a woman whose spirit and intellect have not been crushed by the inevitable disillusionment of romantic love nor by assuming the role of wife and mother. As Makowsky notes, Annie "helps Ruth break away from her hackneyed notions about heterosexuality and maternity" (56). In the most direct assault on the illusions of romantic love expressed in the novel, Annie says,

> "Romantic love is a wonderful thing, . . . I suppose it's the most beautiful thing in the world—while it lasts." She laughed in a queer, grim little way and gave a sharp twist to the knot she was tying.

"Sometimes it opens up to another sort of love—love of another quality—and to companionship. It must be a beautiful thing—when it does that." She hesitated a moment before she finished with a dryness that had that grim quality: "With me—it didn't." (266)

While Annie converses with Ruth, she is working in the garden, and Glaspell uses her "quick, sure motions [as] she made the asparagus into bunches for market" as a metaphor for the way Annie "deftly" does not let any activity "take all of her." She "twists" the "knots"; she is not tied by them. When Ruth wonders how Annie could be happy in a loveless marriage, Glaspell concludes with characteristic wry wit, "It seemed Annie had the same adjustment to him that she had to the asparagus,—something subordinated, not taking up very much of herself" (263–64). There is a sacred part of Annie that she refuses to subordinate to anything and reserves for herself alone. Unlike all the other women in the novel, she has a self apart from her relation to men. "Just what is it you fought for—kept?" Ruth asks. "'To be my own!' Annie flashed back at her, like steel" (267).

It is not accidental that Annie is described in phallic terms such as "hard" and "steel," because she has fought to preserve in herself that quality long thought to be inherently male—an active, intellectual mind. Annie has an "unconquerable" spirit; she speaks in a "fighting voice" and thinks "like a sent arrow." Glaspell is radical in portraying an isolated rural woman, a wife, mother, and farmer, as her herald of early-twentieth-century feminism. "Rich in interests," Annie also opens up the larger world of early-twentieth-century modernism to Ruth: "There were new poets in the world; there were bold new thinkers; there was an amazing new art; science was reinterpreting the world and workers and women were setting themselves free." Compared to Ruth's tragic, romantic bid for freedom, Annie is far freer, even though she has taken on all the practical obligations of a woman's life. She would not trade places with the wealthy, pampered townswomen, for, as she says, "the free don't trade with the bond." Annie's talk "kindled old fires of [Ruth's] girlhood, fanned the old desire to know," and she radically points the way to Ruth's true road to freedom, through her mind: "Nobody holds my thoughts. They travel as far as they themselves have power to travel. They bring me whatever they can bring me—and I shut nothing out. I'm not afraid!" (265–67).

Christine Dymkowski has discussed a metaphor central to Glaspell's drama, as evidenced by titles such as *The Outside* and *The Verge*, the image of "life's margins as central to human experience" that "identifies women as outside the mainstream of life and thus capable of shaping it anew" (91, 92). To symbolize the marginalized existence of women, imagery of "outside" versus "inside" the social circle is developed throughout *Fidelity*, culminating in a striking metaphor for Ruth's position outside, when she is isolated in the mountains with her lover:

> All through that winter something else had marked night, something she tried to keep from looking out at, but which she was not able to hold away from. She was looking at it now, looking off into the adjoining field where the sheep were huddling for the night. . . . With the first dimming of the light, the first wave of new cold that meant coming night, a few of them would get together; others would gather around them, then more and more. Now there was the struggle not to be left on the outside. The outer ones were pushing toward the center; they knew by other nights that this night would be frigid, that they could only keep alive by the warmth they could get from one another. Yet there were always some that must make that outer rim of the big circle, must be left there to the unbroken cold. She watched them; it had become a terrible thing for her to see, but she could not keep from looking. (378)

Ruth is obsessively drawn to and horrified by this nightly vision of helplessly dying animals because in them she sees herself. This powerful image of humanity huddled together for self-preservation, excluding those on the edge who struggle to return to the life-giving warmth, symbolizes one of Glaspell's major themes, common to both her drama and her fiction: the conflict between woman's desire for autonomy and individuality and her need for inclusion in a community that shuts her out, refusing to allow her those qualities. Many of the protagonists of Glaspell's novels are similarly isolated, alienated, and ostracized, and the purpose of the novels is to show, as Glaspell does here with Ruth and Annie, the forging of new communal ties between women that are strengthening and healing.

In her fiction as well as her drama, Susan Glaspell puts women and all the variety of their relationships with each other on center stage. *Fidelity* is the story of a young woman's struggle to free herself from the cultural binarisms that entrap her within her gender and to break through to her unique individuality. But Glaspell shows at the same time how hollow the American romantic ideal of self-definition at the expense of community is for women, because a woman cannot do that alone, without the friendship and support of other women. *Fidelity* is a young woman's novel—a cry of rebellion against the oppressive patriarchal forces of the late Victorian society in which Glaspell grew up and a cry of triumph at her liberation from that society, with the world all before her, waiting to be discovered. Written in Greenwich Village, the novel very much benefits from the writing techniques Glaspell was experimenting with as a playwright. However, it does not show the psychological depth nor the radical expression of a female semiotic that distinguishes her next two novels. It was a woman with much deeper self-knowledge who emerged over a decade later after the breakup of the Provincetown Players, two bizarre years in Greece, the decline and death of her husband, and the long illness of her mother, to write the most striking novels of her maturity.

A woman's body with its thousand and one thresholds of
ardor—once, by smashing yokes and censors, she lets it
articulate the profusion of meanings that run through it in
every direction—will make the old single-grooved mother
tongue reverberate with more than one language.

—*Hélène Cixous*

# 2

# Greece/Greek as Mother's Body in
# *The Road to the Temple* (1927)

In 1922 Susan Glaspell left the Provincetown theater and her Greenwich
Village life behind and joined her husband, George Cram Cook ("Jig"), on
a quixotic two-year stay in Greece that ended with Cook's death in 1924.
In addition, during the years 1923–28 Glaspell returned frequently to her
native Davenport, Iowa, to nurse her increasingly ill and senile mother,
who died in 1929. *Brook Evans*, written during this period and published
in 1928, represents Glaspell's most prolonged and detailed analysis of the
profound ambivalence that, according to feminist psychoanalysts Nancy
Chodorow and Jane Flax, characterizes the mother-daughter relationship.
When Cook died, Glaspell lost the relationship that most closely replicated the mother-child intimacy in her life. *Fugitive's Return*, published in
1929, fictionalizes her experiences living in Delphi with Cook and represents the results of her meditation upon those two great losses.

Directly after her return from Greece, however, Glaspell first wrote a
biographical eulogy to Cook, *The Road to the Temple* (1927). Greatly
concerned that the remaining Provincetown theater members were forgetting the vision of its founder, Glaspell attempted "to valorize Cook as a
great man" despite the fact that he never fulfilled his own expectations as
an artist (Makowsky 91–92). Veronica Makowsky has rightly noted that
*The Road to the Temple* cannot be fitted into "paradigms of masculine

lifewriting." It is a strange and unique document in which Glaspell marginalizes herself in order to reconstruct the George Cram Cook of her dreams. There are, however, telling fragments in the text where she emerges from hiding and we see what Greece meant privately to her, or at any rate to the persona she constructs for herself within this narrative. Glaspell's experience of the temple is revealed covertly in a text ostensibly about Cook to be entirely her own.

For instance, as soon as she and Cook arrive in Greece, as described in chapter 37, they make a pilgrimage to the Parthenon. It is a dramatic moment, and it is all Cook's—reaching his lifelong goal, touching the sacred marble, recalling the great Greek past—while Glaspell refers to herself deprecatingly in the third person as "she who followed" (313). But the beauty of Greece seduces her, particularly after they leave Athens and go to Delphi. She shifts to the first-person plural and the second person to draw the reader into her experience and express her own passion for the place:

Delphi lies steeply on the lower slopes of Parnassos, two thousand feet up from the great olive-groves that wind to the Corinthian Gulf. Our balcony seemed to overhang those two thousand feet, and in the light of Greece we looked across the gulf to the mountains of the Peloponnesos. It is on a scale for gods—exciting and satisfying in form, a breath-taking plunge and lift of the eye—a wideness to which you want to open your arms. But what you are always wondering is how grandeur can have the loveliness of little intimate things, how clarity can be so subtle. 326–27

What does this passage have to do with Cook? Very little. It is Glaspell's entirely, particularly in the feminization of "grandeur" and "clarity" by "the loveliness of little intimate things."

Aside from such fragments, Cook occupies center stage in the biography, while the novel *Fugitive's Return* centers on Glaspell's fictional protagonist Irma, to whom she often gives actions and views attributed to Cook in *The Road to the Temple*. Both renderings of Glaspell's Greek experience are fictions of course, the biography merely posing more ostensibly as truth. Glaspell paints herself in *The Road to the Temple* as a fairly ineffectual observer of an archaic, threateningly patriarchal society, while in *Fugitive's Return* Irma becomes the all-powerful "Kyria of the Archai," a goddess able to counter male violence and patriarchal privilege with one chilling glance. Cast in the binaristic spatial terminology of sexually segregated ancient Greece, *The Road to the Temple* can be read as the polis, or public realm of men, while *Fugitive's Return* gives us the oikos, or private, hidden household of women. Glaspell's brief personalized fragments in *The Road to the Temple* also take the reader, verbally, into the oikos, or female space of her private experience of Greece. They introduce us to the unique style that permeates the novels of this period, a female semiotic in which women read signs quite differently from men.

Cook's typically fin-de-siècle youth was steeped in Platonism, transcendentalism, and Darwinism. Like the young Yeats, he tried to rediscover the lost Christian God in pantheistic visions of nature and in a mysticism that owed a lot to youthful sublimated autoeroticism. After a Harvard education, a year at the University of Heidelberg, a failed marriage, and an abandoned teaching career, Cook returned home to Iowa and found consolation in farming and novel writing until Floyd Dell roused him, introduced him to socialism, and brought him to Chicago where he wrote book reviews for the *Chicago Evening Post*. In 1913 Cook and Glaspell were married. They moved to Greenwich Village and began summering in Provincetown, where they originated the Provincetown Players with friends.

Cook's version of the theater was as a Nietzschean "call upon the vital writers of America to attain a finer culture," a chance for "one hundred artists" to create an "American Renaissance of the Twentieth Century" (*Road* 224–25, 244). All his life Cook identified with Nietzsche. As Makowsky observes, his writing "sound[s] a single note: Cook's overweening ambition to become a Nietzschean superman and lead humanity to greater heights" (96). By the end of his life he was "glad to find that the great Nietzsche is in some ways my inferior," being "always mad, while only a fraction of me is mad" (386). "Always he talked of Greece," Glaspell wrote, and when the Provincetown Players failed, in his view, to "bring to birth in our commercial-minded country a theater whose motive was spiritual," he announced, "It is time to go to Greece" (*Road* 244, 309–11). A fanatical Hellenist, he yearned all his life to rediscover a lost, idyllic past through visiting Greece and through mastery of the Greek language.

A full third of *The Road to the Temple* is devoted to those two years in Greece, as if they were, for Glaspell, the apotheosis of the man. Sadly, however, what emerges through the cracks of her hagiography of these last years is the portrait of a man losing his grasp of reality. Cook would speak only Greek; he grew a long beard and sported the traditional Greek shepherd costume of woolen tights, skirted tunic, and crooked staff; he was subject to sudden rages as well as to moods of silent withdrawal; and his drinking bouts began to frighten even Glaspell, who usually euphemized his drunkenness as Dionysian excess. Indeed, Ozieblo attributes his behavior in Greece, and even his final illness, to the advanced stages of alcoholism (224). Cook's idealism, always incapable of compromising with realities, became an obsessive parody of itself, as he tried to create the "Delphic Players" among the Greek shepherds and villagers. They were to enact his "Cain and Abel" play on the ruins of the ancient Dionysian theater, but Cook could not write the play because he spent his days building stone walls in the woods: "He grew more thin all the time. We could not stop him. What he wanted was to make these walls, fitting stone against stone, sometimes taking down a whole wall to make it better, until they approached the strength and beauty of ancient Greece" (394). These futile walls might stand as a metaphor for the unremitting idealism that drove Cook all his life and walled him off from everyone, virtually ensuring his failure, were it not that he did inspire others to greatness, most notably Susan Glaspell. For despite the increasing worry he must have been for Glaspell at this time and the fact that, had he lived much longer, their relationship would have become untenable, Cook was her Dionysus—drunk, saint, muse, madman. She loved his physicality, his energy and zest for life: "Jig on the beach in his bathing-suit; the muscles of his big beautiful body have power and rhythm. . . . He wets a foot, shakes it indignantly, stands there shaking his head like a lion about to fight. Then suddenly he plunges; one yowl, then he is swimming magnificently" (227).

Cook's obsession with death also moved Glaspell deeply, from his first "mystic religious rapture" at the age of sixteen, reading Plotinus in the University of Iowa Library, to his own bizarre death at the age of fifty from glanders, a rare disease he apparently contracted from their dog when, as Glaspell writes, "he who all his life had felt death, had come to it and did not know" (35, 441). Their transcendent moments as lovers all focused on a shared sense of the imminence of death. Early in their relationship, for instance, they stood together at Black Hawk's Watch Tower in Iowa where "Indian lovers, too, had known the sweetness and no doubt at times the pain and terror." Glaspell felt their love for each other "gave life to the love of vanished women for men long in their graves," and she murmured, "I wish we could die now" (209). Glaspell wrote that the "sense of death was never far from our love" and some fifteen years after the incident in Iowa, two weeks before Cook's own death, during "a night of strange beauty when daylight found us still talking—of love, of death," Cook recalled that earlier moment when Glaspell wished for death as the "greatest beauty I have known on earth" (209–11).

Cook challenged Glaspell as an artist: in 1912 he wrote proposing that she join him as a "co-discoverer and formulator" so they could become "two living growing writers who study, think things out together, sow seeds in each other's minds, keep them warm and growing" (223–24). Later he spurred her to write plays:

"Now Susan," he said to me briskly, "I have announced a play of yours for the next bill."

"But I have no play!"

"Then you will have to sit down tomorrow and begin one."

I protested. I did not know how to write a play. I had never "studied it."

"Nonsense," said Jig. "You've got a stage, haven't you?" [the wharf at Provincetown]. (255)

And finally, Cook took her to Greece. Certainly Glaspell was an established, committed writer long before she met him, but it is debatable whether, without him, she would have lived as fully or written as well. Provincetown and Greece were both transformative experiences that elevated her writing to a much more sophisticated level. For these, Cook was her muse, her own "road to the temple."

Thus I must disagree with Makowsky's conclusion that the experience of Greece was for Glaspell a "deracination" and with Ozieblo's characterization of it as an example of "wifely submission" (198). If Glaspell did have to "renounce the kindred spirits of Greenwich Village" for a while, it resulted in some of her finest writing, so it was a world well lost (Markowsky 83). We must be careful not to unquestioningly accept the statement of Cook's daughter, Nilla, that Glaspell "subordinated herself completely, always to the man of the moment, was anything but a feminist," without allowing for a stepdaughter's possible bias toward the stepmother who broke up her parents' marriage and then, the same year of her father's death, was already involved with another man (Noe 2). But we don't need to theorize about Nilla's motives, since feminist historians have made clear that her postsuffrage generation rejected the feminism of their late-nineteenth-century mothers. In any case, it is a mistake to portray Glaspell as subordinated or victimized by either Cook or her second lover, Norman Matson.

Doubtless Cook was a consummate narcissist. One senses from Glaspell's many long quotations of his writings and jottings in *The Road to the Temple* that what she perceived as a shared philosophic angst over human temporality was really, in his case, an incredulous inability to accept the impending annihilation of his own ego, which he often envisioned on a universal scale: "He, the microcosm, was not different in kind from the great self of which earth and stars were but the multiform shadow" (36). In a telling statement, he wrote Glaspell in 1923 that he wanted "to show you the strange old beauties which are ours. . . . There being no God I, Jig, have become dependent on Susan, as spectator of the world" (211). This reveals the role Glaspell played in his narcissistic fantasy: without father (god), mother and son would exist in an edenic dyad wherein the son would be active and the mother a passive spectator of his world, the fulfiller of his needs.

If we take *Brook Evans* as evidence, we may deduce that the narcissistic, pre-oedipal period remained primary in Glaspell's psychological makeup as well (as I explore in chapter 3). Psychoanalysts have long recognized that, "for girls, just as for boys, mothers are primary love objects" (Chodorow 192). Through intimacy with a narcissistic man, Glaspell could return to "primary love," the oneness of pre-oedipal unity that is the "final aim of all erotic striving" in the only heterosexual way open to her, by becoming the mother to his child (79, 194). The demands of an infantile partner may have become burdensome at times; however, the maternal role she assumed with her childlike lovers (Cook and later Matson) empowered Glaspell and stimulated her both erotically and creatively.[1] Neither relationship ever threatened or detracted from her art, quite the opposite: she produced her greatest work during her years with them.

Glaspell both identified with and separated herself from Cook's lifelong idealization of Greece and ancient Greek civilization. She identified with his nostalgic yearning for a purer American and Greek past because nostalgia for an edenic past expresses buried fantasies of return to the bliss of pre-oedipal union. Idyllic pastoral landscapes and visions of a distant golden age have, since Ovid and Virgil, described "some half-remembered place in archaic terms, a nostalgic reminiscence of an idealized child-scape" (McFarland 30). In the case of Greece, ruins buried deep in the earth under layers of subsequent civilizations reinforce this identification with Greece as the primitive, inner realm of a pre-verbal semiotic, repressed by the civilized, rational realm of symbolic signification. Indeed, in both *The Road to the Temple* and *Fugitive's Return*, Glaspell describes the excavation of the Temple of Apollo by archaeologists who had to move the entire existing town of Delphi because it was situated on top of the ancient stones. In a later novel, *Norma Ashe*, she explicitly connected the two: "Just as there are buried civilizations, so in the span of one lifetime there are buried selves" (59).

Glaspell's key word to signify the buried past is "secret." She uses it to refer to three things that are really all manifestations of one: maternal sexuality, edenic loci, and ancient languages. She employs it so consistently throughout her work that it becomes a metonym for the primarily nonverbal system of signification derived from early mother-child intimacy that Julia Kristeva calls "le semiotique." In "From One Identity to Another," Kristeva stresses its dissimilarity from verbal signification and detects it "in the first echolalias of infants as rhythms and intonations anterior to the first phonemes" (133–36). Carolyn Burke includes both gesture and silence in her interpretation of Kristeva's theory: "The semiotic, then, is in close alliance with the unconscious and expresses itself . . . through the resources of rhythm, intonation, gesture, and melody" (111). Because the semiotic predates symbolic function and is intimately associated with the mother, Burke emphasizes its subversion of patriarchal discourse, particularly when used by women writers: "Such writing creates gaps in meaning, pauses, and silences. It enacts a break from the symbolic within language. The discourse of Logos is literally ruptured to make room for what it has not allowed to be said." Toril Moi agrees that "Kristevan semiotics emphasizes the marginal and the heterogeneous as that which can subvert the central structures of traditional linguistics," and she summarizes its expression as "contradictions, meaninglessness, disruption, silences and absences in the symbolic language" (161–62).

It is in this subversive aspect that Kristeva's semiotic compares with Hélène Cixous's l'écriture feminine. Both locate the unconscious as the source, but whereas Kristeva's semiotic is not gender specific, for Cixous l'écriture feminine is an "antilogos weapon" open only to women (see "Medusa" 245–51). As we shall see, in Brook Evans, Fugitive's Return, and The Morning Is Near Us, mothers and daughters exist within patriarchy under a ban of silence, the "decapitation" so eloquently critiqued by Cixous: "They are decapitated, their tongues cut off and what talks isn't heard because it's the body that talks, and man doesn't hear the body" ("Castration" 49).

It is no wonder then that Glaspell uses the word "secret" so consistently to signify woman's inner life, particularly her sexuality. In Brook Evans, she writes, "If it was all to be secret, then the picture should be secret too" (20). Naomi, the first-generation mother in that novel, hides the photograph of her lover, Joe, since her sexual encounter with him has been forbidden. The picture reappears much later when she passes on the secret to her daughter, Brook, the novel's protagonist. The secrecy of female sexuality shared between mother and daughter is further symbolized by a revealing yellow dress Naomi makes for Brook, who fears "this secret way going into an unknown world" (211). Furthermore, throughout that novel the connection between female sexuality and an edenic locus is maintained, as Brook's son, Evans, discovers the "secret place" by the brook where his mother was conceived. In *The Morning Is Near Us*, the protagonist, Lydia, struggles to find out "the secret of unhappy glances, of troubled looks . . . the secret of this house," which turns out again to be maternal sexuality (104). Going a step further, if we may take "secret" as metonymic for vagina, we see that what Brook and Lydia both fear/desire is sexuality and the consequent return to the mother's body, for, as Adrienne Rich writes, "perhaps all sexual or intimate physical contact brings us back to that first body" (243).

Most significantly, then, in *Brook Evans* Glaspell links Brook's lover, Erik Helge's, study of ancient languages with secrecy: he must go to China because "there was something, some secret" only to be attained "from old manuscripts in China." Likewise Brook thinks of his knowledge of ancient Greek "as if a key that could unlock beautiful secrets" (258). The mystic adept, a feminized man, Erik plumbs the secrets of an ancient (semiotic) language, just as he will access the secret of Brook's sexual desire. (Obviously the actual language of ancient Greek is symbolic logos, but as something ancient, buried, and unspoken, Glaspell portrays it as semiotic.) For Glaspell therefore, the "road to the temple" is the road to the inner recesses, the secret of the mother's body, as she describes the Temple of the Mysteries at Eleusis:

> What did this living rock know that we did not know? What were the secrets told here which no man repeated to an uninitiate? The Temple had fallen now; its initiates were deep in the past; perhaps the rock, so long before them, and so long after, would give us its secret, if we sat believing that it could. (*Road* 318)

From Athens, she and Cook had taken the Sacred Way to Eleusis as initiates did thousands of years ago, and here she refers to the fact that initiates into the Eleusinian Mysteries—the worship of Demeter, earth mother, and her daughter, Persephone, Kore or maiden—were forbidden to tell what was viewed in the temple during the climax of the ceremony. It is probably one of the best kept secrets in all of human history, for even today scholars can only guess (see Mylonas 281). Glaspell describes the initiates as buried deep in the past, embraced by the living rock, earth, the eternal mother. She shared this moment with Cook, who, like Erik Helge, is often characterized by Glaspell as a mystic adept, as they sat together on the temple steps talking "of Demeter, of the seed corn—of how, behind ritual, there may be only one's own truth, and perhaps that itself is the mystery" (*Road* 318).

But the "inmost place" in Greece for Glaspell was the omphalos, the Oracle and temple at old Delphi, home of the ancient sibyls and spiritual center of the ancient world: "It is as a secret place. . . . Something in the form of the place itself lets you understand the stories of how, even before temples, there were strange powers here. It has always been an inmost place" (331). The strange powers Glaspell refers to are those of the earth mother in her various incarnations—Gaia, Themis, Phoebe—ancient matriarchal sibyls that predate both male theological newcomers to the Oracle, Dionysus and Apollo, as the priestess in Aeschylus' *Eumenides* recounts in her brief history of the Oracle:

> First in my prayer before all other gods
> I call on Earth, primaeval prophetess.
> Next Themis on her mother's oracular seat
> Sat, so men say. Third by unforced consent
> Another Titan, daughter too of Earth,
> Phoebe. She gave it as a birthday gift
> To Phoebus [Apollo], and giving called it by her name.
>
> (Harrison, *Prolegomena* 261)

Thus, here and in *Fugitive's Return*, mythology reinforces Glaspell's portrayal of old Delphi—Temple of Apollo, Dionysian theater, and village graveyard— as the locus of the inmost recesses of the mother's body and her buried semiotic.

Above Delphi, where the whole village retreated during the heat of summer, Glaspell depicts an edenic locus in the same terms: "The forest opens and gives us Kalania—the mountain park, that secret beauty, loveliness that is like a heart guarded by mountains of spruce" (*Road* 336). Again, she describes a vaginal space, a heart recessed and guarded, that opens to reveal secret beauty—"a hidden place where has been maintained a way of life through centuries of change" (341). Although Glaspell loved the "little house of spruce boughs" on the mountain where she lived with Cook and Nilla all summer, this idyllic pastoral was disrupted by bandits who terrorized the villagers and extorted money from the shepherds, signifying for Glaspell a rape of the maternal space.

All of these secret loci Glaspell shared with Cook. She quotes his notes after their return from visiting Arakova, a village higher up the mountain from Delphi, describing women spinning wool in the street: "I knew that what I saw in this so-called new Greek town was something older than ancient Greece. I saw, and secretly knew that I was seeing, the basis of our world, the next thing after mother's milk, those women spinning the wool of their lambs" (332). Apparently Cook was in on the secret, but despite his awareness of a more ancient matriarchal substratum to Greek culture, as evidenced by this quotation, and despite Glaspell's frequent rendering of him as feminized (for instance in chapter 33, "Certain Women," where he is portrayed translating Sappho), *The Road to the Temple* reveals that his experience of Greece was fundamentally patriarchal. Cook believed that language as symbolic discourse linked him to the ancient past, which was for him a patriarchal past:

> "For myself I feel if the words I speak came to me from authentic fathers through three thousand years, and were going on three thousand years to children's children, I would then have in my mind something to satisfy our otherwise vain thirst for immortality."
> (330)

Cook's pursuit of Greek was characteristically obsessive. Glaspell describes her exasperation when, instead of helping to pack, two days before their departure Cook was hunting down "a mammoth book" giving the definition of "every Greek word, each with its history from its origin!" Indeed, the book itself reconnected Cook with his father, who had traded away the family copy in 1861. Cook spent the entire journey "studying the Greek that built the Parthenon" and "in the smoking room getting the Greek that returns from America" (316). For him, all the contemporary Greeks he met "exist to carry on the Greek language" (329). Most significantly, he wrote in his book, "It is necessary to master or be mastered by the Greek language" (317). That he viewed learning the language as a struggle for mastery indicates his oedipal engagement with it, for in Lacanian terms, symbolization is the law of the father.[2]

In this context it is worthwhile to apply Virginia Woolf's critique of traditional male education, founded upon mastery of the dead languages, as the entrée to patriarchal power and privilege in *A Room of One's Own* and her parody of it in *Jacob's Room*. Poor as she is, Jacob's widowed mother ensures that her son learns Latin from the local pastor so that he may enter the bastions of privilege, first prep school, then Cambridge. Woolf's own male relations were all "stamped and moulded by that great patriarchal machine," the educational system, to emerge at sixty "a Head

Master, an Admiral, a Cabinet Minister, or the Warden of a college" (*Moments* 153). Her description of Jacob's Cambridge days is virtually identical to Glaspell's description of Cook's life at Harvard—young men lounging in their rooms, reading classics, forming close friendships, debating and arguing at their leisure. "At 37 Thayer [Cook's dorm], Jig sleeps on the couch, to be awakened next morning by a low murmuring and goes into the next room to find Hill half-way through Aeschylus' *Seven Against Thebes*. 'I slipped on Dick's dressing-gown and lay on the couch with a copy in my hand, listening to his translation. After breakfast John joined us and we finished the play'" (*Road* 56–57). As Woolf's Jacob says to his friend Timothy, "Probably, we are the only people in the world who know what the Greeks mean" (76). Even though "Jacob knew no more Greek than served him to stumble through a play," the ancient language gives these young men membership in an elite, exclusively masculine world. Jacob's education imparts to him a "gift from the past" that gives him mastery: "He looked satisfied; indeed masterly . . . the sound of the clock conveying to him (it may be) a sense of old buildings and time; and himself the inheritor" (45). Likewise for Cook, "the Greek letters could take him into a world where he knew who he was" (*Road* 266).

Excluded from the great patriarchal machine, Woolf determinedly studied Greek with tutors, but Glaspell took another route: she refused. Cook scorned her for resorting to French instead of learning Greek, but despite his urging she saw how much time it took and that it would threaten her writing: "I said that what I wanted was to write in the English language" (317, 408). In this way she not only protected her work from the encroachment of Cook's demands, but she separated her experience of Greece from his: she would not subject it to the logos, preferring to keep her experience of Greece semiotic and essentially mystical. Rather than mastering Greek, Glaspell "would learn such words as I liked—the word for lamb, the sea, the shepherd, the trees, the Temple, the spring, the vineyard" (408). Her approach was that of play as opposed to Cook's battle for mastery, a difference that delighted him, something she could not "quite credit" because she did not understand how fundamentally different their approaches to language were. Cook, however, ultimately respected her way of doing things: "Let her begin where she will. I have seen Susan stand before those old stones as if they had something to say to her" (409).

Two striking first-person fragments, crucial to *Fugitive's Return*, are described in *The Road to the Temple*, the first when Glaspell goes alone to the Temple of Apollo (the Delphic Oracle) and the second when she goes to the ruins of the Dionysian theater. Both portray her reading of signs in an essentially female way. She loved the Greek inscriptions on the fallen stones,

> the letters of stone into which were locked secrets from long ago. I felt the letters as a key, and now that the Temple was so much a part of my life, I would have its secrets. I saw the word Delphi, beautiful in Greek letters, and several other words intrigued me. (409)

Here again she equates an ancient language with secrets, and again the secret will turn out to be female sexuality. She traced the inscription onto paper and showed it to Cook, who "bored into" it (a revealing way for her to characterize his act of translation):

> "Woman, what have you brought home?"
>
> "Brought home?"
>
> "This inscription of yours. It is the most indecent thing I have ever seen upon paper—I mean stone."
>
> You could read the inscription one way, the usual way, and it was commending the virtue of a certain hero of Herod. But you could juggle it a little, not violating inscription technique, and behind this perfunctory tribute lurked a sensational accusation of unchastity. (409–10)

For Glaspell, the inscription signifies the repression of an "archaism of the semiotic body," to use Kristevan terminology, (that is, the unchastity behind the tribute) by patriarchal symbolic (that is, "the virtue of a certain hero of Herod"). That Glaspell reads this hidden language as a subversive female semiotic is further indicated by her ensuing characterization of the Oracle:

> What of the other inscriptions? There too did the Oracle hide words within her words? Had these stones held secrets through the centuries? Were they laughing deep laughter? (410)

Truly this represents the "laugh of the Medusa," to refer to Cixous's famous essay, the laugh of the powerful sibyl who knows that her body is not death, as men would characterize it, but alive with a vibrant and profuse sexuality/language. Within the inscription, as Glaspell portrays it, is hidden the "profusion of meanings" to which Cixous refers in the epigraph quoted at the beginning of this chapter. As Glaspell concludes, "The

Oracle must have said a good deal the authorities of the Temple did not care to repeat, yet they would be fearful about refusing it." In Glaspell's rendition, the Oracle's laughing secret is banned but not silenced within the inscription. Her words may have been censored by patriarchal authorities, but they could not refuse her entirely because they feared her power. She speaks the body, disrupting the patriarchal text, just as the Kristevan semiotic is said to "enact a break from the symbolic within language" (Burke 112). Or, to apply Showalter's view, with the Oracle Glaspell creates a metaphor "for a Female Aesthetic, for sisterhood, and for a politics of feminist survival" (*Sister's Choice* 151). This scene represents another striking example of her radical exploration of the "women's language unintelligible to male audiences or readers" that Showalter and Kolodny praised in "Jury of Her Peers" (151). There are many more in the novels that follow.

The second fragment revealing Glaspell's private experience of Greece occurs while Jig and his daughter "were deep in their Greek" and Glaspell goes alone to the theater. She wants to see "the places of the dancers of the odes still marked in unfading stone in the theater of Delphi" (*Road* 418). Again she seeks a nonverbal inscription from the buried past, one that will tell of the earliest beginnings of dramatic art in religious ritual, in the chanting and dancing of Dionysian odes. She notes that "beneath these squares, between which now grow the little plants of soft velvet-gray, the god Dionysus is said to be buried" (418). Here she refers to the tradition that "at Delphi there were rites closely analogous to those of Osiris and concerned with the tearing to pieces, the death and burial of the god Dionysos, and his resurrection and re-birth" (Harrison, *Prolegomena* 439).

Despite Cook's devotion to Nietzsche, Glaspell's understanding of Dionysianism and of the archaeological relics at Delphi came from Jane Ellen Harrison's *Prolegomena to the Study of Greek Religion*, which she had been reading on the boat returning to Greece in 1923 (probably the third edition just reissued in 1922) (Noe 50). Both she and Cook would have learned about the matriarchal or chthonic substratum to Greek religion from this remarkable volume. Harrison was a brilliant lecturer in classical archaeology at Cambridge whose studies of ancient Greek religion, art, and drama had a more profound influence upon modernist writers such as Woolf, Lawrence, and Joyce than did Sir James George Frazer's *Golden Bough*.[3] In the *Prolegomena*, Harrison differentiates between Olympian and chthonic ritual; describes the fertility rituals of the women's festivals; delineates the genesis of matriarchal goddesses from primitive daimones; traces the "superimposition" of the patriarchal Olympian hierarchy over indigenous matriarchal cults of Demeter, Kore, Hera, Aphrodite, and others; and concludes with a study of Orphic and Dionysiac mysticism. Harrison's feminist approach throughout the *Prolegomena*—but particularly in her discussion of Dionysus; his female worshipers, the maenads; and Delphi, where "high on Parnassos Dionysos held his orgies"—enabled Glaspell to imagine old Delphi as an all-female world of strength and healing in *Fugitive's Return* (391).

The source for Glaspell's characterization of the repressive authorities of the Temple is taken from Harrison's description of them as "past masters in the art of glossing over awkward passages in the history of theology" as they drew "a decent veil" over the struggle between the cults of Apollo and Dionysus for control of the Delphic Oracle (391). Likewise, Glaspell's understanding of the Oracle as a female voice silenced by patriarchy originates with Harrison, for Harrison's descriptions of its "three strata"—starting with the original earth goddesses, then the coming of Apollo, and finally Dionysus—consistently vilify Apollo. For Harrison, Apollo was a "woman-hater" and, characterized by Aeschylus as the "utterer of his father's will," he epitomizes patriarchy. "It was not only the Olympian Father Zeus who victoriously took over to himself the cult of the Earth-Mother and the Earth-Maidens. Even more marked is the triumph of the Olympian Son, Apollo" (390–94). Harrison's anger at the erasure of the mother is further evident in her discussion of a votive relief found at Eleusis. "The vase-painter knows quite well that it is really a priestess who utters the oracles. Only a priestess can mount the sacred tripod," yet Apollo is portrayed "seated on the very omphalos itself":

> But even here, so stately and yet so pitiful are the ancient goddesses that our hearts are sore for the outrage on their order. And on the vase-painting, when we remember that the omphalos is the very seat and symbol of the Earth-Mother, that hers was the oracle and hers the holy oracular snake that Apollo slew, the intrusion is hard to bear (319–21).

While Apollo is the symbol for repression and erasure of the maternal, for Harrison the late importation of "the rude immigrant god from Thrace," Dionysus, marks a return to mysticism and to the mother in Greek religion. Harrison is emphatic that "the relation of Dionysos to his father Zeus was slight and artificial. He is . . . essentially the son of his mother, 'child of Semele,'" and Semele "is the Earth" (402). She concludes that "Dionysos is a difficult god to understand. In the end it is only the mystic who penetrates the secrets of mysticism" (363). Similar to Glaspell, Harrison characterizes the mystic as one who penetrates secrets. The very nature of the ecstatic mysticism associated with Dionysus is semiotic in the Kristevan sense—nonverbal, irrational, manifold—and, as Harrison describes it, a "return to nature," a return to mother.

Another vase painting Harrison discusses shows the young Dionysus, welcomed by maenads and satyrs, rising out of the earth in the pictographic tradition of the Kore, who was often portrayed "rising out of the Earth she really is." By this the "vase-painter meant that the god is Earthborn" (404–5). Similarly, Glaspell depicts the "little plants of soft velvet-gray" rising up between the stones of the theater floor as Dionysus. Earlier she had referred to this lichen as "a soft gray plant that is like a memory com[ing] up between the great stones of the old stage" (*Road* 404). Thus Glaspell's rendering of old Delphi signifies the inmost recesses of the mother's body and also represents a map of the unconscious, here and in *Fugitive's Return*. Body and mind are not exclusive but analogous here, for the unconscious is where the repressed semiotic resides, buried but rising up like the fingers of lichen into consciousness as memory, dream, poetry.

The omphalos, overarched by the Temple of Apollo, is the perfect spatial representation of unconsciousness overborne by consciousness, just as "language as symbolic function [Apollo] constitutes itself at the cost of repressing instinctual drive and continuous relation to the mother [Dionysus]" (Kristeva 136). To the Oracle the worshiper comes for the voice of "archaic, instinctual, and maternal territory," the voice of the semiotic body (Kristeva 136). And in Dionysian intoxication, according to Harrison, the "breaking of bonds and limitations and chrystallizations" becomes poetic inspiration, just as for Kristeva the semiotic breaks the bonds of "signification . . . the operating consciousness of a transcendental ego," giving music and rhythm to poetry (Harrison, *Prolegomena* 445; Kristeva 133).

Sitting in the Dionysian theater, Glaspell received the inspiration for *Fugitive's Return*. She describes observing this remarkable tableau of female pathos:

> In this quiet November afternoon I sat there and thought of the Delphi I knew, and of the god Dionysus. The silence was broken— two women were about to cross the stage, the one supporting the other who was crying. When they saw some one was there, they halted. But they saw it was I, and I went up to them. It was the wife

of Alekos Komblss who was crying. We stood there holding each other's hands. (*Road* 418)

Alekos Komblss was a shepherd abducted by bandits who believed his father, Demetrius, had betrayed them to the police. Glaspell and Cook had already spent a rather terrifying night nursing Demetrius in the mountain camp where he had been wounded by the bandits. The Komblss family was ruined by this internecine battle: Demetrius sold off their flocks to pay the ransom, yet Alekos was never returned. In Greece Glaspell witnessed vicariously an archaic culture of domination by violence. The unspoken suffering of women in such a brutal patriarchal society moved her deeply, as her participation in this drama of female comforting indicates. The scene is transcribed into *Fugitive's Return*, when the protagonist, Irma, communicates semiotically in a kind of mime on the Dionysian stage with Stamula, a shepherd's wife. Like Bacchantes or Dionysian maenads, Glaspell's characters enact a silent drama of female solidarity and subversion in a world apart.

As Glaspell returns from the theater on this occasion, she passes the village burial ground, to which she had often felt drawn yet avoided: "I turned away now, but it was as if I had to go back. Reluctantly, yet not resisting a curious compulsion, I opened the gate and went in there among the dead" (418). One might say, indeed, that Glaspell had a compulsion about graveyards. They figure in almost all her novels. Key scenes in *Fidelity* and *The Morning Is Near Us* involve the protagonist's searching and crying out for her dead parents in a graveyard, while the burial of Ambrose Holt in the family plot among his ancestors concludes *Ambrose Holt and Family*. In *The Road to the Temple*, Glaspell's ambivalence toward the graveyard—drawn yet repelled—replicates the ambivalence toward the internalized, omnipotent mother typical of the pre-oedipal period (see Chodorow 82) and projected onto mother earth. The graveyard symbolizes the mother's body, particularly in its fearful or devouring aspect. When Glaspell enters and sees that graves have been dug up, her reaction is startling:

> I saw things I did not understand, and they filled me with an excitement I understood even less. There were graves which seemed to have been dug into; crude little wooden shrines were thrown into half-filled graves. Jig and Nilla were astonished by the emotion which surprised me when I began to tell about the place. It was an outrage, I said—and what did it mean? (418–19)

That Cook and his daughter were astonished by her reaction indicates its vehemence; that she, usually so analytical, seems equally baffled by it indicates how deep its roots are in her unconscious. The only two words she uses to describe her feelings in this passage are "excitement" and "outrage." She is first excited, then outraged by this violation of the mother's body. Although Cook explains that it is the local custom to dig up remains after seven years to make room for more burials, to Glaspell it seems like rape. Here she shares Harrison's sense of outrage at the sacrilegious intrusion on the ancient goddesses. Again the customs of an archaic, patriarchal society have jolted her deeply and inspired her imagination, for rape also figures in *Fugitive's Return*.

Glaspell was so shaken that she dreamed a few nights later that she was dead and had been "thrown into a sort of ditch, and no one knew I was there" until her dog comes and tugs at her skirt. She tells the dog they will not walk in the temple again (420). Glaspell follows this frightening experience of the engulfing mother with an image of herself playing a nurturing maternal role. She describes herself standing outside on the balcony at night, with the dog "sleeping on his own little bed, Nilla in her room working at Greek, and Jig at his big table, books and papers around him":

> I liked the feeling that my household was safe; that they were doing the things it seemed their part to do; that Athanasius and I had talked of what there would be for them to eat tomorrow. . . . That sense of a household which one keeps safe, that it may move on its destined way, is satisfying, it is more than other satisfactions. (420)

In feeding her loved ones, in reenacting pre-oedipal closeness with them by encompassing them safely within the oikos, Glaspell felt her deepest satisfaction. Her private, first-person fragments embedded in *The Road to the Temple* movingly reaffirm the beneficent power of the semiotic mother, as do the endings of both *Brook Evans* and *Fugitive's Return*.

The loss of the daughter to the mother, the mother to the daughter, is the essential female tragedy.

—*Adrienne Rich*

# 3

# Mother-Daughter "Tensity" in *Brook Evans* (1928)

Susan Glaspell's novels, from *Brook Evans* through *Norma Ashe*, represent a profound contemplation of the parent-child relationship from the daughter's point of view. However, although her work is psychoanalytic, Glaspell was no Freudian. Her 1915 play, *Suppressed Desires*, written with her husband, George Cram Cook, for the Provincetown Players, parodied the "current Freudian frenzy" that had hit bohemian Greenwich Village. Marcia Noe quotes Glaspell as recalling of the time, "You could not go out to buy a bun without hearing of someone's complex" (29). Glaspell mocked the popularization of Freudian theory, not Freudian theory itself, the general outlines of which she was obviously familiar with, as were most of her contemporaries. While there is no evidence that she consciously attempted to incorporate Freud's theories into her work, like Freud, Glaspell portrays a binaristic patriarchal culture in which little girls, no less than little boys, must choose between their mothers and their fathers, must give up the mother as primary object and turn to the father. Where Glaspell departs from Freud is that she does not depict oedipal conflict as an inherent destiny. Rather, it is shown in her novels as culturally induced, the result of a patriarchal society that holds female sexuality hostage. Glaspell's idealism has been much commented on, and in contrast to Freud's deterministic view of humanity, she presents the possibility for amelioration of oedipal and pre-oedipal conflict for both sexes, particularly with the passing of each generation and the increasing freedom for women from the 1880s through the 1920s.

Because of Glaspell's intense focus in *Brook Evans* on mother-daughter relations, Nancy Chodorow's *Reproduction of Mothering* provides an apt theoretical key to unlock the meaning of this novel.[1] Chodorow modifies Freudian theory by focusing on object-relations and the importance of the pre-oedipal mother-child dyad in the development of gender. The exclusive and prolonged mothering of the "male-dominant, father-absent family" endemic in Western industrialized society causes both boys and girls to reject the mother and devalue femininity, not merely because of patriarchal socialization but as a form of ego survival against an internalized omnipotent mother (40). The pre-oedipal period is a time of primary identification with the caregiver and primary narcissism in which the infant cannot distinguish between itself and the mother who fulfills its needs (61). With growth, this period gives way to one of greater mobility and the creation of ego boundaries separating child from mother, but the separation remains essentially ambivalent: "Children wish to remain one with their mother, and expect that she will never have different interests from them; yet they define development in terms of growing away from her. In the face of their dependence, lack of certainty of her emotional permanence, fear of merging, and overwhelming love and attachment, a mother looms large and powerful" (82). Gender differentiation culminates in the oedipal period, and in adolescence children attempt to finalize their gender in conformity with the heterosexual demands of the culture. Boys can separate from the mother more easily because of their sexual difference, while a "girl remains preoccupied for a long time with her mother alone." The pre-oedipal attachment of daughter to mother persists into adolescence, sustaining "the intensity, ambivalence, and boundary confusion of the child still preoccupied with issues of dependence and individuation" (96–97).

It is exactly this mother-daughter intensity and ambivalence that Glaspell portrays so dramatically in *Brook Evans*. The central mother-daughter relationship in the novel is that of Brook and her mother, Naomi.[2] Structured as tautly as a three-act play, the novel begins in 1888 when Naomi is eighteen, focuses intensely on the period when Brook is eighteen and Naomi thirty-eight, and ends a generation later when Brook's son, Evans, is eighteen and she herself is thirty-eight. This tripartite chronological structure allows Glaspell to show how neurosis is generationally perpetuated in families. The historical overview she gives to familial and gender conflict indicates that she would agree with

Chodorow that "society constitutes itself psychologically in the individual," even though she believed that people can make individual choices to change their destiny (50).

The opening scenes of Glaspell's novels are often strikingly metaphoric, revealing through the carefully crafted moment the themes that will dominate the novel:

> Her mother came into the kitchen, looked at the peas which did not yet cover the bottom of the yellow dish, at the basket still heaped with peas in pod, laughed indulgently: "Naomi!" When indulgent the o in her daughter's name was round and long. "What in the world you thinking about?" (3)

The passage suggests the ambivalence that Glaspell, in great detail, will go on to show characterizes the mother-daughter relationship. Mother and daughter are as if "peas in pod," sharing the natural world as symbolized by the fresh produce of their garden. There is love indicated in the mother's indulgence and in the caressing pronunciation of the daughter's name, but there is also disapproval hovering at the edges of her question, for not enough peas have been shelled. Naomi has been daydreaming of her lover, Joe Copeland, and the mother's disapproval foreshadows her later condemnation of the daughter's sexual fall.

Book One tells the story of Naomi's fall from grace in edenic terms, as the scene of her lovemaking with Joe is a mossy bed by a tree-bowered brook, "the world asleep—not knowing—alone here together, this freshness in the trees above the sweet sound of the clear brook, the far-away gentle stars" (12). The following passage refers not only to the locus of Naomi and Joe's lovemaking by the brook, now passed from spring to fall, but also to Naomi's "swollenness"—her pregnancy, which is, like the brook itself, symbolic of natural continuity. She names the child in tribute to this symbol:

> Rains had swollen the brook. A more powerful stream than the brook which knew her and Joe. And yet, the same brook—something that had been then, was now. Something that went on. Something that went on after Joe had stopped; would go on when she herself was no more. (33)

The day following this night with Joe, while looking at herself in the mirror and undressing, Naomi sees her body in terms of male desire, for "that which made her beautiful" is the memory of Joe's desire (20). She looks at pictures of Italy in a magazine before drifting into a doze, her mind filled with images of "a land of romance," but wakes up to her father's agitated voice, telling of an accident with the new haying machine that has killed Joe. Glaspell shows in this scene that Naomi remains emotionally arrested for the rest of her life in an adolescent stage of development. Her sexual union with Joe becomes the only moment of her life truly lived for herself, and the rest of her life is sacrificed to the daring of that moment. Just as Glaspell used the language of sappy magazine romances to characterize Ruth's love for Stuart in *Fidelity*, here she uses romantic clichés of Italy to characterize Naomi's fantasies and to emphasize that an impossibly romantic dream of erotic love remains her only saving grace in a doomed life of enforced obedience: "They were lovers, the Italians. . . . centuries they had sung songs of love, fought and died for it. The nightingale. Venice. Murmuring of water and the ardent whisperings" (21). This is the dream Naomi obsessively tries to pass on to her daughter, despite the fact that there is no evidence that Joe would have married her, quite the opposite. Class differences separated her from the wealthy Copelands, and Joe's mother's vehement condemnation of her as a "trollop" when she tells of her pregnancy after Joe's death indicates that he, afraid of his mother, would probably have abandoned her and the baby (9, 30–31).

Instead, three patriarchs decide Naomi's fate: her father; her pious and unattractive suitor, Caleb Evans; and Brother Baldwin, the minister. When Caleb, whom she despises, offers to marry her, she begs to be allowed to stay in her home, asking her father, "If you would—for my sake—stand a little disgrace?" but no one in this world sacrifices for a woman, particularly for her sexuality; it is she who must sacrifice for others, and what she sacrifices is her sexuality (44–47). Just as Mrs. Lawrence condemns Ruth's selfishness in *Fidelity*, Naomi's parents make it clear that a woman's duty is to sacrifice herself for others. Her mother urges her to think of

> "the life your child would have. Yes, think of that, Naomi. Now get your stockings out, dear. I want to see that they're mended." . . . There was no use calling from this bad dream to her mother. . . . She knew what Naomi was going into—what the bad dream would become, yet she went on talking cheerily about the stockings, pretending she did not know (44).

Their silenced nonverbal relation, sublimated into clothing, will be repeated in Naomi's relation to her own daughter and is typical of the largely nonlinguistic pre-oedipal period, here replayed during adolescence. According to Chodorow, the body issues central to the pre-oedipal dyad are often expressed during adolescence as shared involvements with food, weight, and clothes (135–36). The next generation, Naomi and Brook, will be similarly estranged, with Naomi only able to express love for her daughter through clothes and food, just as her own mother did. In *Brook Evans*, mothers and daughters exist under patriarchal "decapitation," the silencing of female voice and sexuality previously discussed in chapter 2. They communicate secretly in language that is opaque to men, based on their earlier pre-oedipal closeness, transmitting and reading signs through eye contact, gestures, and objects, just as Mrs. Hale and Mrs. Peters in "Jury of Her Peers" read a poorly stitched quilt (clothes) and a broken bottle of cherry preserves (food) as signs of Minnie Foster's breakdown and defiance.

Book Two begins in 1907 in Colorado, where Caleb has taken Naomi after their marriage. Naomi had to give up her family, her home, and the fertile green fields of Illinois that she loved and that were emblematic of her sexual fertility (17). She now lives isolated in prairies dominated by the distant mountain, Big Chief, with all the paternal referents that name suggests. Brook and her father "share pleasure" in Big Chief, lit up by vivid sunsets, but Naomi feels "shut in" by the mountains just as she is shut in by her marriage. When Brook protests, "You can get over them," her mother replies, "I will never get over them" (64). Brook loves Colorado just as Naomi loved Illinois, because both women associate the landscape of their childhood positively with their fathers, both farmers. Brook's shared pleasure with her father and alienation from her mother's imprisonment foreshadow her rejection of her mother and adherence to her father and to the patriarchal values that will ultimately oppress her just as they have her mother.

Naomi illustrates the exclusive mothering discussed by Chodorow that is so threatening to children. Victimized by a patriarchal form of marriage, economically dependent on her husband, and isolated from others, she is all sacrifice, all service to husband and particularly to child. In every scene Naomi is working—gardening, cooking, sewing, washing, ironing, or on her knees scrubbing the kitchen floor. Barely tolerating her husband, who is often absent from the home working at other farms, her only love object is Brook:

> Often there was "a little saved up" when there was something Brook very much wanted. Sometimes there were quarrels about money. . . . Mother would say she had to have a new dress, some things for the house, a woman couldn't get along with nothing. Then more than likely the old dress would be made over again, and it was surprising

how much there was "put by" when Brook's new room was to be furnished. One night, coming in the kitchen after she was supposed to have gone to bed, she saw her mother going through Father's pocketbook. She pretended not to have seen, and she felt uncomfortable about despising her mother for this, for she knew it was she who profited by it. (70–71)

In addition to Naomi's poverty and self-sacrifice, this passage illustrates the painful ambivalence that characterizes the child's reaction to the pre-oedipal mother. Brook knows that "here was a love that would do anything in the world for her—die for her, suffer, do wrong for her," and yet she cannot help "despising her" (205). Why? That is the central question posed by the novel and the central issue in pre-oedipal maternal-child relations. That early "unity was bliss, yet meant the loss of self and absolute dependence," so mother-love is both desired and feared (Chodorow 194). Chodorow cites the findings of many psychoanalysts in determining that "the pre-oedipal mother, simply as a result of her omnipotence and activity causes a 'narcissistic wound' [that] creates hostility to the mother in a child" (122).

Orality is the primary infantile mode of the pre-oedipal period, so it is appropriate that so much of Naomi's mother-love and Brook's resistance to that love are expressed through food:

"I saved a little of this for you."

Brook frowned as she poured the cream on her oatmeal. It was a habit of her mother's thus to hide the nicest things for her. Sometimes Brook would protest, "I don't want things that Father doesn't have. . . . Why should I have them?". . .

"Mother loves to give them to you, darling. Mother can give you so little." Brook would eat the delicacy saved for her, though she did not like this habit of her mother's. (70)

Brook's behavior, her manner of speaking, and later her sulks and tantrums seem incredibly infantile when we remember that she is eighteen at this time. But that is just the point: Naomi has been so dependent on her daughter as the sole object of her love that Brook has remained infantilized. Brook wants to reject the sensual intimacy of mother and food because it creates a complicity that excludes her father, with whom she desires to be united because her oedipal issues are resurfacing now but also because, as Chodorow states, "a girl's father provides a last ditch escape from maternal omnipotence, so a girl cannot risk driving him away"

(195). The passage portrays again the pathos of Naomi's poverty, but it is also apparent that for Naomi food is a form of control, and she feels satisfaction in seeing Brook "eat the morsel against which she protested" (112). Later, when Brook has achieved more separation, she will not eat the orange Naomi buys for her.

Chodorow summarizes "a variety of ploys which prepubertal girls use to effect their individuation and independence" (137). These include becoming critical of their mother, trying in every way to be unlike her, and idealizing another woman outside the family. The daughter will thus create "arbitrary boundaries by negative identification (I am what she is not)," as Brook does in idealizing a neighbor, Sylvia Waite, a missionary who is home visiting her own mother and who is everything Brook's mother is not, "a good Christian woman," as her father says approvingly:

> It was nice to watch Mrs. Waite, standing erect, as if indeed glad Jesus loved her, confident. Her clothes were good style. Missionaries did not need to be dowdy, as most of them were, in their pictures. Watching her standing there so strong, sure, happy, Brook thrilled to think of how she would return to far places east of Constantinople, where she gave her life to all the little ones who needed her. Mrs. Waite was really older than her mother; she looked years younger, as if God blessed her for her good works. Brook, too, felt blessed, just to be standing near her and singing the same song. (77)

Loved by Jesus and blessed by God, Sylvia Waite belongs to the patriarchy and receives the benefits of her adherence: wealth, community, and relative freedom. She is the archetypal virgin mother, fulfilling the woman's role of caring for children but with "little ones" immaculately conceived, as it were; she bears no taint of association with the maternal body. She stands erect and confident, as opposed to Naomi, who is often pictured as abject and bent; she is beautifully dressed, as opposed to Naomi, who wears "an old-fashioned coat . . . made from the coat Brook had discarded" (71); and she travels freely, apparently without her husband, while Naomi is imprisoned by Big Chief. It is no wonder that Brook tries to identify with her because of these benefits, as well as to escape from primary identification with her mother. However, to achieve such a negative identification Brook must repress her own sexuality, since chastity is the price of patriarchal adherence. Her rejection of the internalized mother's body and consequent denigration of female sexuality will perpetuate the very institutions that have victimized and created her own mother (in other words, Chodorow's reproduction of mothering).

That pre-oedipal issues of maternal-child merger and separation are also present for Naomi in her competition with Sylvia Waite over Brook becomes clear when Sylvia and her mother come over for tea. Because Sylvia's mother, Mrs. Allen, was the midwife who helped deliver Brook, memories of Brook's birth are contrasted in Naomi's mind with her present sense that Brook is drawing away from her, encouraged, she believes, by the very woman who drew her out of the mother's body in the first place. When Caleb joins them and she sees Brook sitting between Caleb and Mrs. Allen, she recalls, "It was Mrs. Allen had taken Brook to Caleb" when she was born, over Naomi's protests (118–20). She sees herself at war with these women who want to turn her baby over to the father. Naomi reasserts her claim by describing the dance Brook attended, dancing being synonymous with sexuality and frowned upon by the evangelical church to which they belong.

> "Isn't it possible," asked Sylvia Waite, with the gentleness one employs toward an unreasonable person, "to put that—youthful feeling into the work we may do for our Lord?" She sat straight, confident and smiling, as to say, "See? Am I not happy? Has my Master's work not given me life?"
>
> Naomi, bent, tense, could say no more, for she would say too much; but she felt with passion that while Sylvia Waite's face was smooth and hers drawn, while that life would seem full and hers not a successful life, felt that in her was the truth, and wanted words and power for the faith that had not died. (119)

Naomi feels passionately and is perceived as unreasonable. She is, indeed, the archetypal "madwoman" in the attic and Sylvia and her mother will later label her as "not quite—steady in her mind" (211). The truth she believes in is the truth of the female body, of sexual love, and she bears the marks of patriarchal punishment for that rebellion, her bent body, drawn face, and failed life, while Sylvia flaunts the "confidence" borne of her "Master's" munificence.

The battle over Brook's soul is thus set up along the traditional dichotomous lines of Western culture: mother/body versus father/spirit, the "classic opposition, dualist and hierarchical" that for Cixous underlies "everything that's spoken, everything that's organized as discourse, art, religion, the family, language . . . [and] all ordered around hierarchical oppositions that come back to the man/woman opposition" which "automatically means great/small, superior/inferior" ("Castration" 44). When a young man, Tony Ross, asks Brook to go to a dance with him, her parents are bitterly opposed to one another along these binaristic lines:

> She noticed how her mother stooped, carrying the bucket of water to the flowers beneath Brook's window. . . . There was always anxiety in her mother's voice, and as if—as if she were more glad [to see you] than she thought she ought to let you know. Mother had looked lonely, carrying the water to the flowers. . . .
>
> "Do you think Father would let me go?"
>
> "Why wouldn't he let you go?" The answer surprised Brook. It seemed to have surprised her mother, too, it had come so quick and harsh. She turned back to the plants.
>
> "Well, you know how he is," said Brook. "Dancing. You know—it's against his principles."
>
> Carefully, bent low, her mother was pouring water on the green things just above the ground. (59–60)

Naomi is pictured here characteristically stooped/oppressed, but she is also Natura, the earth mother giving life, "pouring water on the green things." Glaspell shares with many modernists the view that sexuality and generational continuity represent humanity's true eternity and, like James Joyce and D. H. Lawrence (in his early work such as *The Rainbow*), she elevates the flesh traditionally identified with woman to critique an arid, patriarchal Christian church and the repressive bourgeois proprieties sanctified by that church. Like Molly Bloom, she is "Gae-Tellus," the earth mother, but lacking the adoration of a Leopold Bloom she is condemned as the whore that Molly easily might have been (and indeed often was according to early critics). However, Naomi's loneliness and emotional dependence on Brook are also evident in this passage. At one moment Brook "wanted to hug her mother" but she cannot: "Why didn't she? She so seldom did anything like that, and her mother would have loved it. Somehow, it wasn't natural to do it, though she half knew her mother was starving for it. Perhaps that was why she couldn't" (70). Glaspell's psychological observation here is acute. Naomi's starving need is exactly why Brook cannot give in and hug her. Brook must struggle against her to define separation and autonomy, but at the same time she feels guilty for denying her mother, whom she loves.

Pre-oedipal conflicts are now complicated by a pubertal resurgence of oedipal issues intensified by Brook's relationship with Tony. As Chodorow stresses, during the oedipal period "a girl does not give up this pre-oedipal relationship completely, but rather builds whatever happens later upon this pre-oedipal base," as she "oscillates between attachment to her mother and to her father," exactly the relation Glaspell portrays (115, 129). That Brook's sexuality is strongly identified with her mother is illustrated by Glaspell's clever use of mirror scenes that replicate each other in each generation. On the day of Joe's death, Naomi had returned from school and observed that "the cherries her mother was putting up were rich red," reminding her of "the feel of the moss on which her hand had rested the night before." She saw that her mother "looked tired" and "stooped" and offered to help with supper preparations, but her mother told her to rest. Naomi went into her bedroom and, undressing before a mirror, "put her arms behind her head, stretching, then her throat, her head thrown back, looking at herself with half-closed eyes," she recalled "it"—the "secret" of her sexual experience with Joe, "that which made her beautiful" (19–20). Brook, too, notices that Naomi looks "tired" and "stooped," volunteers to help with supper, and is similarly told to rest. In both generations we see the mother's exhaustion and sacrifice for her daughter's well-being. As her mother before her, Brook, instead of helping, goes into her room and basks in the sensuality of her reflected image: "Hands behind her head, she looked in the glass. Her chemise had slipped from one shoulder. One wore a low-neck dress to a dance. She arranged her chemise as if it were a dress to wear in the evening. She knew that her shoulders and her throat were beautiful" (60).

Glaspell's replication of these mirror scenes shows the close mutual identification of mother and daughter in their sexuality, as the adolescent girl discovers herself as object in the mirror: "it is she-as-object suddenly confronting herself" (Beauvoir 338). This means two things for the girl, both of which are portrayed by Glaspell in these passages. First, up to this time she has been an autonomous individual: now she must renounce her "sovereignty," to use Simone de Beauvoir's term, by accepting her erotic and social status as object. To become sexual means to become the mother's body. The girl is unaware that her body's degraded future is inherent in its budding sexuality, for by becoming the object of desire she exchanges a girl's protected autonomy for the mother's life of toil and sacrifice. Second, there is a basic confusion in her eroticism that Beauvoir points out: incarnated as the "absolute object of desire," she narcissistically desires herself (336–40). She cannot distinguish the desire of the man from the love of her own ego, hence the lavish homage Naomi and Brook pay to their own reflections in these passages. When Naomi enters the room and sees Brook's reflection, she recalls her own past image and starts to cry, indicating her "narcissistic over-identification" with her daughter (Chodorow 104). She will push Brook to fill the sexual role she idealizes, symbolized by the low-cut yellow dress she makes for her to wear to the dance, an image symbolizing their union in the female body.

Brook's quasi-sensual spirituality shows that she does not yet perceive the endemic cultural split between body and spirit, nor the sequestering of woman in the body that maintains male transcendence. Brook believes it is "quite right and natural" to daydream about her lover while attending church with her father (79). Church "made her feel lifted up," and she had a sense "of being taken in where she was one with others" (76). Returning home and seeing the yellow ruffle of the dress her mother had hidden "under a towel that did not entirely cover it," she is thrilled and holds it up, admiring herself and singing happily, "Holy, Holy, Holy, Lord God Almighty!" (80). In Brook's childlike innocence, body and spirit are still unified. She can admire the hidden yellow dress, secret symbol of the sexual body she shares with her mother, and in the same moment sing a hymn of praise to the father. Prelapsarian, she still belongs "one with others," an accepted part of the patriarchal church community that excludes her mother. She has not yet learned the lesson her mother has so painfully paid for: that female sexuality is banned from patriarchal community. As a sign of the sexual female body, the dress, like the dance, is forbidden by her father. Brook storms when Caleb insists that Naomi add a yoke and sleeves onto the revealing dress, but her mother consoles: "Nevermind. Don't you see? I'll make it as a separate waist. . . . You can show it to him that way, and then—take it out." Uncomfortable with this illicit complicity, Brook begins to feel the culturally induced rift that will ultimately force her to choose between father and mother, spirit and body.

Racism, xenophobia, class snobbery, and religious intolerance are added to sexual repression as Caleb's reasons to forbid Brook's association with Tony Ross, whose original name he discovers is Rossi. Not only is Tony descended from poor Italian laborers, but he is Catholic and has "Indian blood" (88). He is clearly sexualized Other. Brook's parents are deadlocked in opposition over whether she may go to the dance. It is the first time Naomi has ever defied her husband, and her aggression in defense of her daughter's right to experience love and sexual passion shocks and frightens Brook. While Brook can see the injustice and bigotry behind her father's refusal, she knows the father's word is law, and in her heart she wants to obey it: "Oh, she would go, all right, and yet she was on Father's side. It wasn't right to deceive him like that" (95–96). After Naomi sneaks Brook out to the dance, Caleb catches Brook returning and forbids her to see Tony:

"Look here, Brook. I'm your father. Isn't that true?"

"Of course," said Brook, sullenly.

"And this is my house. Is that true?"

"Yours and Mother's."

"And yours," he added, changing. "But I'm master in my own house. And I say you cannot go to dances. I say you cannot keep company with this fellow." (101)

For all her constant caretaking, the mother has no real power in determining her child's destiny because she has no economic power. As Caleb makes clear, the "master" owns the wealth and thus controls the fate of his possessions.

Ironically, however, Brook wants to obey her father. Her change of object from mother to father during the oedipal stage has been partially successful, but unconscious pre-oedipal desire for the mother as first love object continues to pull on the daughter at the same time. She looks to the father as a way to define her autonomy against the narcissistic mother, but in addition, according to Chodorow, a mother's heterosexual preference for men "leads a girl to devalue her own genitals," so she "turns to her father in defense, feeling angry, like a rejected lover" (123–25). Jane Flax has commented that the daughter sees the father "as the gatekeeper to both autonomy and the outside, nonfamilial world. Yet the price of identifying with the father is high. It means acknowledging his (at least sexual) control over and privileged access to the mother. The daughter must give up her own pre-oedipal tie to the mother and often take on the father's devaluation of and contemptuous attitude for the mother and, by extension, for women as a group" ("Relationships" 37). Glaspell has shown that a woman can possess the phallus, the power and independence Brook wants, in the character of Sylvia Waite, but only if she rejects the mother and abjures the female body, as Brook will do.

In desperation, Naomi tells Brook that she does not have to obey Caleb because he is not her real father (102). While Naomi thinks her confession of love with Brook's biological father, Joe, will unite Brook on her side, it has the opposite effect, driving Brook to side finally with Caleb.

So Mother had "gone wrong." Mother. She was telling about it, as they sat across the table from one another. . . . It didn't seem nice to be talking about it, Father right here in the house. Tony must be almost home now. Was he thinking about her? Would he be thinking of her—after he had gone to bed? (104–5)

Brook's seemingly unrelated association with Tony is actually quite related: will I, like my mother, be the object of male desire—with the same consequences? Naomi is trying to lead Brook to discover the joy of her sexual body, her jouissance, but for eighteen years she has shown more effectively through her abject poverty, unpaid labor, isolation, and self-sacrifice the price of that joy. When Naomi describes Joe as a lover, Brook "felt embarrassed. It was as if Mother had taken off too many of her clothes. Father, asleep there upstairs—in that was naturalness, safety . . . yes, it was right a father should be strict" (105).

Brook's embarrassment is multidetermined. Just as when she wanted to hug her mother but could not, she is made uncomfortable by the seductive intimacy of her mother's confessional nakedness. She senses in the safety of her father that "last ditch escape from maternal omnipotence," a heterosexual preservation from the threat to selfhood posed by pre-oedipal narcissistic unity with her mother (Chodorow 194–95). Brook also discovers that she is not, and has never been, her mother's sole love object, a place she has felt confident in occupying since her birth. Like a rejected lover, she turns to her father, whom she now perceives as having loved only her. "Not then, nor at any time in all her life, had look or word of his hinted, 'You are not my child.' With the deepest feeling of eighteen years Brook Evans whispered, 'Father!'" (107)

Naomi's confession that Caleb is not Brook's biological father allows Brook to give her oedipal desire full reign, since now her mother has no legitimate claim. She begins to distance herself from Naomi and unite with her father in everything, fawning on him adoringly: "'Bread, Father?' Brook asked gently, sitting at supper. . . . She said 'Father' a number of times, lingering over the word as she had not done before. 'Mother' she said only when she must" (122). Brook relishes her oedipal defeat of her mother, rubbing it in that she possesses the father, and shares with him the bread symbolic of communion in the patriarchal church. Her relationship with her father is developed at every step "while looking back at her mother—to see if her mother is envious, to make sure she is in fact separate, to see if she can in this way win her mother, to see if she is really independent" (Chodorow 126). "If I should have to give my whole life to

Father," Brook says to Naomi, drawing herself up, "as in heroic feeling, . . . that would not be too great a return for what he has done for me. . . . I must give him the gratitude—love—you never gave him." Brook idealizes her father's "sacrifice" in marrying Naomi and "letting another child pass for his" but, as Naomi tries to protest, Caleb has received only joy from Brook's presence in his life, and he married Naomi "because he wanted me, and could have me no other way" (130–32). Rather, as Glaspell stresses in the next chapter, it is Naomi who has sacrificed, who has "paid her way, and Brook's way" by "submitting with loathing" to the "violation" and "defilement" of Caleb's "attempt to be man with his wife" (134–36). Eager to supplant Naomi, Brook of course cannot accept her father's sexual desire for her mother.

Naomi urges her daughter to give up the old man for the young. But when Tony comes to visit Brook, who is studying the Bible with her father, she refuses to see him. Naomi tells Tony not to give up: "This—this other—her father—that will pass" (127). She knows instinctively that the father must give way for the daughter to have a loving sexual relationship with another man. Naomi believes that Tony, the handsome young lover, will persuade where she can only alienate, so she arranges a secret rendezvous between Brook and him. However, she is so narcissistically identified with her daughter that she sets up her own meeting with Tony by a brook in the woods, replicating her tryst with Joe. In telling Tony the story of her past and that Caleb is not Brook's father, Naomi risks exposing her daughter to just that branding of "whore" that has destroyed her own life: "Now that he knew she herself had not waited for marriage did he think . . . What was she putting in his mind! She—a mother" (154–55).

This is more evidence of the irony and ambivalence that characterize the mother-daughter relationship for Glaspell. In planning a way for her daughter to elope to California with Tony, Naomi must give up her life's only consolation, its only joy, her daughter, Brook. As Flax puts it, "she will cease to exist when her daughter leaves because she cannot be a mother without her reciprocal partner, a child" ("Relationships" 33). She is willing to do "this lonely, lonely thing—more lonely than all her life" to ensure that Brook will not have to live as she has, but simultaneously she risks exposing Brook to exactly the fall from patriarchal grace that has destroyed her own life (147). When Caleb leaves for a week to bring the cattle to graze in the mountains, Naomi's plan takes shape. She sends Brook out to the field one evening, where she knows Tony will be waiting. Torn between her desire to keep Brook safely by her side and her desire to push Brook into sexual experience, Naomi expresses her "creed": "Anything that life can do to you is better than not having lived" (167).

Just as in her relationship with her own mother, Naomi's relationship to Brook is bound by silence. She senses that Brook has made a compact with Tony to elope, and together they wash and mend her clothes just as her own mother once did with her, but the illusion that Brook is still "on her father's side . . . must be guarded for her," and neither mentions the impending elopement (173). Mother and daughter both perpetuate the hidden, nonverbal world of women's lives, for which Naomi once condemned her own mother. Both suffer from the gulf between them that, for Flax, reconfirms woman's "devaluation of the female world, denies her a chance to mitigate the mother-daughter conflicts, and forces her to turn more exclusively to men" ("Conflict" 182).

At their last meal together Naomi offers Brook cherries to eat, clearly a vividly symbolic fruit for Glaspell. As Susan Stanford Friedman has remarked, this fruit suggests "an evocative image of the ripening sexuality" of young women (218). Naomi associated the cherries her mother was preserving with the mossy bed on which she made love with Joe; thus her offering of cherries is another sign of her narcissistic attempt to replicate her own life in her daughter, as she now replicates her own mother. But it can also be seen as the mother's offering of the female sexual organ, and of the potential for jouissance, to her daughter. Significantly, the two foods Naomi offers her daughter are cream and cherries—the two colors traditionally symbolic of womanhood, the white of virginity (and, as milk, maternity) the red of sexuality. Luce Irigaray seeks to unite these culturally dichotomized female colors as a metaphor for union with, rather than severance from, the mother's body: "I love you: body shared, undivided. Neither you nor I are severed. . . . You are quite red, and still so white. Both at once. You are pure because you have stayed close to the blood. Because we are both white and red, we give birth to all the colors" (70). Brook is unable, however, to acknowledge any such union. She does not finish eating the cherries but abruptly leaves the table, signifying her ambivalence about accepting the mother's fruit and identifying with her sexuality (173).

Brook's rejection of her mother and the subsequent parting of mother and daughter are portrayed in a marvelous tableau of semiotic gesture, without a word spoken.

> There was a moment when she wanted to say, "Mother, you understand, don't you?" But she had not said it, and the mother who was to be left there alone, knowing, gave no sign. . . . seeing her mother standing there alone she had almost run back in horror, for she knew to what it was she left her. . . . At that her mother's arms extended—

reached—reaching far as they could toward the child—child she had never reached. Brook's arms went as to reach out now, across more than the prairie, but she covered her face, trying to shut out this picture of the brave lonely mother she never saw again. (209–10)

The mother does not speak the language of sign and syntax here but rather an eloquent bodily semiotic, and the daughter's attempt to repress this painful memory diminishes her own capacity for nonverbal communication.

Brook's final cutting of the cord is fittingly accomplished through symbolic signification in a letter she mails to her father. She knows he will read the words to her mother:

Dear Father: I will not see you again. Maybe not for a long time. I had a great temptation, and I was going to do what you did not want me to do, and what I knew myself was not right. Then, at the last minute, I found out . . . that a trap had been set for me—that my own—that some one very close to me, who should protect me, had given out ideas of evil against me, so that he could say—No, I cannot explain, Father. I feel too shamed. (179–80)

The letter leads both Naomi and the reader to believe that Naomi's creed of sexual love has proved to be false. By "trapping" Brook in the female body, Naomi has trapped her in "evil" because it appears from the letter that Tony, given license by the mother's fall, has branded the daughter a whore, if not, as the reader most dreads, tried to rape her. But we find out later, in Brook's reflections as a mature woman, that the written word was a lie. When Tony simply revealed, "Your mother knows. It is what she wants," Brook ran away from him, declaring, "I will not be tricked! I will not be trapped like this!" (211). What is the trap but sexual intimacy, which Brook dreads as a violation of her autonomy, dating back to her pre-oedipal relation to her mother? Tony, as the mother's champion, is actually the mother's surrogate. Ironically, the intensity of Brook's first object-relational tie with her mother prevents her from the sexual intimacy her mother so desperately wants her to have with a young man. Glaspell's tale offers moving evidence of Chodorow's assertion that preoedipal issues of merger and separation dominate women's lives.

Why does Brook lie? By intimating that Tony has attempted to rape her, she has destroyed her mother's faith in romantic love, while at the same time blaming her for the violation of that love. Brook has rejected the sexual mother and replaced her with the patriarchal virgin, Sylvia Waite, who "said she would be my mother and take me away with her." Further, she in turning to Sylvia, she "knew that nothing could hurt her mother more" (212). Thus Brook commits a symbolic matricide that is indirectly effective: her mother lives "in a daze" until she dies some years later (203). The only way Brook can achieve selfhood is to "kill" the mother, but simultaneously killing the mother's body in herself renders her incapable of sexual and emotional intimacy in adult life.

Book Four explores Brook's guilt over this matricide and her eventual reconnection with her dead mother and her own sexuality. It begins with her son, Evans Leonard, now eighteen, waiting for his mother in a café in the Gare du Nord in Paris, self-consciously ordering her a drink as if for a lover, as Glaspell illustrates the too-intimate pre-oedipal and oedipal attachment handed down to yet another generation:

> Mother's beautiful brown hair—gold in it—thick, wavy, yet close-lying, giving that handsome form of her head. He let his thought linger on it with pleasure, pleasure just a little resolute, closing over the thought that it hadn't gone on turning gray, that she needn't have cried. Frowning against what threatened—the wondering, would it have gone on turning gray, if Father hadn't . . . Nonsense! Why shouldn't Mother look young? Younger? Younger now than then? Father gone and Mother looking younger? (185)

Evans's enigmatic thoughts here refer to his belief that his father, terminally ill after injuries resulting from World War I, committed suicide by taking an overdose of his medication on a day when his mother—who had spent nine years nursing him (a sacrificing caretaker, just like her own mother)—found some gray hairs on her head and started to cry. It is natural that Evans would feel ambivalent about this event, since it fulfills his unconscious desire to get rid of his father and replace him in his mother's affections. However, the thought that most threatened—"Father gone and Mother looking younger?"—reveals a deeper fear of maternal omnipotence. He tries to repress thoughts that his father died so that his mother could live, thus making his mother responsible for killing his father, devouring the father, in effect, to renew her youth. This derives from his own pre-oedipal fear of engulfment by the omnipotent mother. Glaspell shows that the structure of Evans's early family life, with a father absent in war and then weakened by illness and a mother who has repressed her own sexuality and individuality in a life of service to husband and son, will produce yet another generation of misogynistic fathers in Evans unless there is some radical change, unless Brook accepts her sexual energy and redirects it toward a man other than her son.

Evans is waiting to meet his mother to accompany her on her first return home. Her father, Caleb, now back in Illinois living with Naomi's brother and his family, is dying and wants to see Brook. But she postpones the trip, ostensibly because she has discovered in a Paris shop a yellow dress reminiscent of the one her mother made for her so many years ago, but in actuality because she now stands at a crossroad facing a decision that repeats and resurrects her decision at eighteen between father/chastity and mother/sexuality. She is torn between two men: one, Colonel Fowler, an elderly, benevolent yet authoritative patriarch; the other, a youthful, sensuous, rebellious scholar, Erik Helge. At thirty-eight, Brook renews the mother-daughter identification she once abandoned in facing a choice that could redeem her matricide and her mother's life of sacrifice. Should she choose Colonel Fowler, the "reasonable thing, making a home for herself and her boy," even though life with him would offer "little that to her was life"? (247) Should she repeat her youthful decision, choosing the safety of father and a life of self-sacrifice for her child, or should she choose the fearful sexual intimacy of mother?

In her golden dress, Brook is whisked away from a musical soiree by Erik, who takes her dancing. While driving home through the forest, the car breaks down, and they spend the whole night talking together. He does not want her to return to America to visit her father, but instead hopes that she will go to China with him on his research grant money. The Colonel tries to argue her out of this "little fling," takes "command" of her life, and makes all the arrangements for her visit to America, a paternalism Brook has finally come to resent. When the Colonel wants to know whether Erik intends to marry her, Brook questions his right to ask: "She was not a child, to have her affairs taken out of her hands" (253).

Erik's opposition to her planned trip to America echoes her mother's similar pleas to give up her father. When Brook says, "Even my son feels I must go to my father," Erik argues passionately that her father is old, "at the end of things," while "these are the years for love and love is here. . . . It is now—or die not having lived! Oh, how can one argue it?" That Glaspell intends to parallel Erik with Naomi is further evident when Brook thinks, "Where had she heard that before? Some one had said that before!" (269). During this discussion Erik and Brook are again "deep in the forest, as if they were alone on earth," the edenic locus of sexual love. Like her mother so many years before with Joe, it is here that they consummate their love (270).

Brook's choice of Erik may be a problematic one for feminists attempting to place Glaspell's novels within a feminist tradition. Brook, who has no work to give her own life meaning, gives up visiting her father to accommodate Erik's "passion in his work." Like her mother, she appears to find her creed in the traditional romantic myth of woman sacrificing self for the ecstasy of love. Furthermore, she has been permitted to pursue a liberated sexuality by her husband's suicide. He "rescues" her, almost as if she were a princess in a fairy tale, from a life of drudgery caring for him because, as he states, "You were for something else. You were for life" (217). It seems that Brook can only achieve sexual liberation through the agency, and with the permission of, men. However, that *Brook Evans*, written in 1928, focuses on sexual liberation may reflect both cultural and biographical reasons specific to the time. As Elaine Showalter has shown, during the feminist "crash" of the 1920s following the failure of women's suffrage "to change the basic patterns of sex-role conditioning," women's energies were rerouted primarily to relationships with men (10–16). Nevertheless, it is important not to underestimate or devalue what that sexual liberation meant to women of Glaspell's generation, emerging from the repression of their parents' late-Victorian mores. The freedom for women to experience sexual pleasure was a significant gain, and Glaspell presents it as such here.

In addition, at this time in her life Glaspell was concerned with reaffirming sexual vitality in a mature protagonist because of her own love affair with a younger man, Norman Matson. Brook reflects anxieties about aging and a justification of the older woman's right to sexual expression. She voices fears that a woman's "youth was gone at thirty-eight" and dreads becoming "one of those silly women, running around alone, trying to seem younger than she was" (200). Further, although *Brook Evans* is dedicated to Norman Matson, and Erik Helge's Nordic background is derived from Matson's Norwegian descent, Erik's characterization is pure Cook. Critics have been puzzled by Glaspell's apparent adoration of Jig Cook, a narcissistic, infantile man, seemingly incapable of maturity in either life or work and even at times "megalomaniacal" (Makowsky 89). Of course, narcissistic men like Cook (and Erik) make excessive demands upon their mother-lover, but coming out of the oppressively paternalistic late nineteenth century, Glaspell could only experience, and portray in her novels, sexually vital relationships with childish men. Her choice of the infantile man, as opposed to the paternalistic, is a bid for freedom within those historical parameters, as much as it may appear to be a failure of feminism. For Glaspell, childlike men encourage female freedom of expression, and they have what Glaspell most prized in Cook—a joi de vivre, a sense of adventure that the dour fathers of her parents' generation could only repress. "If I were limited to telling just one thing," she wrote about Cook, "I think I would say it was the play in him—rich, unashamed play" (*Road* 303).

In a novel that has vividly illustrated the sacrifice of female sexuality at patriarchal insistence, it is significant that, in Brook's husband's suicide, Glaspell portrays an instance of male sacrifice so that female sexuality may thrive. She reverses the oppressive gender dichotomy that has "decapitated" Naomi and Brook thus far: the unwritten law that female sexuality must be bound and that woman must sacrifice herself for others. In this novel, as in several others, Glaspell points to the necessity for a more feminized male, one who will accept female sexuality and put the needs of woman before his own, rather than expecting the opposite relation as normative. Like Tony, Erik is a mother surrogate. In choosing him, Brook chooses the feminized male or, rather, a relation that will reestablish the primacy of the mother-child dyad through its sexual intimacy. In having rejected her mother, "a powerful source of women's sexuality—the memories of early infantile gratification—is denied," which "correspondingly reduces sensuality as a whole" (Flax, "Conflict" 183). Brook is not sacrificing herself to go with Erik to China but giving up the visit to her father in America. In effect, as her mother predicted, Brook is finally relinquishing her oedipal attachment to father so that she might love another man. She is returning to her mother.

But in order to do so, Brook must confront the guilt of her matricide and her deep longing for the absent mother she banished: "'Heartbreak, yes. I broke her heart,' Brook said, sitting very still before her desk, facing it as she had never faced it, wanting now to know" (204–5). She faces here, in a climactic chapter, the central question of the novel:

> Why had there not been ease between her and her mother? . . . She had soon come to know that her mother did not exist for herself, but existed for Brook. Why should this, of all things, exasperate one? Why was it so hard for her to show love in response to the completeness of this love? . . . There was a tensity in her mother's love. Was that what irked her? Did she resent the knowledge it was she alone her mother loved—as if this were a responsibility, making her the other part of something not of her choosing? (205–6)

Glaspell's neologism, "tensity," captures all the conflict and ambivalence of the pre-oedipal mother-daughter tie. The mother's love is too intense and creates tension in the child. The child, male or female, cannot fulfill a lover's role for the lonely, isolated mother. This responsibility makes it impossible for the child to show love in response to the mother's totally engulfing love. Her autonomy violated by the mother's need, the daughter feels manipulated into becoming the "other part of something not of her choosing." This is the "essential female tragedy" Adrienne Rich refers to, that the patriarchal institution of motherhood forces daughters to reject their mothers since, in order to survive, the daughter must cut the most important nurturing tie in her life. Brook now realizes that in the past she "could not go ahead if she went as one with her mother. So she left her out, though taking all she could get from her!" (208)

This insight allows her to acknowledge and mourn her abandonment of her mother, and it revives her ability to read the signs of a female semiotic. Once again Glaspell expresses renewed mother-daughter identification appropriately through mirror images, as Brook looks at herself in the mirror wearing the new yellow dress, a sign of her reunion with the mother's sexual body:

> Still by the mirror, hair not made orderly, still flushed by that feeling of dancing with the strong Northerner [Erik], . . . she met the life in her own eyes, saw the thought in them before she quite knew what she was thinking of—that she was as old now as her mother had been when she last saw her. This woman at whom she looked, in the dress her mother had wanted for her, radiant, eager in the thought of dancing with that man all life, she—Brook—was as old now as the woman who stood by the side of the house extending her arms to the daughter who left her alone (202).

Through reliving the silent moment of parting from her mother and, in effect, becoming her mother, Brook returns to the semiotic bodily knowing that predates the verbal logos. She sees before she cognitively knows and is "charged" with sexuality, experiencing a joyful recovery of jouissance. Then, momentarily losing the courage to go on thinking of her mother, she thinks that she ought to write to her father, but symbolic signification is quickly overborne by the power of an alogical, affective semiotic that can be verbalized only by the amorphous word "it," but that is clearly the resurgence of her connection to mother: "'Dear Father,' she began, but after a little found she was making aimless marks on the paper. She crumpled it and took another. 'Dear—' She sat looking down at it. 'Mother,' something within her said. It rose, took her, 'Mother!'" (202).

*Brook Evans* does not conclude with Brook and Erik riding happily off into the sunset, however, as Glaspell again violates the norms of romance fiction, just as she did in *Fidelity*. Book Five focuses on Evans's return to America alone, to bring the reconnection with Naomi full circle. Thus the major theme in this novel is not romantic love but generational continuity and the amelioration of destructive familial patterns founded in the cultural repression of female sexuality. Evans ostensibly returns to see his grandfather, but continuity with the past is established through his foremothers.[3] Evans's connection with the past is initiated by seeing Naomi's picture in the family photo album, itself a locus of semiotic expression through its image of his grandmother's eyes that speak of "felt things" rather than "exact" knowing: "It was there for Evans—the gentle look of one who saw, felt things. So she was here, too, behind him. . . . those eyes that looked up at him from the old album—Naomi—his grandmother. What did they say? He did not know. He did not exactly know" (300, 312).

When Evans goes for a walk he discovers the "secret place . . . where the brook became as a curving arm," the locus of the primal scene between his grandparents. How fitting that here, lying as it were in his grandmother's curving arm, he becomes initiated into the secret of his mother's sexuality, as he reads the letter in which she informs him of her marriage to Erik. Evans's first reaction is, just as Brook's once was, the pain of the rejected lover. He identifies with his dead father "in one of those graves—forgotten" and rages against his mother: "So Mother had kicked it all over— Father, him, her own father, the Colonel—given up the whole past—gone off by herself—this stranger" (307). Just as Brook once did, he sides with his father, seeing him as the sacrificial victim, "The rotten time Father had had!" and identifying with him as well: "He'd live in England—be like his father—the kind of person who didn't throw everybody down for— for—" (308). Long his mother's sole love object, Evans feels abandoned and outraged that his mother should suddenly stop sacrificing her own happiness and sexuality for him. He walks off his anger, then returns to the brook and is calmed by the maternal lullaby of "that place he liked—it was as if he came back to a secret place he had known a long time. He lay on the moss by the oak-tree, closed his eyes, and the brook was like a friend" (309).

Here, through the "intimations" of the brook's music, Evans hears his dead father's voice: "Who had a long hard time? Your mother had a long hard time" (310). Evans continues to read his mother's letter and, with his imagined father's approbation, comes to feel that "Father had guarded her. Then he must guard her now. All right. All right, then. Sure. He would stand by Mother" (312). This ending may seem equivocal to a feminist view at first. In the traditionally patriarchal way, Evans appears to accept and "guard" his mother's sexuality, thus taking on his father's possessive role. But it must be remembered that what is being guarded is not possession of the mother but her freedom of sexual expression with "that stranger," the man of her choice. In addition, the father's voice is heard through the brook, and the brook *is* Brook. Similar to Erik, Evans's father is a feminized male, and his voice is merged with that of the boy's foremothers. Evans perceives parental union in the commingling of symbolic signification (letter) with semiotic intimation (brook). Thus Evans gives up his pre-oedipal and oedipal pretensions to sole possession of his mother, and he does so with his father's support. Glaspell shows that a mother who accepts her own sexuality and a father who accepts female sexuality are both necessary to engender a son who will not repress autonomy and sexuality in his future wife and daughters, who will, in effect, break the cycle. As Chodorow and Dinnerstein emphasize, patriarchal dominance must be relinquished to unbind children from the oppressive aspects of their mother's love.

Glaspell's use of the word "intimations" refers to a book of poems by a young American poet entitled *Intimations*, which Evans bought on the Left Bank and was reading at the train station in the opening of Book Four (183). She appears to have invented this book, but it indicates that, like Kristeva, she connects the semiotic with avant-garde poetic language. Further, Glaspell may be alluding to Wordsworth's "Intimations of Immortality" ode, a poem she will use with far more ironic intent years later in her last novel, *Judd Rankin's Daughter*. The ending of *Brook Evans* does suggest images of Romantic pantheism:

> He smelled drying grass—the new hay. The brook and the trees— this pure clear sound of the brook within the more freely moving sound of the trees—music—intimations. . . . Yes, he would stand by his mother. Love. He didn't know it yet. Some day. Yes, perhaps. He felt close to all who were in their graves. He closed his eyes and listened. The wind passed over his face. Through all the future it would flow softly—with deep sweet meaning—with mystery—this hour—intimations from the brook. (312)

Filled with mystery and nonverbal "deep sweet meaning," this voice of immortality is too grounded in earth, in the mother's body, to coincide with Wordsworth's "visionary gleam" which, while it exalts nature, is embued with a Victorian nostalgia for the loss of heaven, a patriarchal eternity, and is dominated by images of sunlight, an amorphous but certainly paternal godhead. This is a more modernist vision of an eternity found in sexual and natural regeneration. All the natural beauty—from the new hay to the trees, the brook, and the music—repeats precisely Naomi's exalted experience of sexual love with Joe and her communion with nature that her grandson here relives, becoming one with the mother and uniting past with future. This is Glaspell's feminist vision of maternal reconnections healing divisive patriarchal binarisms, reuniting mother/father, body/spirit, semiotic/symbolic.

A long and psychologically intense novel, *Brook Evans* is one of the bravest and most searching literary explorations of the mother-daughter relationship that we have. It portrays female adolescent development in detail and would contribute greatly to any college course on women's literature, history of feminism, or the psychology of women. In her next novel, *Fugitive's Return*, Glaspell continues to explore the mother-daughter relationship, but by using Greece as her setting, she widens the psychological parameters of that novel to a mythic level.

> We are at the very least forced to recognize that the suppression of
> women's writing is historically and psychologically directly related to
> male sexual violence against women, that men have cut out the tongues
> of speaking women and cut off the hands of the writing woman for fear
> of what she will say about them and about the world. If we arrest
> the alphabet we wrest from the tapestry and translate the voice of
> the stick in the sand, the poem is a four-letter word, RAPE.
>
> —*Jane Marcus*

# 4

## *Fugitive's Return* (1929) Part I

### Flight to the Past

*Fugitive's Return*, Glaspell's most sophisticated and complex novel, requires the same psychoanalytic methodology as used in the previous chapter to make sense of the protagonist's exploration of her past; however, set in Greece, it also requires myth criticism to delineate the mythological allusions that enrich it. In addition, Glaspell continues to focus intensely on differences in language, giving female ways of speaking and knowing their most poetic evocation in this novel and necessitating further application of the Kristevan female semiotic. Similar to *Brook Evans*, the novel can be divided into three sections, but whereas the earlier novel traces intergenerational growth toward sexual liberation, *Fugitive's Return* focuses on the psychological regeneration of one woman, Irma Lee Shraeder, as she recovers from an attempted suicide by traveling to Greece and reexamining her past. *Fugitive's Return* charts the fugitive's flight from a self that has become a living death, her slow process of return to the lost child buried within, and thence to rebirth.

Since her divorce from husband, Dan, and the death of her young daughter, Birdie, from infantile paralysis, Irma has retreated "down into the safety of her nothingness, where she could see without being" (33). Catastrophically divorced from self and world, her "immunity" from pain is preserved by never allowing conscious access to the buried past. Irma represents a telling portrait of the alienating effect of repression, referring to herself as "that which looked on" and wondering, "Was it indeed herself, watching something walking through a life arranged for it?" (92). Irma is another self-sacrificing mother; as with Naomi in *Brook Evans*, her child "was all: reason for Irma Shraeder, reason for the universe" (4). Without her reason for existence and now that "even the suffering was dead," Irma tries to kill herself (7).

In one of Glaspell's most striking in medias res openings, the novel begins with Irma bathing and observing her body in the mirror, preparing to commit suicide by taking sleeping pills. This mirror scene and the first mirror scene in *Brook Evans* bracket the tragedy of woman's life when it is defined solely in terms of male desire. The youthful Naomi feels "the beauty of one who has been ardently loved," and when she looks into the mirror, she sees "that which made her beautiful"—the memory of Joe's desire for her (13, 20). But in Irma, Glaspell portrays an older woman, "less desirable now, breasts, hips fuller." She can hardly bear to look at herself in the mirror because "a man who wanted this body . . . had ceased to want. Now she herself had ceased to want it" (2). With the loss of male desire comes an almost total loss of identity.

The second chapter, as Irma carefully dresses herself for death, expands on themes announced in the first. Combing her hair, she recalls her first meeting with Dan, and the reader begins to glimpse one cause of the repressed rage that motivates her self-destructive impulses. Her one "gift from beauty" is her "luxuriant, lustrous" hair, and of course hair is the symbol par excellence of male-inscribed female sexuality. She recalls her first meeting with Dan: "'I saw it across the room' Dan said, 'Whose hair is that?'" For him she was merely hair. As Glaspell reveals later, he had no notion of her as a person, and he was bitterly disappointed when she did not fulfill the sexual promise of her hair. Indeed, one might follow the changes to Irma's hair throughout the novel as a précis of the changes in her self-development. Here she coils it about her head, making "her face more than ever as a mask." Her cool, masklike calm is her repressive defense against the "chaos" and "panic" she knows is "right there" (5).

This novel is one of Glaspell's most overtly feminist works; like "Jury of Her Peers," it represents a subtle exploration of female rage and revenge and, ultimately, a tale of women uniting in opposition to patriarchal law, for Irma is saved from death and restored to life by "sisters." First, her cousin, Janet, interrupts the death ritual, finding Irma attempting to write a suicide note but unable to begin because she can't write her name: "To write one's name is an assertion of one's self. When you write your name, you know who you are" (11). Another apt symbol of Irma's loss of identity is a psychosomatic muteness, which is soon evident to both of them: "She thought she had spoken, but she heard nothing, nothing but Janet, saying: 'Yes, Irma? Yes?' Then they had gone, her words" (17). Disoriented, Irma cannot tell if she has drunk the dissolved sleeping pills or not. At any rate, something has been killed, along with the identity of Irma Shraeder, wife and mother, and that is her "words"—the voice of symbolic signification. She is Cixous's decapitated woman, whose tongue has been cut off but whose "body talks" ("Castration" 49). Her surrogate sister, Janet, "opens the door from life" by bringing a friend, Myra Freeman, who gives Irma her passport and a ticket to Greece she is unable to use (11). With her former identity silenced and erased by the name of another, Irma sails to Greece to begin a new life.

The nurturance of sisterhood echoes the pre-oedipal mother-daughter intimacy. This is particularly evident in Irma's relationship with Janet, which dates to childhood. Irma feels "she had never been intimate with any one. She did not know how. She had not learned it," but then she immediately recalls "she and Janet, little girls together, scolding imaginary children in the apple boughs" (14). Like many of Glaspell's heroines, Irma's isolation and alienation from self, sexuality, and humanity relates back to a crucial disjunction from the pre-oedipal mother and from mother earth. It is key that her one and only intimate relationship, with Janet, is recalled in memories of play that enact an edenic maternal world and a vaginal space:

> Janet. Irma. Playing house together in the apple-trees back of the barn. You can make houses of fallen leaves, too—rooms opening into one another; you can turn a corner, making a doorway, a threshold. . . . and between the grove and the house, the covered well. You let down the bucket. (12)

Irma's two other mentors, Myra and Anna Mead, an archaeologist who befriends her on the boat to Greece, are women dissociated from men—a suffragist and a scholar, both unmarried. They are her first guides to a new source of identity independent of male definition. Janet brings Myra, "who worked so hard for suffrage . . . and instead of taking passage for the Piraeus she has to go West for the Party," and Irma thinks, "In her life there had been no 'work'—no party" (15–16). In taking on the identity of a woman who is defined by work instead of sexuality and/or maternity, Irma is cleansed of her past identity, allowing her to question other possibilities: "If you are Miss, then you have never been married at all," she thinks. "Who are you, when you are Miss Myra Freeman?" (25). Anna Mead, the archaeologist, is also a worker; Irma thinks of her as engaged in a "fervor of rescue work." But Irma is ambivalent, for obvious reasons, about one who unearths the buried past, "busily scratching for old secrets" (40).

Significantly, Janet and Myra have chopped off Irma's hair to make her look something like Myra's passport picture. Upon their arrival in Greece, Anna confides, "You have an atrocious hair-cut!" She takes Irma to "Louis of the Grande Bretagne," who "trimmed it very short—indeed cropped it" (43–44). The symbolism of cutting her hair is fairly obvious: her beneficent mothers begin to free her from man as she becomes Myra Freeman.[1] The second cut, however, marks a return to beauty, but a beauty that is identified with the timelessness of ancient Greece and the dignity of mature womanhood as opposed to the doll-like ideal with the "vividly penciled mouth" of the modern age (20). Irma's hair appears now "as something worn a long time gone," and she can look at herself in the mirror, "for she did not see there one she had known before" (44).

Irma's physical transformation is completed by being taken to a shop where the Greek women weave silk and she is draped in "the folds of an old beauty": "She watched them at their looms. She would like to do this too, liking the rhythm of these movements, as the beautiful fabric, heavy, supple, grew" (45). A key word in this passage is "rhythm." Similar to Ruth in *Fidelity* and to so many of Glaspell's protagonists, Irma is an outsider; she has no home, no place where she belongs: "She moved just outside a rhythm in which others moved facilely, and which she, outside, felt, often with resentment, but sometimes with a wistfulness that gave it a beauty they who were within did not seem to find" (3). In Greece she finds a rhythm, that is, a place to belong, a home among a people (primarily women) whose rhythms she eventually shares. Further, as Kristeva repeats in several contexts, rhythm is one of the basic attributes of the semiotic (133–34). Glaspell is so artful, therefore, in making muteness the psychosomatic expression of Irma's alienation. In Greece she will learn to speak the body, to weave the semiotic rhythms of a new language, a women's language, and the story she will share tells of rape and of the saving strength and joy of female bonds.

Glaspell's mythical allusion here is appropriately to Procne and Philomela.[2] As Jane Marcus has remarked about Woolf's use of this myth in *Between the Acts*, "The voice of the nightingale, the voice of the shuttle weaving its story of oppression, is the voice which cries for freedom."

Marcus equates Woolf with Procne, as an interpreter of the signs of Philomel's text, the "feminist reader of the peplos, the woven story of her silenced sister's rape," and Glaspell may be said to play the same role here ("Still Practice" 215). This marvelously rich first section of the novel illustrates Glaspell's modernism in her facility with the "mythical method," to use T. S. Eliot's term. Like Joyce, Glaspell here unites the present with the past through mythic parallels as a way of "giving a shape and a significance" to her art (Eliot 178). Like Joyce, she suggests that humanity experiences a kind of cyclical eternity through children and through "metempsychosis," to use the Joycean word, moments in which the past is reincarnated in the present. Since Irma has lost a daughter, a daughter she replaces through adoption by the end of the novel, another important classical allusion is to the myth of Demeter and Persephone and the ritual celebration of their reunion, the Eleusinian Mysteries. In addition, Glaspell contrasts Dionysianism and Apollonianism throughout the novel.

Chapter 9 begins two years after Irma has settled at Delphi in the same setting Glaspell described in *The Road to the Temple*, although here the house she inhabits is within the sacred precinct of temple, oracle, and theater. As Glaspell and Cook did, Irma lives among shepherding peasants intimately tied to the land, much as their ancient ancestors were. Irma's Delphi, however, is primarily that of the oikos; she is surrounded by women in a healing all-female world, like an echo in the present of that long-vanished Greek past, as described by Jane Harrison, of matriarchal priestesses conducting chthonic rituals. As Veronica Makowsky points out, the women Irma encounters here "exhibit aspects of Irma's past and the roles of all women" (109). They mythically and symbolically act out Irma's inner conflicts, as well as the binaristic roles that confine women in patriarchal culture.

The women's names and perhaps their characters were suggested by Glaspell's actual experience in Greece, but *Fugitive's Return* is an elaborately stylized work of art in which actual experience serves Glaspell's fictional purposes. As in *The Road to the Temple*, where Glaspell describes Athanasius ("Thanasie"), a waiter who left his job at the Pythian Apollo Hotel "and took up the business of giving us the kind of life we wanted in Delphi" (325), so Irma is served by "old Elias who did so well for himself at the Phythian Apollo" (*Fugitive's Return* 47–48). Athanasius's sister was Stamula, who lived with her family "in the house just above us" (*Road* 436). In *The Road to the Temple*, we do not find out anything more about this woman, but in *Fugitive's Return*, Elias's sister,

Stamula, becomes Irma's closest friend. However, the fictional Elias has another sister, Vascelo, whom he installs with her two children "to live below in the house and cook" for Irma (53). These two women personify the Dionysian and Apollonian selves that battle within Irma. Vascelo is the abandoned woman, a Medea who rages and beats her son, while Stamula is the calm and loving Penelope:

> Not easily did Vascelo live without a husband, as she had lived now these four years. She would not get a husband, either—not with her misshapen boy Jannes, and her little girl. Plenty of young girls in Greece going without husbands these days. So they would laugh when Vascelo went into her rages and screamed in the village street. . . . Stamula was gentle and goodness looked from her face. But Stamula had her own house, where every board shone. . . . The distaff and loom were happy with Stamula. In her calm fingers thread did not break or tangle. (53–54)

As the Dionysian aspect, Vascelo represents Irma's repressed rage, just as she lives "below" in the house. Secretly, Vascelo would "steal over to the village and indulge herself in anger as another would in wine," whereas "it seemed almost in the center of the Temple of Apollo Stamula had been born" (70). Bearing all the marks of patriarchal favor, Stamula is Irma's Apollonian ego ideal, the woman she would like to be, a beloved wife and respected mother who is untroubled by buried passions and whose place in the community is assured.

Another Dionysian element is introduced when Elias brings Theodora, a Greek refugee from war with the Turks in Smyrna, to be Irma's maid. Theodora is the beautiful, exotic dancing woman desired by men, and she embodies Irma's sexuality. When Irma hesitates to accept her services, Theodora begins to dance before her and babbles stories "in a torrent of words" (73). This character is modeled closely on Glaspell's and Cook's actual refugee servant, Theodora, whose antics entertained them hugely. In the mountain camp they had to supply her with a bonfire each evening:

> We found the purpose of this evening fire was that Theodora jump over it—or through it, indeed. It was as some mad rite in which she could not be restrained. Around this fire she told us stories of her village beyond the Bosphorus. . . . In some of them Jig recognized the most ancient stories of Greece. (*Road* 383–84)

Symbolically, Glaspell's fictional Theodora is a bridge figure who exhibits both Dionysian and Apollonian elements: she is "courteous" yet "defiant," "humble and proud." Her sexuality is aggressive, like Vascelo's anger, yet she will become engaged to marry; she will be accepted into the patriarchal system because of her physical beauty.

In chapter 12, Glaspell portrays a tableau illustrating the symbolic relation of these women. First Irma tries to unite her battling selves, Vascelo and Theodora, by holding out "a hand to the one, to the other, thus asking them to be at peace" (76). Irma as ego and Stamula as idealized ego (symbolized by their spatial position in the house above Vascelo) are trying to keep peace among the libidinous drives, rage and sexuality. Yet Vascelo's abuse, as Elias would "shake and beat" her into submission, remains a painful reminder of the consequences of female transgression (53, 71). As Vascelo in turn berates her son, Glaspell illustrates the origin and replication of familial violence in a patriarchal system.

Finally, there is Constantina, who represents the motherless daughter. She is modeled on an "eleven-year-old shepherd girl, Constantina, who, since she was seven years old, had many nights been alone on the mountain with the sheep" (*Road* 348). Cook was "thrilled" at this little living exemplar of the past, and the solitary girl certainly must have touched Glaspell. "Looking into her face as she leaned to our fire," she wrote, "we would feel something older than Greece" (*Road* 348). The fictional Constantina indeed becomes identified with something older than Greece, the ancient matriarchal voice of the Delphic Oracle. She also signifies the buried child within Irma, for her story "was never all told to [Irma] in words; it came to her in what happened to her own life" (*Fugitive's Return* 57).

"Woe unto the Greek whose children are all daughters" (57). A fifth daughter instead of the desperately wanted son, Constantina was disowned by her father, and her birth caused her mother's death. Her father refused to give her a dowry and cursed her, "You are not a boy, but you are not a girl. You are feet—and a voice!" (59). Without beauty, "little more than a dwarf, so dry and wizened she looked as much an old woman as a girl," Constantina "would not become a woman any man would marry," and without a dowry she lives "outside the lives of others," laughed at and stoned by the group, a reflection of Irma's own alienation (60). Genderless, she is also wordless, again like Irma: "Even to Stamula, Constantina said little, as if she knew her life was not with others, as if she did not have words" (61). She retreats to the mountain to herd her father's flocks, but her attempt to take up a male role exhibits a kind of hubris that must be struck down. A tall shepherd youth, Andreas, "the most beautiful youth of the mountain, he whom a stranger had called the new Apollo" rapes her, then prefers to go to prison for it rather than be forced by her father into marrying her. That settles her fate: "No one would marry her now. She was not a woman. She was a shepherd" (63). Like Irma, undesired by men, she cannot be a woman. Motherless, she has no succor and no recourse.

The significance of the shepherd's nickname, "new Apollo," should be obvious, echoing again Jane Harrison's characterization of Apollo as a "woman-hater" and as the apogee of patriarchy.[3] The rape of Constantina takes place in or near the Temple of Apollo, as Stamula shows Irma:

> They reached the Sacred Way [to Eleusis], but turned from it and followed the wall before the temple. Ascending steps, climbing over fallen stones and through grasses, Stamula pointed into a lowered place, as a cellar, though small; as a grave, though large. (69)

Glaspell's description is ambiguous as to whether this hole is "before" the temple, by the wall, or "in the temple" (69). It is ambiguous because Glaspell is conflating the actual temple and the graveyard described in *The Road to the Temple* (there is no graveyard in *Fugitive's Return*) in order to express her outrage at the rape of the graves she observed there (see chapter 2) through the rape of Constantina.

Constantina is therefore identified with the Oracle, as her rape below ground enacts Apollo's "victorious" usurpation of the chthonic "cult of the Earth-Mother and the Earth-Maidens" at the omphalos, as described by Harrison (*Prolegomena* 319). This identification is also suggested by her father's characterization of her as "a voice," and it becomes even more explicit later in the novel (264). But the mythological allusions of Constantina's characterization are manifold. In this silenced rape victim Glaspell portrays another Philomela, and as a motherless daughter raped underground, Constantina also signifies Persephone. Irma will become her Demeter; although she needs to be reunited with the silenced child within herself, Irma also needs to rediscover the lost mother-daughter intimacy in order to love and to live fully.

In *The Road to the Temple*, the villagers referred to Cook and Glaspell as "Kyrios Kouk and Kyria." One senses in that text that the feminized title, although one of respect, erased Glaspell's identity. Publicly she played the role of wife to Kyrios Kouk, a role in which she was powerless to change things she did not like, such as the desecration of the graves or Cook's drinking bouts at the wine shop that made even Thanasie "shake his head at me darkly" (412, 426). In *Fugitive's Return*, however, as Irma's identity transforms again, from Myra into "the Kyria of the

Archai," the impersonal title empowers her, just as her silence does. The villagers begin to regard her with the superstitious awe reserved for a goddess, and indeed Glaspell intends her incarnation into "the prophetess of the temple," where she is identified with the Oracle just as Constantina is:

> The dress she wore was so near the color of stones that had once been the temple that when she walked among them she seemed of them. . . . Her hair was longer than when she came, and she was more beautiful now than at first, as if she had grown in grace, alone with the antiquities and the fields watered by the Castalian Spring. (50–52)

Irma has come a long way from the naked, powerless, self-destructive woman of the novel's opening. But her stonelike reserve is another mask, a seeming Apollonianism still hiding the repressed Dionysian self. Stamula's Apollonianism, too, is largely a pose, for she teaches Irma to weave and in doing so teaches her to speak an intimate, subversive female tongue.

> Though the Kyria did not speak, and understood but little Greek, she and Stamula would communicate with each other at the loom. These difficulties had made them companions, sharing, not only the difficulty, but pleasure when the handicap was overcome and communication flowed between them. (64)

Chapter 11 presents a truly remarkable piece of l'écriture feminine, one of those passages of Glaspell's writing that leaves the reader wondering how she could have written a text that so embodies feminist theories of six decades later, and one that is at the same time so richly allusive mythologically that it should stand as a classic example of modernism. It is a chapter that celebrates a joyful female semiotic, opening readers to an erotic "female aesthetic of reading," to use Jane Marcus's terms. "If we use Kristeva's concept of the difference between the symbolic and the semiotic, in which the semiotic is laughter, rhythm, sounds without meaning, that which is outside discourse . . . we may define a female aesthetic of reading as 'semiotic' as opposed to male 'symbolic' aesthetic, with fixed meanings and 'correct' orderly relations between words and meanings" ("Still Practice" 239).

Through sisterhood with Stamula, Irma begins to reconnect with the body. Glaspell makes it very clear at the beginning of the novel that Irma was divorced from physicality, particularly through her inability to dance and her alienation from rhythm (3, 29). When we realize that their looms are placed on the Dionysian stage, the semiotic as well as the mythological allusions proliferate:

> To express what they meant they would often have to act things out. There was place for this around the loom, on the huge flat stones before the curve of ascending seats where no one sat. Stamula —always in her dark peasant dress of the tight waist and long full skirt, her head cloth of dark red, had more things to tell, and many gestures for her stories. The Kyria, wearing a dress of supple wool, the color of the old stones when the light falls upon them, the waist line just below the breasts, hair bound with bands to keep it from falling about her face as she worked, had fewer movements, and it had at first been hard for her to express in this manner. But her face had become—was it happier?—warmer, perhaps, in working with Stamula, and it was as if in learning to work at the loom she had found how to let her hands, her body, do the other things for her. (64–65)

The detailed description of their dresses links Irma and Stamula with Demeter and Persephone as they are so often represented in the statuary, votive reliefs, and vase paintings that Glaspell saw in the museum at Eleusis and in the National Museum in Athens, as well as in Harrison's illustrations. These goddesses are distinguished by their stately robes, the simple sleeveless chiton with the graceful peplos draped over it (see figs. 1 and 2). Irma and Stamula vividly express Cixous's belief that woman speaks the body, physically materializing her thought, as Stamula enacts "a little play" of feeding her husband and manipulating him through his piggish appetite, and they both laugh together—the exultant laughter of Medusa. Their pleasure as the "communication flowed between them" is surely an erotically charged "jouissance of profound desire" (Marcus, "Still Practice" 246). Irma's face becomes warmer as she finds out "how to let her hands, her body, do the other things for her," and she rediscovers bodily joy through communicative union with Stamula:

> Both women would laugh—that is Stamula would laugh and the Kyria would smile. Talking to each other in this way made them more humorously and more deeply acquainted than if they had been able to talk with words. A thing said by acting seemed to mean, not only the thing said, but something of which it was a part, something underneath. (65)

Fig. 1. The Grand Relief of Eleusis. From George Mylonas, *Eleusis and the Eleusinian Mysteries*. Copyright 1961 by Princeton University Press. Reprinted by permission of Princeton University Press.

Fig. 2. Relief of Demeter and Hekate. From George Mylonas, *Eleusis and the Eleusinian Mysteries.* Copyright 1961 by Princeton University Press. Reprinted by permission of Princeton University Press.

This passage beautifully exemplifies a female semiotic with its laughter, rhythm, and sounds without fixed meaning ("a thing said by acting seemed to mean"), as well as a "female reading aesthetic," defined by Marcus as "a sensual experience of return to the mother's womb, and a dangerous secret experience of loss of self," as the women enact "something underneath" that is larger than both of them and of which their semiotic is only a part (246).

With its allusions to Philomela as well as to Penelope, weaving provides a metaphor for women's bodily speaking that is mythologically and historically rich. Feminist critics such as Rachel Blau DuPlessis, Elaine Hedges, and Elaine Showalter have discussed an aesthetic revival of needlework in American women's writing since the 1960s.[4] Showalter begins her chapter "Common Threads" with a tribute to Glaspell's use of quilting in "Jury of Her Peers," but DuPlessis and Hedges completely overlook it. However, "Jury of Her Peers" is not the only Glaspell text in which needlework—weaving, quilting, or sewing—is significant. She consistently uses it to represent the way silenced women communicate their heritage, sexuality, and solidarity with one another. In *Brook Evans*, the yellow dress hand-sewn by Brook's mother symbolizes the forbidden sexuality she wants to pass on to her daughter. In *The Morning Is Near Us*, Lydia discovers a chest of needlework that links her to her dead mother, to which she is led through sewing a doll's dress with her daughter. As Showalter describes, sewing "helped forge bonds between women" and "parallels between piecing and writing" were exploited by American women writers from the 1840s to the 1880s (*Sister's Choice* 148–56). While other modernist women writers disparaged needlework as a sign of their mothers' subjection to the home, Glaspell was able to integrate what she regarded as good fictional technique from nineteenth-century women's writing with the aspects of modernism that were meaningful to her. Her connection of needlework with female sexuality and a female semiotic is radical for her time and remarkably prescient in foreshadowing the resurrection of this metaphor by women writers in the 1970s.

Mythological allusions in chapter 11 continue to proliferate. The placement of Irma and Stamula on the Dionysian stage on Parnassos, plus their illicit, exclusively female jouissance, links them with the maenads as described by Harrison, who went "every other year with the Delphian women to Parnassos" to hold exclusively female revelries (*Prolegomena* 391). Dionysus also provides another link to mythological parallels with Demeter and Persephone. We know from *The Road to the Temple* that Glaspell and Cook visited Eleusis and were knowledgeable, probably via Harrison, about the sacred rituals enacted there, and the fact that "they became affiliated with the mysteries of Dionysos" (150). Among much other evidence, Harrison analyzes a vase painting in which Dionysus is seated on the omphalos, next to Demeter on her throne and Persephone carrying her characteristic torches. She concludes, "To the ancient mind no symbolism could speak more clearly; Dionysos is accepted at Eleusis; he has come from Delphi and brought his omphalos with him" (556–57).[5]

The essentials of the Demeter-Persephone myth undergird *Fugitive's Return*: a mother betrayed by patriarchy, grieving for a lost daughter; a daughter, raped and motherless; a third woman who brings them together.[6] Bracketed at the beginning and end by images of the buried child, Constantina, the chapter portrays a trinity of women that represents different aspects of female life. As Harrison explains, matriarchal goddesses reflect the life of women in each of its phases; in particular, Demeter and Kore are "merely the older and younger form of the same person," just as Irma and Constantina are essentially one, while at the same time being grieving mother (Demeter) and raped daughter (Persephone) (262). But what about Stamula? Harrison continues, "Greek religion has besides the twofold Mother and Maiden a number of triple forms. . . . Dualities and trinities alike seem to be characteristic of the old matriarchal goddesses" (286). Stamula is the third goddess who makes reunion of Demeter and Persephone possible—Hekate, the witch. She also plays another character traditionally associated with Demeter, the servant Iamb, who enables the mother to laugh again.

The worship of Demeter and Persephone at the Eleusinian Mysteries, the most widespread religious cult in ancient Greece, grew out of age-old localized women's harvest festivals such as the Thesmophoria and the Haloa. The scene enacted in chapter 11 between Irma and Stamula seems inspired in part by Harrison's description of the Thesmophoria. Glaspell's chapter takes place in early October during the grape harvest, just as the Thesmophoria, a harvest festival, also occurred during October. Elements of these ancient harvest rituals melded over time with elements of the Demeter-Persephone myth, according to Harrison, and some appear in Glaspell's version. Women at the Thesmophoria fasted while seated on the bare ground to mimic Demeter's fasting, and on the third day they reveled with great license, telling "scurrilous jests" that reenacted Iamb's joking to lift Demeter's spirits (136). Harrison quotes a similar description of the Haloa from an ancient source: "The women . . . celebrated alone, in order that they might have perfect freedom of speech. The sacred symbols of both sexes were handled, the priestesses secretly whispered into the ears of the women present words that might not be uttered aloud, and the women themselves uttered all manner of what seemed to him unseemly quips and jests" (148). This is the scene Glaspell echoes as Stamula makes the Kyria laugh for the first time:

When she understood this she was so pleased with what Stamula had done, with herself for understanding, that Stamula heard what she had not heard before. She heard the Kyria laugh. Delighted, though always in her gentle way, she caught her friend's hands and shook them up and down, herself laughing all the while, and almost as if she would have the Kyria dance with her. Again the Kyria laughed, but stopped, her face strange, as if she had heard a sound to which she was unaccustomed. (66)

Bodily, nonverbal communication with Stamula enables the Kyria to laugh and nearly dance before she stops herself. As Cixous describes, woman's decensored language gives her back her pleasures and her "immense bodily territories which have been kept under seal" (250). Even in ancient Greece, women's language was regarded as "scurrilous," in other words, as the sexually explicit voice of the female body. For example, in some versions of the Demeter myth, the character who makes her laugh is Baubo, who does so by exposing her genitals.[7]

A ritual "downgoing and uprising" at the Thesmophoria, where priestesses would descend into great clefts in the earth with the remains of sacrificed pigs as fertility charms, was mythologized, according to Harrison, as Persephone being dragged down under the earth by Hades. The priestesses would later enact an "uprising," just as Persephone returns in the spring (the anodos of the Kore), to bring up the relics of the previous year's ceremony and magically fertilize the fields. This "downgoing and uprising" is an image Glaspell exploits, using the hole in the temple floor where Constantina was raped and another underground tunnel beneath the theater where she hides. Chapter 11 begins with the Kyria glimpsing the "small gray eyes of Constantina peering through the fig tree that hung over the old theater" (64). At the end of the chapter, in a passage I have already discussed, Irma and Stamula leave the Sacred Way to Eleusis so that Stamula can point out the "grave" where Constantina was raped. "She could not make the story clear, but the feeling from it was as something that flowed between them, so they did not wish to separate but remained in the temple until after the sun had set" (69). Again, their understanding is experienced in a semiotic "something" that flows between them, perhaps the unspoken experience of women through the ages. They have, as Marcus puts it, translated the "voice of the stick in the sand," and the "poem is a four-letter word, RAPE." They do not want to separate, but seek consolation and strength in each other.

The Kyria tries to reach out to Constantina by wrapping a scarf around the girl. Local women had woven the scarf "for the Kyria, and dyed it the color of the soft little plant that comes up between the stones of the ancient stage. A gray softer than silver, and as if it held the memory of other colors" (69). Obviously, this color links the scarf with Dionysus, as Glaspell twice characterized him in *The Road to the Temple*. Thus the Kyria tries to draw Constantina into the maenads, into a strong, healing sisterhood. Constantina, however, rejects the gesture, throwing the scarf away. "But as if her eyes could not reject, she watched it, coiled on the stage" (69). The scarf, coiled like a snake, is also therefore associated with the great python of the Oracle, the voice of the Pythian Priestess, slain by Apollo. In fear, Constantina rejects womanhood; she is still bound by her pain and needs a mother to guide her. But Constantina's eyes are gray, as is the lichen symbolic of Dionysus: the maenads and the voice of the Oracle are her female heritage and she will be joined with them. Not yet, however. The chapter ends with the image of Vascelo, her rage silenced by Elias, "as one beaten" (71).

Chapters 13–18 conclude the first section of the novel, bringing Irma to the brink of an intense self-analysis of her past in the second section. These chapters are deliberately repetitive and build in intensity. They focus on the Kyria's protection of three small animals—a lamb, a bird, and a dog—that symbolize the abandoned child within her. Her repressed pathways to emotion are reopened through this series of needy "children" that will culminate, in the third section of the novel, in Constantina. No longer a victim, Irma finds the power now to oppose patriarchal persecution of the weak by the strong:

> She had come to know she had a strange power. It was not in what she did; it was something went on within her gave this authority. . . . It was in the presence of cruelty this thing was wrought which gave her power. It was before pain, though not pain alone, but pleasure in pain. If she met boys torturing a bird, beating the beast that carried for them, she had only to stand there, entirely still, she had not even to look at them, and this happened which gave her authority. (98)

This was a role she assigned to Cook in *The Road to the Temple*. In the actual Delphi, Kyrios Kouk had the power to stop the boys and men from killing birds with stones, and she portrays him almost as a Saint Francis in his miraculous ability to befriend a wild bird in the mountains, tame it, and communicate with it (344–45). One wonders sometimes to what extent Cook inspired Glaspell, and to what extent she made him into the image of her desire. Was Jig her inspiration for Irma, or did she project herself into the fictional creation of Jig, just as she did into Irma? Or did they, in the way of lovers of many years, begin to meld into one another? At any rate, it is obvious in *The Road to the Temple* that they both loved animals, particularly dogs, far beyond the norm: "We were peculiarly close in this feeling we shared, and which we knew few people would understand" (429). The cliché about pets was true in their case: their dogs were their children. Glaspell describes the drawn-out illnesses and deaths of their dogs, first Nezer in Provincetown and then ToPuppy in Delphi, in wrenching detail. As usual, when Glaspell and Cook loved deeply, it was bound up with the imminence of death: "He put his arm around me. 'Do you know what I would like—what I would really like—and I can say it to you. I wish we could all be buried together—you and I, and Nezer, and ToPuppy'" (432).

It is Easter time when the Kyria tries to save the lambs from sacrificial slaughter for Easter dinner, and the allusions to both pagan ritual and Christianity are manifold. The Greek children "are accustomed to this— that the pet lamb be slain in the spring," alluding to the ancient ritual sacrifice of the pharmakos, or scapegoat, as well as to the more contemporary preparations for Easter dinner (81). Like the children, Irma befriends the lamb, and it follows her around. One day it wandered "into that lowered place in the temple—the place Stamula had shown the Kyria, where Constantina used to hide, and where misfortune befell her." Constantina, her innocence betrayed, is identified with the lamb as it descends into the locus of her rape. When Irma descends into the hole, like a priestess of chthonic ritual, to rescue the lamb, Vascelo observes her sitting "there on a stone, as if thinking about something" (81). Thus Irma and Constantina are both identified with the Oracle, for the omphalos is traditionally characterized as a large stone, like that upon which Irma sits contemplating the girl's rape.

Irma saves this lamb by purchasing it from Elias. More children arrive, asking the Kyria "to spare the life of their lamb" (82). She is thus associated with Christ—"Suffer little children, and forbid them not, to come unto me: for of such is the kingdom of heaven" (Matthew 19:14)—a connection that becomes more explicit in the next chapter. Obviously she cannot stop the slaughter of all the lambs in Delphi, but "that Easter the Kyria ate no meat" (84). However, there is an allusion to Demeter here, too. Harrison stresses that ancient matriarchal rituals were meatless, in contrast to Homeric, patriarchal rituals, involving the slaughter, roasting, and shared feasting with the gods of a beast. The pharmakos, like the pigs at the Thesmophoria, was sacrificed for purposes of purification and fertility, and it was never eaten. Demeter's ritual celebrated the grains of the earth; likewise Glaspell's priestess rejects meat and in so doing rejects patriarchal slaughter of the innocents.

These images of the ostracized child culminate in the stray dog the Kyria saves. This episode is clearly derived from ToPuppy, the dog Glaspell and Cook adopted in Delphi. He belonged to their landlord, Demos, who lived below them, and he had been starved and abused (*Road* 369). When they were preparing to depart for Kalania, the landlord requested they return the dog. What follows is another brief "fragment," a moment extraordinarily revealing of Glaspell:

> Locking ToPuppy in a room with Nilla, Jig and I went below. Jig was angry enough, but I have never in my life known anger like this. That ToPuppy, after knowing life with us, should be returned to the kind of life he would have with them—to ask you to "return" the dog you have saved and come to love. . . . The interview was short.
>
> That evening Demos was saying Americans were bad people. Even the women would shake a fist in your face and threaten to kill—just for something you had said about a dog. But what could you do with people like that, he wanted to know. They were dangerous. You had to let them have their own way. (381)

It seems the wife of Kyrios Kouk could shake a fist, finding power and authority when it really mattered to her—when it involved maternal protection of the weak. Glaspell describes the fictional Kyria as "one mighty with wrath" at the villagers' persecution of a stray dog, apparently a wrath she derived from first-hand experience. Like D. H. Lawrence, Glaspell was raised in an evangelical Protestant faith, and like him, she could invest her prose with resounding biblical phraseology when it suited her purpose. She had also described Cook in *The Road to the Temple* as "mighty with wrath" at perceived injustices, yet another instance of their melding identities in her re-creation of him (348).

Again, the stray dog in *Fugitive's Return* suggests a ritual pharmakos. The villagers throw stones at him, and on festival day they pursue "the starving beast" with a rope, crying, "Hang him! Hang him!" Vascelo and Theodora join in the "chant," another word that links this episode with primitive ritual (87–88). This is a symbolic representation of the ritual "hanging god" to which Frazer devotes so much of *The Golden Bough* and which Eliot exploited so thoroughly in *The Waste Land*. In a lengthy discussion, Harrison explains the ceremony of the pharmakos as a communal purification, an expulsion of evil through "leading out," beating with medicinal herbs, and finally killing the scapegoat, chosen from among criminal outcasts (*Prolegomena* 95–109). "The pharmakos is killed then, not because his death is a vicarious sacrifice, but because he is so infected and tabooed that his life is a practical impossibility" (104). At the end of the novel, before she leaves Greece, Irma herself kills the dog as an act of mercy and a ritual purgation of her past, but here the Kyria regards the group persecution of an innocent as sadistic and puts an end to it by invoking Christ. Very dramatically, this is the first time she uses her voice since the onset of her psychosomatic muteness:

> Then it happened. The Kyria spoke. In their own tongue she spoke. Each word was spoken with care, and it was as the voice of heaven speaking the language of earth.
>
> "Was it for this Jesus died?" (89)

Three contemplative chapters follow: Irma's thoughts on Christ, on the Oracle, and on her own life, ending in a repetition of the preceding scene in her memory. For the Kyria (and, one senses, for Glaspell), "the unpermitted was pleasure in pain." "Trembling with anger," she recalls seeing a "hot red light" and hearing "a voice. It said: 'Was it for this Jesus died?'" (106). The emphasis given by this repetition elicits consideration of the significance of Christ in this text. Glaspell stopped attending church in Davenport, Iowa, during the intellectual ferment of the early years of the twentieth century when she became a member of the Monist Society, a group devoted to unifying the cultural binarisms caused, in large part, by Christian doctrine. Portrayals of Christianity in her novels, particularly *Brook Evans*, satirize the small-minded, sanctimonious hypocrisy of many churchgoers, as she saw them. But she remained, at heart, a Christian. She did this by dissociating Christ from the church and associating him instead with ancient Greece. Irma in *Fugitive's Return* and Norma in *Norma Ashe* both experience a moment of divine revelation in which they sense the presence of Christ. In *Norma Ashe*, Christ is identified with Plato, "a great companion," whose thoughts reach "across the centuries" (324). In *Fugitive's Return*, he is, like Dionysus, envisioned as a feminized god.

A binarism that Glaspell seems to have accepted is the association of male with sadism and female with masochism, but she envisions a masochism, modeled on Christ, that is a triumph of the meek over the mighty. In *The Road to the Temple*, she interprets a rather garbled poem of Cook's about Christ. In her view, "this god, hating the will to destroy, embodied the more feminine will to be destroyed," and she describes Jesus saying, "Rather than be thruster of that knife, I will be lamb" (350–52). This is again strikingly similar to Lawrence's views, who also envisioned the lamb of Christ as passive and masochistic. In *The Rainbow,* Ursula finally rejects her Christian training in such terms:

> Her God was not mild and gentle, neither Lamb nor Dove. He was the lion and the eagle. . . . they were not passive subjects of some shepherd, or pets of some loving woman, or sacrifices of some priest. She was weary to death of mild, passive lambs and monotonous doves. . . . She did not see now lambs could love. Lambs could only be loved. They could only be afraid, and tremblingly submit to fear, and become sacrificial; or they could submit to love, and become beloveds. (389–90)

Ironically, by pitting herself against sadism ("pleasure in pain"), by adopting the voice of a feminized masochistic Christ, Irma, like Ursula, is relinquishing passivity and opposing sacrifice. Jesus awakens Irma's voice and an active power to love that frightens her. She is learning to love aggressively, rather than submit to love, the sacrificial female role that ended in her utter powerlessness portrayed at the beginning of the novel. For Glaspell, Jesus speaks for the silenced ones: "Out of those mists he had come—out of his silence, compelled to raise voice because they were cruel to one another, driven to speech because the beasts could not speak" (91).

But what about that other voice that also speaks for the silenced—the Oracle? The same chapter 15 contains a fascinating contemplation of the meaning of the Oracle and portrays Irma's dialogue with it. Irma thinks of the Oracle in two phases, similar to Harrison's view: a later patriarchal phase when it was controlled by "man's" ambition and an earlier matriarchal phase when it spoke "like Constantina . . . this long story of voices":

> The Oracle. That was a childish idea. Man wanting to be directed. Man getting up a play. Give me wisdom, man said. Show me the way. Yes, the way. Wisdom was to point the way for himself, and he did not know that wisdom is that which looks on. The Oracle was a fraud, using man's desire to advance himself, and calling this wisdom. And yet . . .
>
> There was a hollowed place in the temple. One climbed down the stones into tall grasses and thistles. There the little shepherd girl, Constantina, had been ravished. There the Oracle once spoke. (93–94)

Marcus describes Virginia Woolf's charwomen (also inspired by Jane Harrison), like Mrs. McNab in *To the Lighthouse*, as the "voice of the semiotic" ("Introduction" 7, 14). For Marcus, Woolf "sees in the charwomen's rhythms and words, tunneling a channel into the obscure origins of language, a place where . . . language follows the rhythms of the body. She is searching for the female logos" (13). So, too, Glaspell is trying to return to semiotic origins, to tunnel beneath the patriarchal burial of the voice of the female body. However, Glaspell portrays this tunneling both as a return to the maternal origins of language and as an actual return to the mother's body, to the earth. Irma recalls the day when she "let herself down" into the "hollowed place in the temple" to rescue the lamb. He had "remained below, in his foolish voice demanding succor. Mindless little animal—alive but helpless, needing always to be directed, believing all is well where there is one to tell him what to do" (94). Her description identifies the lamb with a helpless baby: the lamb is Constantina, but it is also the child Irma lost, and the lost child within Irma herself. Fittingly, she descends into the vaginal space and discovers a child.

This is not only a place of birth, however, but also a place of death—it is the grave where Constantina was ravished. Glaspell reveals through this symbolic space what the voice said before it was silenced by men seeking ambition: the "four-letter word, RAPE." After this Irma would "go down into this place and herself silent, put questions to the long-silent Oracle." She sits "until it was as if something opened underneath that would have been her voice, as if an old way opened" (95). Thus Irma communicates with the Oracle as she did with Stamula, in a wordless semiotic that opens "something underneath"—the buried, unconscious voice of the female past.

In the culminating chapter of this first section, Irma realizes with dawning terror that emotion has broken through her repressive defenses. She can no longer stand outside of life because "she was feeling!"—first, love for the unloved dog (child/self), then rage (108). Speaking with the righteous voice of Christ has allowed her finally to express her wrath, and that opens the floodgates to her past. She begins to understand her identification with the puppy as she recalls seeing him trotting home from the fields behind the donkey:

> He was tied to the animal that had heretofore borne him, and must keep up. She saw him coming back at night, tired, but he must keep up, or he would strangle. Being trained—so young—too young. So is one trained, so compelled, when in life. He did not understand. He was frightened. He was tired. (92)

Like the lamb, the puppy symbolizes a child. Tied to the body that had borne him, the body of the mother, compelled to conform, learning too young that he must keep up or die—all parallel Irma's own development. If she should return, even in her own mind, to the life she has abandoned, she will lose the distance that protects her from feeling, but ironically the dog that reflects herself has initiated her "doom" because she loves it (102). She now knows there is "no escape" (109). In the next section of the novel, Glaspell will chart a rebirth in which memories come alive and seeing finally becomes knowing.

With Dionysos, god of trees and plants as well as human
life, there came a 'return to nature,' a breaking of bonds
and limitations and crystallizations, a desire for the life
rather of the emotions than of the reason. . . .

—*Jane Ellen Harrison*

# 5

## *Fugitive's Return* Part II

### The Nostos of the Mother

A nostos is a homecoming, the most famous being Odysseus' ten-year
return voyage to Ithaca. Irma begins her return voyage to home and motherhood by recalling the home buried deep in her memories of childhood
and by performing the psychological self-analysis that indelibly marks all
of Glaspell's novels. The intensely modernist mythic method of the first
section of *Fugitive's Return* gives way in the second to concerns with social
class and American socioeconomic change that will increasingly preoc-
cupy Glaspell in her later novels. Thus the second part of *Fugitive's Return*
returns to Glaspell's home turf, the American Midwest, at the turn of the
century: "The Lees lived on the outskirts of town, which would seem
desirable, but in this town it was not desired" (110). Irma's sense of being
an outsider derived originally from her childhood in which rural poverty
marked her as "different" and excluded her from the middle-class "uptown girls" (110–11).

Through Irma's childhood memories, Glaspell portrays a triadic family
structure common to most of her novels, with a more or less culpable
father whose dominance and, in this case, well-meaning improvidence
have made her mother's life one of constant labor and struggle, and a

mother who was "afraid things weren't right, yet helpless to make them right" (111). Like Naomi in *Brook Evans*, Irma's mother is blighted by her marriage, but unlike that novel, here the father is a more sympathetic character who has brought his wife down in class and social status, distinctions Glaspell critiques. Strains of the naturalistic class analysis that will be more fully developed in *Norma Ashe* begin to show in this novel. Her parents' conflict is basically one of labor versus capital, and Irma is torn between her father's laborious efforts at economic survival—"the day's work done, supper eaten, sitting on at the table, figuring in his little book"—and her mother's endurance—"how long Mother had kept pleasant," that is, had put a good face on her déclassé status (118–19). Irma loves her father yet identifies with her mother, taking on her yearning for a lost world of wealth and privilege, even though the values of that world are more superficial than those of her father.

As a girl, Irma finds the chaos of their poor home intolerable and longs for the order and stability she naïvely associates with wealth. She envies her cousin, Janet's, home:

> for here was a house that did things in a certain manner, a position unquestioned. It was this definiteness Irma wanted for herself, the security of accepted ways; though she did not so think it then—a form in which to move . . . where things stood always in the same relation to one another. (124)

Irma seeks form because social change, coupled with her father's ineptitude, has divorced her from the stability of an ancestral past. As she confesses later in the novel, the endurance of the traditions of ancient Greece evident in the archai (ruins) and in Stamula's weaving like the "generations of women behind her" taught Irma that she, too, "had wanted an ordered life" and was "homesick for a form in which to move" (214–15, 276).

Irma survives these conflicts only through repression, learning early "that way of trying not to know certain things there were to feel" (119). She thus inhabits "two different worlds," and repression of her inner turmoil makes "her surface more and more impassive," soon hardening into the mask she habitually wears as an adult (125). But Irma finds solace in "play acting," an escape she shares with her father because he also lives largely in a fantasy world: "'If I had the money of all the men in this town who've worked for my father,' Father would go on. . . . Here was something she knew. Father was making up a play" (118, 128). Her brother, Ed, not identifying with their mother, does not experience such a conflict.

He locates himself according to their actual economic status as belonging "to the neighborhood gang," the underclass of German immigrants and laborers (113–14). As Irma parades around their home like a "princess," he feels insulted by her disdain and mocks, "'Think you're in a play?' Yes, often she did feel she was in a play" (126). Idealized versions of her father figure largely in her fantasies. When he does contract work for the town, usually confounding himself by underbidding, Irma pretends he plays a paternal role she can look up to: "happy on the job, jovial with everyone, Father would seem like a good-natured king," and she "would get the feeling of her father as a commander. . . . Yet this was insecure ground. A good deal of the time Father worked with the men. The commander was also a laborer" (120–21). Irma is ashamed to take her father's dinner to him like the German immigrant girls she and her mother deprecate, and at the same time she is heartbroken to be disdaining the father she loves when he wants to share the dinner with her, making it into a picnic (122).

Her mother "understood" all of Irma's conflict; in fact, she is complicit in it because Irma manifests her own disappointment in her husband and disinheritance from an economically secure past. Similar to Naomi, her mother's greatest fear was "that the daughter she idolized, for whom she would have worked to the death, might be sucked into a life from which she could not escape" through marriage, as she herself had been (139). Glaspell is adept at showing how daughters become their mothers, despite their resistance. In *Brook Evans*, this identification is ultimately a positive one, but here, ironically, pursuing her mother's world of wealth and stability, Irma enters into a marriage and a leisured lifestyle that is as much a prison as her mother's life of poverty. Like Brook, Irma is caught in a miasma of pre-oedipal and oedipal conflicts. Although intimately tied to her mother and sympathetic to the hardship of her life, she is also enraged at the ways in which her mother has turned her against her father and feels a hostility toward her mother that she cannot understand: "From what awful place came the satisfaction in hurting one who sympathized with you?" (129) After Irma goes away to school, "each month her mother longed for that time when Irma would come home," but when she visits, "it would be to her father Irma would go, as for refuge" (139). As in *Brook Evans*, the "tensity" of her mother's emotional demands upon her is stifling, and she turns to her father for relief. Nevertheless, Irma is also enraged at her father for disappointing her dreams of him as omnipotent and for dissipating her rightful paternal inheritance. His power to determine her and her mother's destiny, as well as his weakness and failure in business, constitutes a betrayal of the romantic, good-natured king of her oedipal fantasies.

Rage against men is a significant theme throughout the novel. This is played out symbolically when Irma's father is injured in the fire that burns down the old Lee homestead. Although her father fights to save the house, when the barn catches fire he is "terrified as he had not yet been" because of his beloved horses, his last remaining connection to the land his ancestors had worked. He rushes in to save Judge, his favorite horse, who bolts and knocks him down. Irma tries to run in and help him but is turned away by a firefighter. As her father is taken away to the hospital, Irma reassures him that Judge escaped unharmed (127). The fire and her attempt to run into the barn after her father express Irma's ambivalent rage against, and desire for, him. The "wild horse," Judge, also ambivalently symbolizes her sexual passion as well as her judgment upon her father for his failures. As Irma will discover by the end of this section, her sexuality is bound up with her rage, and one cannot be freed without unloosing the other.

With the loss of the homestead, all pretenses to their old family status are gone. They must move into one of the flimsy row houses that Irma used to pretend were part of her "domain," built by her father for the workers, and live there in cramped quarters among the immigrants (123). Although her father is permanently injured, what he cares about most is the welfare of the horse and convincing his wife and daughter of its blamelessness. Irma shares her mother's resentment at this new and final descent in status, but she also understands her father's motives, his love of the horse and his tie to the land. Once again she is impossibly torn between her parents (139).

Typical of her generation, Irma wants to reject the old agrarian ways of life and be accepted into the new wealth of a growing professional bourgeoisie. Through Irma, Glaspell is also portraying an America in the process of rejecting its agrarian past, moving to cities, and turning to industrial development and investment of capital founded upon the cheap labor provided by immigration, a theme she will develop even more fully in *Norma Ashe*. Ironically, Irma sees this "uptown" world as the stable one, when in reality these cataclysmic economic changes are disrupting a long, stable history of life upon the land, as she eventually learns. Irma's father, although more tied to the land than her mother was, could not maintain that connection; thus Irma has suffered a crucial disjunction from the earth, symbolized by the vineyard of her grandfathers:

She passed through the vineyard Grandfather Lee had planted and cared for, which Father too had cared for, though with less devotion, for Father had turned to other things. The vines looked strong and happy, here on the sunny hillside. They did not know there was no one to care for them now. The foundations of the house were un-damaged—strong. A few charred timbers rose. This house had been built to last, to house for generations. . . . Home was gone, gone without her having loved it enough. Now she knew, but now it was too late. (130–31)

The vineyard is a dominant metaphor in this novel, a form of garden resonant with Dionysian and Christian allusions. It signifies Irma's disconnection from the stability of a long ancestral past and the eternal rhythms of a life rooted in nature and dependent upon seasonal change. Until Irma is rejoined to mother earth and reunited with her paternal heritage, she will always be "play acting," alienated from her true self and lost in the rootless transience of modern industrial life.

While her cousin, Janet, goes to finishing school, Irma, like the immigrant young women, goes to "training school," preparing to teach in the public schools (133). When she becomes a teacher, she boards with a farm family and falls in love with the eldest son, Horace. She finds in him and in the farm life he loves "a fullness, richness, beauty in which there was also pain" because of her deeply conflicted past (137). Horace is too much of the earth and too much like her father, so she fears a replay of oedipal betrayal. Glaspell portrays Irma's connection to the earth and its rhythms as the source of her sexual vitality, which Horace arouses: "The country itself wooed her back, for it was all alive, she who moved through it was alive . . . her body rhythmic with youth and power, flushed with the sense of being desired" (141–42). But, ashamed of her sexuality, she turns her back on this earthy life with its many reminders of her parents' tortured marriage: "'No,' she said—denying, betraying" life (145). Repressing pain, Irma also denies joy, life, and her own sexuality.

Soon both her parents are dead, so at last Irma goes to live "uptown" with her aunt and cousin, while her brother marries a Swedish immigrant woman and continues to live in the row houses and work as a laborer (149). "Janet was of the gayest, smartest crowd in town" and tries to draw Irma into the incessant social whirl of the leisured class, but Irma is too burdened by her past, both by a sense of the poverty that marks her difference and by a sense of the more meaningful values of her parents' life on the land. Typically, Irma covers the chaos within by projecting a distant, elusive exterior, "cool as the water lilies," which attracts Dan Shraeder, a young architect. Her seeming iciness makes her the inaccessible object, "something to be reached. Something to be battered down," that, in accordance with his gender, he must possess (164).

For her, marriage to Dan is the fulfillment of her "childish desire." She is finally "released from that uncertain social position which had brought unhappiness from the time she was a little girl. Dan was sure enough of himself to give an assured place to her. It was something into which she could step, which was uncontested" (160). And "he saw in her what the others did not see, desiring as they did not desire. Thus he made her desirable. He made her a woman" (163). In Glaspell's novels, any time a woman's self-definition is derived solely from male desire, she is in trouble. Irma's entree into the bourgeoisie must be paid for by her conformity to gender and to a "formless" lifestyle of postwar boozing and sexual game playing in which she must be the visible accessory to her husband's wealth and ambition. Regarding women primarily as sexual objects, soon Dan desires her only after "the stimulus of drinking, of dancing with other women" at cocktail parties (162). As a response, Irma finds "her love for Dan enclosed her within herself," and she withdraws more and more into a world of her own private pleasures, primarily gardening and, after the birth of their baby, mothering (164). Janet counsels her that she will lose her husband if she does not conform to expectations, that is, play the role of sexual object: "There isn't a woman around you wouldn't get your husband if she could. . . . You have to get him anew every week or so. . . . You have to keep him loving you" (178–79). When Irma rejects this view of marriage—"I couldn't live that way. . . . You speak as if I were a courtesan"—Janet responds, "Why not? The wife who isn't something of a courtesan is something of a flop." But for Irma, marriage should be about "something else" (178–82).

Irma has to believe that Dan "had loved her as herself, and he took her for herself," but of course he did not. He fell in love with an image, just as she did, and now he misses the "excitement" of the courtesan wife. But neither has Irma permitted him the chance of knowing her, as she represses everything that is meaningful to her, even trying to keep her pregnancy a secret from him. "Are you going to put off our ever—ever—really knowing each other?" he asks (172). Irma continues to express her resentment toward her father by excluding Dan from intimacy with herself and with their child. She can't understand why Janet and Dan don't realize that "nothing the noisy party offered compared with the happiness of getting home to her baby" (177). She finds a fulfillment in mothering that leaves no room for her husband, as he accuses: "You don't need a husband. Anyway, you don't need me. Probably you don't need any one—except Berta. . . . She is mine, you know—though you haven't seemed to think so" (200–201).

As Glaspell has shown in Constantina, when boys are born it is a sign of the father's virility, and when girls are born it is the mother's fault. Dan was sure he would "be more likely to have a boy." Irma, too, wanted a boy because she feared the repetition of her own pain in a daughter's life, just as her mother did for her. But when she has a daughter, she adores her with all the power of her sublimated disappointments and sexuality, just as her mother did her and as Naomi did in *Brook Evans:*

> It was only that at times she loved Birdie with a passion too large, loving her both for herself and for the release, the salvation, that came through her. . . . Nor did she indulge this adoration. It was too much. It could not be liberated. When she ached to snatch the little girl lying naked in the sun—kiss her—kiss every lovely little curve— she would only roll her over, playfully spank what they called the cushions. . . . She wanted her child to be free. Free of her. "She is not just something for me. She is her self". . . . She gave every care, but she was calm, cool. (176, 218)

Irma's effort to curb her sexual feelings toward her child and permit Birdie's autonomy is perhaps admirable, but ironically the girl's death is indirectly due to a "passionate and austere desire to give life to her child" that includes the moralistic self-denials typical of Irma (221). Irma's over-compensation to ensure that her life is not replicated in her daughter's life is a form of atonement for her own past that brings horrible consequences. One day when Birdie wants to go play with the wealthier girls who have "two automobiles and a governess!" Irma makes her honor a previous date to play with the daughter of a local farm family. Pleased with herself, she wonders, "Could one live one's life over in the life of one's child— making up for at least some of the mistakes?" But Glaspell's answer is repeatedly, in every novel in which a mother tries to relive her life through her daughter, an emphatic *no* (220–23). From this girl Birdie contracts the fever that kills her. Irma has not only lost the only being she loves but also feels responsible for her death, "as if her feeling for order, for the past, has wrought destruction" (216).

All of Glaspell's portraits of marriage show both sexes' imprisonment in gender, and this one is no exception. The demise of Irma's marriage is portrayed as a power struggle. Every step she takes toward reconnection to a house of her own, to the land, and to an ancestral past empowers her and undermines her husband's masculinity, which is based on supporting a dependent wife with no source of autonomous being. She and Dan live in Boston, and when Irma remembers "that her father's mother's people had come from Cape Cod, that Great-grandfather Chippman's father had gone there in the first days of America," she brings Dan to the Cape where, in an "old burying-ground," she makes out "names she had read in her grandmother's Bible" (165). Characteristically, Glaspell symbolizes generational continuity through a graveyard. Irma immediately feels love for the land of the Cape, "so unlike the wider, richer country that had nurtured her" in the Midwest (165). She wants to buy one of the old houses, but Dan prefers to build a house for her. In accordance with his gender conformation, he wants her to be the passive recipient of his active providence. He feels undermined when she prevails and they buy a house that "was off the highway, on a side road beyond the marshes," expressing the solitude of her nature rather than the gregariousness and social dependency of his (167).

Irma's plans for gardening as they walk among the tangled, unkempt flowers of the old house empower her, making her feel "suddenly capable" (168). With obvious significance, she discovers a vineyard that "was not too far gone; she could restore it, and then it would not so much be on her conscience that the old vineyard at home—Grandfather Lee's vineyard—was neglected and would die" (168–69). She finds an imaginative escape in reading about the "old days" and reconstructing a background tied to the natural rhythms of "that older America" (166):

> and when she restored her vineyard she was holding an older way of life in this confused after-the-war life around her. In this older past, this longer rhythm that which was immediately behind her was somehow less close. Things further back took to themselves the reality. (171)

But Irma feels some fraudulence in this resurrection. She is playacting again because she has not really confronted the pain and chaos of her past; "she had not earned her right to this longer rhythm in which she moved" (171). Yet it is a step in the right direction, as "the days alone with her baby, her flowers, her house gave a new poise, an authority" (183). She finds a deep satisfaction in "doing things she was sure those before had done" because she again participates in the ancient rhythms of a life with form and meaning (214).

This new sense of authority and self-esteem deriving from a connection to the land is augmented by an inheritance from her aunt, who willed the family money equally between Irma and her cousin, Janet: "Janet feels you are her sister. She not only agrees, but desires that you share with her" (184). Irma's aunt treating her "as a beloved daughter" and her renewed sisterhood with Janet give her even more "confidence, a richness, in the sense of their loving her like this" (185). The legacy reestablishes her place in a maternal line and restores the money and power that had been stripped from her mother by her father. Like Woolf's famous five hundred pounds a year, the money gives Irma "a feeling of greater freedom, a wider place in which to move," allowing her to study German (ironically, the language of the much-disdained immigrants) and art (187).

Of course it undermines Dan even further and completes the collapse of their marriage, as he feels that "the house never was mine, anyway. . . . I didn't build it, and now I am not even going to pay for it" (186). He cannot tolerate that she has created a world for herself that is not dependent upon him: "You move around in your little place, and you don't know anything else. You're perfectly in command because for you—that's all there is" (199). He finds consolation with another woman and soon leaves Irma. Recalling Dan's desertion, Irma feels all the passion she had repressed, denied both to herself and to him, and discovers that her sexuality is bound up with her rage against men. She now understands the Vascelo and the Theodora within her (210–11):

> But what it brought was passion—a thirst, lust, to quarrel with him—fight with her hands—beating her fists against him! . . . Now she could have surprised him with her passion—passion against him. She would have said it—where he failed—how he had left her unsatisfied because he did not know—feel—because he was not enough! . . . Flooded with this passion to be near him to hurt, to rend—she did indeed want to be near him. The heat and the power that had risen against him went to him—wanting him—wanting— until the nights consumed her, and she was afraid. (208–9)

The third section of the novel, beginning with chapter 35, returns to the present and resumes the mythological allusions of the first section. Irma's reflections have reached the point of coming to terms with the death of her child, the most painful memory to accept. As she sits in the Dionysian theater "sobbing, crying out her anguish, the mother mourning for her child," something surreal happens that she at first believes must be a dream (217): "A head had appeared there before her—right there on the old stage before which she sat—as if it had come up through the stones" (229). She knows it is not a dream when the head disappears and she realizes it was Constantina emerging from the hidden passage underneath the old stage. She calls to the girl, but there is no response. This bizarre image, a head emerging from a cleft in the earth, signifies a birth from the vaginal space of mother earth. Irma herself experiences a rebirth at this moment, another step in her return from playacting to life: "Now she knew who and where she was. Constantina had told her it was not a dream. Constantina had told her it was life" (230).

The image also has mythological significance. Harrison discusses the anodos (the uprising) of Kore (Persephone) from the earth and provides several illustrations of this image from vases and plates (see figs. 3–5). In one, Harrison notes, "out of the artificial mound, which symbolizes the earth itself, rises the figure of a woman. At first sight we might be inclined to call her Ge, the Earth-Mother, but the figure is slight and maidenly. . . . It is the Anodos of Kore" (277). Again Harrison stresses that matriarchal goddesses reflect the life cycle of women and that "primitive art never clearly distinguished between the Mother and the Maid, never lost hold of the truth that they were one goddess" (274). This is why Constantina can represent both a daughter born to Irma and Irma herself reborn as a child. In consistently identifying each of them with the Oracle, Glaspell conflates

Figs. 3–5. The Anodos of the Kore (Persephone rising up out of the earth).
From Jane Harrison, *Prolegomena to the Study of Greek Religion* (Cambridge
University Press, 1903, pp. 277–81). Reprinted by permission of Cambridge
University Press.

them. While Constantina's anodos in this scene aligns her with Persephone's return from the underworld and Irma's protective attitude toward the girl shows that she is Demeter, the moment is simultaneously one of rebirth for the child within Irma herself.

Over the summer Irma goes up the mountain to Kalania with the villagers, as Glaspell and Cook did, although "her hut was higher than the others, deeper in the trees." In this embedded edenic locus, also a vaginal space, Irma "could rest, as if taken by a great mother" (235). Here she begins to make a closer connection to Constantina, the "child of the mountain, belonging here more surely than any other" (238). Her psychological wounds begin to heal as she lets go of the egotism of personal suffering and grasps a vaster vision of the meaning of life: "Now I know that life is very old, and will go on when I am not. Now I know I am in the great stream, though I do not understand this stream, nor know where it may be tending" (241). After healing in this nonverbal, maternal space, Irma can return to the patriarchal world of symbolic signification with "a new feeling about language—a feeling of wonder there should be language at all, and a wondering why it so often makes us commonplace, when it could make us more as gods." She herself has "more often used it to conceal, defraud, than to disclose," but now she is ready to give up playacting and "use language more reverently" (242).

Returning to the village, Irma begins reading the books she finds in the house, such as Pindar, "for she who lived within the sacred precinct at Delphi should know the Pythian Odes," Aeschylus, Sophocles, Euripides, and Plato (242). She discovers that the books and the house she has been renting belong to a man she had observed on the boat that brought her to Greece, John Knight. His return to Delphi and their dialogue mark her return to the logos, "her own voice speaking her own tongue" (243). Like Cook, he is intimately connected to symbolic signification, language and abstract thought: "She had never seen a face into which thought came as purely" (245). Also like Cook, he is feminized by Glaspell's characterization of him as a mystic adept, one who wants to plumb the secrets of the semiotic voice, the Pythian Oracle. He has absolute faith in the actuality of the voices of the sibyls at the Oracle, yet "we have never found out the secret . . . of why Delphi was." So he has been writing a book about it, because it seems to him that "the place itself holds the secret, and if one tried patiently, trustingly, it would give up its secret" (246–47).

John Knight identifies Irma with a priestess of the Oracle, but she corrects him, again conflating her identity with Constantina's: "If the Pythian Priestess is here, she is Constantina. . . . Was it not a shepherd girl in the beginning?" (247) Irma's relationship with John is "a companionship such as she had never known" (251). He tells her the myths about the Oracle as a more ancient, female voice overtaken by patriarchal interests during Apollo's tenure. As a feminized man, he reaffirms for Irma the eternal reality of the buried semiotic voice:

> "Of course the Oracle was always a gold mine for the Delphians. . . . It went on for centuries. A fraud at times; serving political interest, mercenary, that was bound to be. The priests were often full of tricks, and the Pythia's convulsions would seem pretty vulgar to us. . . . But there was something here. . . . something as pure and strong as the Castalia itself, so nearly quenchless it could go on for centuries—often meanly used, but itself there—in very truth the heart of Greece. . . . I believe it is here yet." (252)

When they go to the museum and see columns of dancing maenads, "those devotees who in the snows of high Parnassos would dance themselves into a frenzy for their god Dionysos," John identifies Theodora as Dionysian. Irma agrees, adding that "Vascelo too would have been one of the dancing women of Dionysos," while her ego ideal Stamula "would have been of the temple, . . . Handmaiden of Apollo" (253). On another day they walk to the theater, and John remarks that "the heart of Dionysos is buried under this stage," referring to the tradition of dismemberment and burial of the god at Delphi. John cannot answer when Irma asks whether he would have been "a follower of Apollo, or follower of Dionysos," but he states that she would have been Apollonian. Irma agrees, "I fear so." She is drawn to Dionysianism because "so much of life seems with Dionysos. He wanted life—for them all. Fullness of life and joy," but she learned early to repress her passions (255). When John attempts to defend Apollo as "a noble god . . . despite a good deal of treachery and dirty work," Irma cites the example of Christ as a morally pure deity. When John asks whether she is a Christian, again she responds equivocally, "I fear so" (255).

All her life Irma has longed for Apollonian form and order and has repressed Dionysian rage and sexuality, but now she is ambivalent toward these dichotomies. She fears her identification with the patriarchal faiths of Apollo and Christ because she is discovering that their rigidly prescribed roles for woman divorce her from sexuality and female power ("raping" her in effect, as the nickname of Constantina's rapist, "Young Apollo," indicates). Glaspell has already revealed the female subtext communicated between Irma and Stamula on the Dionysian stage that brings Irma closer to the fullness of life and joy, and she has shown how Irma's self-analysis in the second section brings her a new understanding of the rage within her. Here, her relationship with John also evokes her Dionysian side because he arouses her dormant sexuality. "Call yourself a Christian if it pleases you," he concludes, "but it is here you belong," on the Dionysian stage (256).

Irma's relationship with John is played out in two ritualistic scenes, one of purgation and purification and one of sexual rebirth, both located in the vineyard during the grape harvest, paralleling the ancient women's harvest festivals Harrison describes and the Eleusinian Mysteries. The Thargelia is "a festival of the offering of first-fruits on the occasion of harvest," as is the Thesmophoria, which includes rituals involving the viewing and handling of sacra, sacred objects, fertility images made of cereal cakes "in token of the growth of fruits and human beings, as a thank-offering to Demeter" (*Prolegomena* 79, 123). The Eleusinian Mysteries included a celebration of first fruits in the form of a barley drink shared by initiates from a communal vessel and a viewing of sacra (157–60). The Haloa, also a harvest festival, included sacra in tribute to Demeter, but "the name Haloa is given to the feast on account of the fruit of Dionysos—for the growths of the vine are called Aloai" (149). Once Demeter would not have accepted wine, but with the merging of their cults, Dionysus "possessed himself completely of the festivals of Demeter, took over her threshing-floor" and contributed wine to the feast (147–48).

In the first scene, chapter 42, Irma sits by the Castalian spring, watching groups of villagers returning from the vineyards and eating "a large perfect cluster" of grapes (269). As Irma partakes of the "fruit the earth" that "had grown for her when she was estranged from the earth," she is sharing in the ritual communion of Demeter and Dionysus and celebrating her return to mother earth (269). Purification in water was an essential feature of the Eleusinian Mysteries. As Irma sits beside the Castalian spring, John joins her and takes her to its source, "an ancient pool in which pilgrims had bathed," where he makes her wash her hands and drink of "the water that opened from the rock" (271). After this ritual cleansing, Irma finally purges herself of her guilt over Birdie's death, for which she still feels responsible. She begins by telling John about her life "as a story:" "It seemed as far back as if a story of old Greece. Distance liberated her, and something in this place itself cleansed her of shame" (272). Her tale culminates in an emotional catharsis in which she cries out for her lost child and slips into the water that washes over her (277). This is a Dionysian breakthrough for Irma, and it is also resonant with the

Eleusinian and Christian significance of purification and baptism. She is cleansed and, as she kisses John, she feels "with wonder" the return of her sexual vitality (278).

The second ritualistic scene occurs in the following chapter when Irma goes again to Stamula's vineyard where "they were still treading the grapes" (282). She tells John about her grandfather's vineyard, "that far hillside, neglected now" (283), and after the others leave she and John make love in the vineyard:

> And when she had here—this night, in the vineyard of Delphi, known love, all that had died in shame or grief was resuscitated in beauty. There was not one old moment but was charged with life. Every bird she had ever loved, each flower, each tree, was living fragrant music now. (285)

Irma's sexual regeneration is described in images of vegetative fertility as a culminating spiritual renewal, linking her with the eternity of all natural cycles, as the initiates at Eleusis believed. Glaspell's mythic method here is exactly as Joyce's or Eliot's or Lawrence's, an attempt to give form and meaning to contemporary life through a reincarnation in the present of a mythic, eternal human past. In the revelation of the sacra and in the symbolic birth enacted at Eleusis, initiates were assured of the eternity of all natural cycles, and "now that life had taken her back," Irma, too, becomes an "apostle to life" (295).

Glaspell's reputation as a sentimental writer is astounding, for there isn't a single novel in which she doesn't reveal romantic love to be illusory, and *Fugitive's Return* is no exception. Although these cathartic revelations are crucial to Irma's development, John's role in them is passive. While she is "newly returned to life," she soon finds that he is "dedicated to hopelessness." As she had observed on the ship, he is in love with a married woman. He returned to Greece because, although the woman left her husband, she fell in love with another man, not John. Nevertheless, he continues to "do homage to what was beautiful, but unalive," to "deify" his sadness as "a shrine inviolate." He is, as his name indicates, a knight who seeks what knights typically seek, the inaccessible lady, in an acting out of oedipal desire for the forbidden object. He is static, as frozen in time as an Apollonian work of art or as the lover on Keats's vase:

> His whole life within was an arrangement, as a piece of music, a work of art, a drama, is an arrangement. He found an esthetic pleasure in this arrangement; with gentleness, and with austerity, he

guarded it, but she who had lived long with hopelessness was unable not to know that his holy of holies was a death chamber. (267)

John Knight is not an "active wanderer and seeker" in Glaspell's terms (Makowsky 113). Quests in Glaspell's novels are not active searches in the world outside the self but voyages inward—a return to self, to homeland, and to intimacy with others. John is trapped in a rigid psychological stasis clinging to an "unchangeable" love and will not allow Irma to "violate—cloud—that perfected love" (291). She points out that such an existence is sterile, for nothing unchangeable can participate in life; "it is death" (287). Despite his attraction to the voice of the Oracle and the positive role he plays in Irma's regeneration, John is a patriarchal Olympian, just as Harrison characterizes them: "All life and that which is life and reality —Change and Movement—the Olympian renounces. Instead he chooses Deathlessness and Immutability—a seeming Immortality which is really the denial of life, for life is change" (*Themis* 468). For Harrison, just as for Glaspell, the matriarchal mystery faiths of Demeter and Dionysus express "the impulse of life through all things, perennial, indivisible" (476).

In asking Irma to be his "great understanding mother" and identifying her with the "great one," John affirms Irma's mythic status as Demeter and her active participation in the perennial stream of life from which he has, sadly, excluded himself (286–88). Irma accepts the maternal role, believing that she can change the unchangeable, in yet another of Glaspell's portrayals of heterosexual love as essentially a maternal/infantile relationship. But it is clear that Irma thinks less of him now, "secretly gloating" over the inevitable deflation of his fantasies should the woman he adores ever return his love (289–90). Glaspell also questions whether the intensity of romantic and sexual love is not always tinged with hopelessness because the desire to "be as one," to return to pre-oedipal union, cannot ever be realized: "The urge in love is not only to bring the lovers together; it is to throw themselves against the impossible—to break down that last barrier—breaking down loneliness. This cannot be" (293). Furthermore, as Irma will soon find out, Demeter's allegiance is never to man or to gods, but first and foremost to her daughter.

Irma's sexual awakening and romantic involvement with John increasingly identify her with Theodora, whose lover is Andreas, Constantina's rapist. As they return from midnight trysts with their lovers, Irma is "startled" when Theodora says, "Like you, I thought it too beautiful to stay in." Irma thinks, "'Like you,' . . . Theodora had been somewhere with Andreas. And she had been in the stadium with John Knight" (253). When

Theodora asks the Kyria to pay a dowry for her to marry Andreas, who had gone to prison rather than marry Constantina, "fatally humiliating the girl," Irma is torn between the two aspects of herself that Theodora and Constantina represent. To give into her desire for heterosexual love and acceptance into patriarchal monogamy would be a betrayal of the little girl within, "raped" by those same patriarchal familial structures. The woman in Irma who seeks, like Theodora, "what it is all women have in common—loving, and the need to be loved; their own home and children, that place among others" is at this point still in conflict with "the figure of a lonely little girl, beside a spruce tree, looking down upon life of which she did not partake" (264–65).

But the very terms in which Theodora puts her request incriminate the patriarchal system in which she yearns to take her place:

> "Had the great disaster not come upon the Greeks . . . had my home not been destroyed, my father and my brothers killed by Turks, my mother killed by want and grief, I should not be in this far place, speaking of my life to a foreigner, asking help of the good and gracious Kyria who took me in. . . . My life would have been arranged. . . . And, Kyria, Andreas loves me." (260)

While Theodora views her situation in the rosy light of romantic love, it is clearly one of compulsion and economic survival. As Irma is well aware, "it would not be all happiness for Theodora; hard work was ahead, and this boy would not love her always as he loved her today" (265). Theodora has no other choice but marriage: "But what would my life be, Kyria, if I could not marry? . . . I ask not because I am greedy, but only because there is no other way, and because without this my whole life will be as nothing" (261). Irma understands that "it was only two hundred and ten dollars stood between Theodora and happiness—between Theodora and despair. . . . But in doing this for Theodora, what did she do to Constantina?" (262). Nevertheless, Irma decides to give the dowry. When "Theodora's joyous singing came up to her," she smiles, "forgetting Constantina; in this wild hymn to life she was one with Theodora" (280). But sexual desire must contend with buried rage against men, as Vascelo's "angry face" reminds her. Irma reprimands Vascelo for trying to "stop the singing by loud railing," but she sees in the bitter woman's face "so much passion that it was hard to hold it back, as she saw now she must" (280).

Glaspell resolves these issues in a strikingly dramatic and mythologically appropriate way. Constantina had been leaning over a ledge watching the two lovers, Theodora and Andreas, regularly (270). Hearing "a thin, long wail" from "out of the temple," Irma finds that on this night Constantina had pushed a huge stone over the ledge onto Andreas's head, as Theodora screams over and over again: "His head! His head!" (296). "Constantina has killed Andreas," Vascelo tells them, unable to keep the "triumph" from her voice as she sits down upon the stone and "at once took up her moaning, rocking back and forth" (279). As Theodora screams to Vascelo, "The stone! The great stone! Oh! You are sitting on it!" the symbolism of this ritual murder becomes abundantly clear. The great stone is a manifestation of the omphalos, the semiotic voice of the silenced, ravished mother/daughter, and Constantina's "severing" of the head of the "new Apollo" is a castration of her rapist (301). It is an act of revenge against patriarchal violation of women on a mythological scale comparable to the Bacchantes's rending of Pentheus or Philomela's murder of her son and serving him to his father to eat. But Constantina's revenge not only has mythic and cultural significance. Psychologically, it expresses, and thus resolves, Irma's rage against her father.

Of course "there was no punishment too great for a woman who killed a man in Greece" (299). If Constantina is found, she will be brutally killed. In expressing her violence toward men, Constantina has become a maenad, as is made clear by her hiding place in the hole beneath the Dionysian stage. Searching for Constantina, Irma thinks, "The heart of Dionysos was buried under this stage. . . . Would it be good to her —strange heart of Dionysos?" (303). Stamula and Irma plot to rescue Constantina while sitting alone together in the temple on the Sacred Way to Eleusis. Stamula will lead them across the mountain pass to a village where they will board a train and Irma will return to America with her adopted daughter, ironically using the "nine large notes that would have made Theodora's dowry" for their passage (310). Irma and Stamula part, reaffirming their sisterhood, "nodding, as in pledge—the love, understanding, loyalty, that can be between women" (322). On the train, "holding this child who had been cursed at birth," Irma hears the sibylline voice of the Oracle "from the very heart of that which was herself, and the voice said, 'I am going home'":

> Slowly it rose—that which gave meaning to all her days. The old house on the hill. . . . the hill waited—patient, ready. On that far hillside she saw a vineyard—place for Constantina, and for herself. . . . She did not see all that was in between, but the goal she saw— inevitable, benign, as day. She would labor in her vineyard. In her own vineyard she would labor. (324)

When she leaves Greece at the conclusion of *Fugitive's Return* to re-build her ancestral house on the hill with a new daughter, Irma chooses the pre-oedipal mother-daughter dyad over a continued relationship with her lover, John, whom she must leave behind. Thus she rejects heterosexual love for a return to mother-daughter intimacy. For Glaspell, no less than for James Joyce or D. H. Lawrence, sexual union between man and woman is "life's sacrament in the face of death," but, as a woman and as a feminist, she finds the mother-daughter relationship even more primary, more eternal (226). Irma hopes that John "might one day walk, a seeker, drawn by the truth of it," into the "reality" of the home she will create, but this dream is predicated upon a growth in his character that Glaspell has given no indica-tion will occur (324). Remaining with John, Irma realizes, would have been to continue playacting, for romantic love is not her ultimate reality: "She had wanted to remain here with him and . . . with her love, her words, draw him to life. But what are eloquent words about reality—if one is not real? She could say, It is life must triumph, but would it triumph, if in her very self it did not triumph?" (316). Life triumphs in this text exactly as it does at Eleusis, through the reunion of Demeter and Persephone and through reconnection to the land with its eternal, natural rhythms.

Irma returns as a mother to the awaiting hillside, which is itself a return to the mother's body, but she also returns to her father, as the old house on the hill and the vineyard are her patrimony from both her Cape Cod and Iowa grandfathers. The biblical phrasing of the conclusion, "She would labor in her vineyard," alludes to the work of the apostles spreading the word of Christ. Glaspell seems to meld Christianity (father) with Dio-nysianism (mother) as Irma, the fugitive of the title, returns home, "an apostle to life," to cultivate her garden. Thus her nostos represents a vic-tory over the paralyzing psychological conflicts that drove her away and a unique resolution of complex familial and gender issues.

In all of her novels Glaspell portrays the process of breaking through the barriers of repression and liberating the self from the stranglehold of the past. *Fugitive's Return* is a magnificent expression of this theme. In Irma, Glaspell has given a moving portrait of psychological catharsis; she has shown how relationships between women can heal and empower, and she has universalized these themes through her adept use of mythological allusions. After such an achievement, it would not be a surprise if the next novel were somewhat anticlimactic, and that is the case, as Glaspell at-tempts something new and, one senses, not as natural to her vision in *Ambrose Holt and Family*, a comic novel about the father-daughter rela-tionship.

# 6

## The Daughter with Two Fathers in *Ambrose Holt and Family* (1931)

Perhaps Glaspell felt that the intense mother-daughter analyses of *Brook Evans* and *Fugitive's Return* had left something neglected that she needed to explore in greater detail: the relationship between father and daughter. In *Ambrose Holt and Family*, she vividly portrays the predicament of a daughter economically and psychologically bound by the law of the father, and she contrasts two fathers in order to attempt her vision of what better fathering might encompass. Blossom Holt's biological father, a pompous industrial magnate, is contrasted with her father-in-law, Ambrose Holt, a renegade who refused the paternal role and abandoned his family, thus reintroducing Glaspell's characteristic opposition of the repressive, paternalistic man versus the childlike, playful, feminized man. Naturally, in a novel about daughters and fathers, oedipal issues play a role, but *Ambrose Holt and Family* marks the beginning of a movement outward for Glaspell, beyond intimate psychoanalytic portraits to a wider social, even socialist, critique of class and wealth as well as gender. Glaspell exposes the bourgeois family structure as based on economic control of women, capitalistic exploitation of nature, and preservation of patrilineal descent through the domination of daughters. Because her focus is on a patriarchal familial and social system that restricts the individuality of both men and women, and because mothers play such a minor role in this novel, I have abandoned the psychoanalytic, object-relational theoretical model used to explicate the previous two novels. Instead, Lynda Boose's discussion in *Daughters and Fathers* of daughters as objects of exchange in Western culture provides a helpful critical paradigm for a novel that ponders the father-daughter relationship so deeply.

As always in a Glaspell novel, the opening chapter is metaphoric and adeptly crafted in order to set out the problem posed by the novel as a whole. In Glaspell's most thorough exploration of the garden metaphor, we meet Blossom Holt, the daughter of wealth and privilege, attempting as a married woman to express herself through her garden:

> What Blossom wanted . . . was her own garden. She grew up sur-
> rounded by her father's expensive floriculture, and had enjoyed it as
> one may enjoy a park. When she tried to do something the gardeners
> were annoyed, or pained. No fun trying this with experts looking on,
> counting the mistakes. So this garden, when she began it a few years
> ago, was as novel as if she had never seen a flower before. It was
> work, but never having worked, that was rather like a vacation. (2)

The garden symbolizes Blossom's rebellion against the strictures of class and gender that have confined her existence. As Glaspell explores in depth throughout the novel, women in patriarchal bourgeois family structure are incapacitated by being protected from work and from hardship; they are then belittled and made to feel like "fools" because they are inexperienced, as this excerpt illustrates.

When her father sends his Dutch gardener to her in an attempt to control the garden, as all other aspects of his daughter's existence, the gardener does "not approve what she was doing" and tries to correct her. It would be better, he says, to "mass" the flowers together. "I know," she replies. "That is proper. I thought I would be improper" (2). Instead, Blossom has planted a "tall proud delphinium . . . cupped by the long formal leaves" right in the middle of the bank of iris. It is an improper phallic image that aptly expresses her phallicism, in other words, her usurpation of male control. It is also an expression of her individuality. The tall delphinium in the middle of the mass of iris symbolizes the theme of autonomy versus community, individuality versus conformity, at the heart of this novel, just as in *Fidelity*. When Blossom questions the gardener, "Don't you ever get tired of doing things the right way? Just following the right way?" and he affirms, "It has been found best," she realizes that

"Father would raise his salary" as the reward for his conformity. Although she can regard her father with some cynicism here and seems to recognize that wealth controls "right" in capitalist culture, she has been raised to believe that her father's will is law. She must learn in the course of the novel that wealth cannot determine moral right. And when the gardener states about the flowers, "each must have its own place," Blossom thinks, "It might have been her father, talking about classes of society. Having always had her own place it pleased her to put something out of place" (3). Again Blossom reveals an incipient desire to rebel against the rigid bourgeois notions of class determined by her father, but although she might desire to "put something out of place," she is nowhere near abandoning her own place. Glaspell compares her to the "social experimenter who goes a little way but stays safe in the main body" (2).

Although this garden could be all her own, a "secret" place like Glaspell's other edenic loci and vaginal spaces where nature can give a "wider or freer" world, Blossom is a "loving, but uncertain" gardener. Unlike Brook and Irma, she cannot access the secret, semiotic realm of the mother. Intimidated and "wearied" by paternal domination, she reluctantly accepts the gardener's aid (3). At the heart of her passivity and powerlessness is the sense of inferiority that has been inculcated in her:

> Surveying [her garden] with pleasure she considered that this was perhaps like the pleasure people got who could really do things, could paint, or write—combining, putting things together so they were nice in themselves, and also had a meaning. She wished she could do something like that, for then she would understand more, have confidence to say what she thought. It seemed the only time she had confidence was when she was by herself. . . . The trouble was, she was supposed not to feel it, and somehow she hadn't the authority to prove, by saying it, that she did feel it. (6)

Not being male, she lacks the confidence to be an actively creative person, and she lacks the authority to prove that her feelings have value. She is further undermined by the fact that she is physically beautiful.

As Glaspell portrayed in Irma and Constantina in *Fugitive's Return*, aging or unattractive women are rejected by men and socially ostracized, leading to their corrosive bitterness and rage. Beauty would seem to be a source of female power in patriarchal culture, although Glaspell undermined this by showing that, without money, even the beautiful Theodora was powerless to affect her own destiny. In this novel and in her next, Glaspell shows that in a patriarchal culture in which beauty raises a woman's value as object of exchange and desire, female beauty is not power but entrapment.

As Blossom enters the house, she catches a glimpse of herself in the pier glass between two windows. Unlike Naomi, who revels in her sensuality imaged in the mirror, but similar to Irma, who feels betrayed by the reflected body image, Blossom "had never become used to looking like this. It did not seem it was herself looked back at her" (7). The external image alienates her from her inner self because her beauty—golden curls, blue eyes, delicate upturned nose, curved lips, fair skin "in texture lovely as a petal," and head rising "from a slender neck, indeed as a flower on its stem"—is childlike and belies the mature thirty-year-old woman that she feels herself to be. "No wonder I have that silly name," she thinks. Even her real name, Harriette, is doubly feminized by the "-te" ending, but she prefers it to her nickname, which she cannot live down, hard as she tries. The name "Blossom" is the sign of her possession by men, first her father and then her husband, and of their infantilization of her:

> Her father began it, when she kicked in her cradle. Before she married Lincoln, when he said—"Blossom! My Blossom!" she would sometimes say, "My name is Harriette." But earnestness only brought more color to her fair skin . . . only gave her eyes the depth of shadowed blue, so he would pull her curly hair, kiss that tender curve of her mouth, until she was farther than ever from the name Harriette.
>
> But Blossom felt her name was Harriette, and that there must be something wrong with her or she would be able to maintain it.
>
> She had about given up, for when she objected to Blossom her husband called her Dolly, or Kitten; if there was one name worse than Blossom it was Kitten, and even worse than looking like a blossom was the idea of looking like a doll.
>
> But she was not a flower, or a kitten, or a doll; she was a woman who thought and felt. She had never succeeded in making anyone else know this; it must be her fault. (8)

How anyone can read passages such as this and assert that Glaspell was not a feminist surpasses understanding.

Here, in yet another variation on her signature mirror scene, Glaspell shows once again that for women, plain or beautiful, young or old, physical appearance is the all-important determinant of identity and status, since they are regarded not as people who think and feel but as objects to be possessed or discarded. Typically, too, Blossom does not blame the culture or the men in her life for infantilizing her but masochistically internalizes it as yet another sign of her own failure and weakness. She participates in her infantilization, something she must come to terms with as the novel progresses, by hiding her inner self in conformity to the image of her as irrational and unintelligent that the men in her life need to maintain. She "secretly read Shelley, though she preferred the secretly read Keats," but when she "talked to the poet with whom she lived about understanding his poetry . . . he laughed and . . . said,—run along and play, or what amounted to that" (9).

For Blossom, men own thought, particularly her poet-husband, Lincoln, and she has no right to it. As she sits in Lincoln's study thinking, she "came to with a start, as if her thoughts had no business to be here; this place was for Lincoln's thoughts. Was it possible that anything of her thoughts remained here, as intruders? She had queer ideas like that at times, but she decided her thoughts were harmless; they weren't strong enough to set up anything against Lincoln's thoughts" (17–18). Despite Blossom's wish to be Harriette, she is undermined by her essential belief in gender as it has been imposed upon her. She censors herself "as if all thought should be his" and idolizes her husband, regarding his poetry as sacrosanct, for it represents the sublimation of her own repressed creativity.

Lincoln Holt, Blossom's husband, is Glaspell's most detailed portrait of a man diminished by the dictates of his gender. He is a parodic caricature of the patriarchal, narcissistic husband and, at the same time, a tragicomic portrayal of a man unable to realize his dreams as an artist because he is compelled to fulfill his socially inscribed gender role as moneymaker and supporter of women. Lincoln has been, in effect, castrated by his father's abdication of the masculine role: "I had less than all the boys around me. I was teacher's son, and their mothers didn't work" (23). His whole life is dedicated to an oedipal struggle to compensate for his father and to resurrect the phallus. In marrying Blossom and managing his father-in-law's cement business, he has opposed his rebel father, Ambrose Holt, by aligning himself with patriarchy and with capitalism. Unfortunately, his conformity to gender and patriarchal family structure constitutes a betrayal of his inner self and his art, as he reveals to Blossom:

> "One thing I like, is woods. These woods up the river here, back from the Mississippi. I liked them when I was a boy. And what am I

doing to them? How am I repaying? I'm tearing them up. Because they belong to your father, and there's clay underneath the woods the Indians loved first, and I loved after them. And your poor father has only three millions—he confesses to three, personally I believe it's five—and when you have millions you must have another million, the sooner the better, for that's the way the game is played." (22)

Here Glaspell equates industrialism with patriarchy in the figure of Blossom's father, and both with the rapine of nature, equated with mother as in her other novels. Lincoln's dilemma is clearly a moral one: "It's a tragedy, and a crime, and I'm in it, like an evil spirit. . . . I am in the business of changing deep old woods into ugly new cities. . . . I support my family by destroying beauty" (22, 24). Lincoln's Faustian bargain is driven by his oedipal need to replace the father he views as inadequate and he justifies it by his rigorous upholding of a masculinity founded upon the economic possession ("support") of women and children: "you could not support James Atwood's daughter by way of the Indians, so now the poet was a business man, supporting his wife, his children, his mother" (33).

In marrying Lincoln, Blossom has essentially married her own father, who as a young man had wanted to be an inventor but got a "hold at the steel works" and started a concrete business after marrying a wealthy man's daughter from South Carolina (54–55). Glaspell shows family structure to be basically the preservation of patrilineal descent through the exogamous exchange of daughters, who only gain presence by becoming mothers, vessels "through which the father reproduces himself" (Boose 25). When Blossom, sensing that her father "should have been a great inventor—not just cashed in so easily," suggests that he give money to aid poor inventors, he replies, "It was a man's business to leave things to his family—build up something for the future, for grandsons and their sons" (55).

In Levi-Straussian terms, the gift of the daughter should "connect the male exchange partners as affines," which would seem to be the case in Lincoln's accession to his father-in-law's business and adoption of his values (25). But as Lynda Boose points out in her critique of the anthropological model, "the problem with the bestowed daughter being the conjunction between antithetical male subjects" is that "the pattern signifies an inherently violent text of desire and competition, not one of mutual cooperation" (29). It merely masks competition over the possession of women, as Glaspell illustrates in Lincoln's resentment of the car Blossom's father has given her. Her husband does not want her taking expensive presents from her father since "that would be just another way of supporting you . . . as if I couldn't—in the manner to which you are accustomed" (52). Just as her father, in competition with his own father-in-law, felt smug satisfaction in his excessive garden and opulent house "because, he said, it was better than the houses he had seen in Charleston, so now he needn't hear so much about the Charleston houses" (53–54).

No wonder Lincoln is outraged when Blossom dares to suggest that she ask her wealthy father to support them so Lincoln can write: "If you ever do it, I'll never forgive you," he tells her with "cold . . . abrupt authority," for he sees it as a violation of his masculinity (25). Her father instructs her in the same patrilineal ideology when she does suggest that he should be proud to support Lincoln and his family, to "contribute to making a great American poet": "A man, my dear, has something that is called self-respect. And that self-respect makes it necessary a man support his family." For Blossom, these gender constraints "seem so silly . . . so wrong," but her father authoritatively stamps her as "a very silly woman. Sillier than I thought. Women are silly, and that makes a great deal of trouble." She feels utterly helpless, rendered powerless by both husband and father to change a system that not only infantilizes her but enslaves them. "Why had she thought she could talk to her father? He sat there entrenched in power" (91–92).

Glaspell shows that men are thus chained to the capitalist system in order to preserve their power. They must sacrifice freedom and individuality in order to stockpile patrimony and perpetuate patrilineal descent. It is with typical Glaspell irony then that Lincoln's new series of poems, inspired by his violation of the woods, should be entitled "The Sacrifice" (35). The woods must be sacrificed for cement, just as art must be sacrificed for money and men must sacrifice to support women, according to Lincoln's view. Prior to this, Glaspell has portrayed sacrifice as a female role, an expression of female victimization, as in Ruth in *Fidelity*, who sacrifices all for love, and in various mothers, particularly Naomi in *Brook Evans*, who sacrifices everything for her daughter. Here Glaspell penetrates further into the whole concept of sacrifice, delving beneath its apparent surface as an abnegation of self to the manipulative passive-aggressive ego gratification that sacrificing for others gives. Just as she portrayed masochism as a form of power in *Fugitive's Return*, here, too, she unmasks sacrifice as the perquisite of the powerful over the weak.

This theme is illustrated through Blossom and Lincoln's two children, Lincoln Jr. and Paul. Although both are boys, they mirror their parents' relationship because the younger, Paul, has a physical disability. Seen as weak and helpless, he is feminized by his father, and Lincoln wants his eldest son to assume the masculine gender role he himself upholds. "Junior" must give up gifts and toys to his younger brother because he "has a great deal that Paul doesn't have,"such as power, strength, and mobility (78). Although Blossom would sacrifice any comfort or pleasure to aid Lincoln's writing, she "did not like the idea of sacrifice, though she could not have said why, or rather, would not have permitted herself to know why" (10, 17). When she protests that perhaps it is an injustice to ask Lincoln Jr. to sacrifice for Paul, their father responds:

"Oh—injustice. One has to learn to bear injustice. The strong must be chivalrous". . . .

"I fear that's not good for his character," said Blossom.

"What a funny way to look at it. His character is just what it is good for. Don't you believe in learning to sacrifice?"

"No," said Blossom, so hastily that she modified it to, "At least I'm not sure."

"I should think you would take it back. Though the reason you don't believe in sacrifice is that you've never had to do it." (78)

Of course Blossom has done it; she has sacrificed her autonomy and identity to conform to a chivalric code in which she must play the passive recipient of sacrifice from the men in her life. And how well Glaspell portrays Lincoln's pleasure in resenting the idle, pampered doll he has constructed.

What Blossom does not permit herself to know early on, she later begins to grasp as the novel progresses: sacrifice teaches one boy that he is all-powerful and the other that he is weak and helpless, making both "insufferable" (69, 189). Watching the boys sleeping, she feels for a moment that it is right to sacrifice, to "keep your place" even if you weren't true to "what you felt yourself to be" for the sake of children (140). But she has begun to doubt whether this is the best way to raise children. "What if she had to be Blossom, if that kept things right for Paul?" She begins to realize that in accepting victimization she perpetuates it, raising Paul to be, like herself, a victim of sacrifice on the part of everyone else, to be dependent and weak. She then urges her elder son to "hold on to what you really are, through it all" (141). As Blossom's awareness grows throughout the novel, she will discover she really wants to keep a better balance between the boys, to disrupt the sacrifice/victim, active/passive dichotomy that Lincoln has established as the pattern for raising them (187–89).

As so often, Glaspell portrays marriage as a power struggle. In this case, Blossom and Lincoln's relationship becomes a battle over who will sacrifice for whom, who will infantilize whom. Between the two cultural roles open to her, daughter or mother, the only empowered stand Blossom can take in relation to men is a maternal one. She dares to act aggressively only in a maternal effort to "shield" Lincoln's writing. When she cancels their attendance at a cocktail party to that end, Lincoln is furious (43–44). He sees Blossom's intervention in his effort to fulfill all his roles—businessman, poet, bon vivant—as an attack on his masculinity: "Why do you humiliate me by making me feel I can't carry the whole thing?" It is indeed presumptuous to manage another's life; Blossom's infantilization of him is as unjust as his of her. But in addition, Lincoln resents her attempt to be "firm" and instructs her to "stick to her own thing—which was outside the important thing" (45). Blossom must not have a "thing" of any importance, in other words, she must abdicate the phallus—work, money, expression, autonomy, independence. Her success can only reside in being beautiful, playing bridge, and giving delightful parties, while "serious" achievements are off-limits (83–84). And Lincoln can categorically refuse to be infantilized, a privilege she does not have. He silences her protests— "she could not speak, his kisses would not let her"—and wins this battle to "bring her back—to Blossom" through asserting his sexual dominance (46). She realizes "she must let him feel he was doing something for her, and especially she must not let him feel she wanted to do something for him," thus accepting the passive role he requires of her in order to fulfill the demands of his gender (48).

Mothers in this text play, for Glaspell, an unusually minor role, as does the semiotic style that so enriches the previous two novels. That in itself is a significant statement in a novel about fathers. Blossom, her mother, and her mother-in-law are all effectively silenced by the patriarchal familial and social structure under which they live. Blossom's biological mother has entirely conformed to her role as pea-brained symbol of her husband's wealth and only wants her daughter to follow suit and be a social success. She sublimates her own drives through overeating, her little hands "so fat they seemed helpless," signifying her indolence and captivity (57). Blossom's mother-in-law, the "Mater" as Lincoln calls her in an Anglophiliac affectation that coldly distances him from maternal intimacy, lives with them and is "a strange woman—shut up within herself" (70). Blossom admires the Mater for going to work and raising her son after her husband's desertion, and she would like to love her, "had there not been this irritating thing in her reticence, something remotely mocking" (29). What irritates Blossom is that her mother-in-law mocks Lincoln, seeing through his poses and refusing to baby him. However, her indifference toward her son masks her resentment at having to conform to the same passive role he requires of Blossom.

"The Mater supported me, now I must support her," Lincoln boasts. After her "hard life" he wants her to "have an easy time of it," laudable perhaps, but in this case, under the guise of a gift to her, he deprives her of work and independence. He characterizes her as "old" and "tragic," which confuses Blossom, who finds her "very active for her years" and "somber" but certainly not tragic (29–30). Lincoln paints her as his mater dolorosa because of his father's desertion, and he sees her consequent taking on of the male role as an aberration he must right now that he is a man, thus supplanting his father (31). He cannot perceive her strength and vitality nor her love of teaching:

> She told Blossom she had really loved to teach. She had proposed that she be teacher to the boys, but her son objected. "No indeed, Mother, that's all in the past. You don't have to work anymore."
>
> "I would enjoy it," his mother said.
>
> "You did that years enough. You did it for me, and now I can do things for you. You don't have to lift your hand, does she Blossom?"
>
> "But suppose I want to lift my hand?" his mother asked mildly.
>
> "Oh, then lift it," he laughed. "Pick up a cup of tea, or the cards, or a book, or your sewing."
>
> Blossom saw Mrs. Holt look strangely at her son, then quickly look away. (71)

Lincoln forces gender upon his mother just as he does his wife, demanding her passivity in order to fulfill his triumph over his father. Even Blossom senses that Lincoln's writing is a form of oedipal displacement of his father, since Ambrose Holt had been a reporter and an editor for the local newspaper before his bolt. The reason Lincoln gives for having become a poet is compensatory. He had to live less extravagantly than the other Harvard boys "so, unable to share their pleasures, he created one of his own—poetry, a poor man's pastime." But Blossom wonders if there isn't even more of a wish to supplant his father than that: "His father had been a writer, of a sort, and not gone very far with it. The son would be a real writer, and support the family" (32, 96). She concludes, correctly, that Lincoln "had built up a life, a personality, from this thing of his father having run away. Then the return of his father might shake the whole structure," as indeed it does (73).

Blossom finds out through her mother that Ambrose Holt, that "impudent man," is back, living in a boardinghouse next to the lumberyard (59). Her primary concern is to keep the news from Lincoln, to shield him from emotional turmoil and protect his work on the exciting new poems. But their secret knowledge of the renegade father's return empowers both Blossom and her mother-in-law, undermining Lincoln's sense of superiority over them. Secretly visiting Ambrose has given the Mater some of her "pep" back, and she uses it to mock her son (77). One of the more humorous scenes in the novel occurs in chapter 9 when Lincoln swaggers in "in high fettle" at the end of the day, inquiring smugly, "'Well, what have the ladies of my household been doing this afternoon?' . . . as if knowing in advance they had not been doing anything very important, as if amused by the things they took seriously" (74). Blossom knows they could deflate Lincoln in an instant by telling about his father, but she believes it is "unjust" to profit by knowing something he doesn't, and she feels sorry for him. Not the Mater, however:

> Instead of turning her to a fierce loyalty to her son, who took the husband's place in supporting her, she seemed to have gained some sort of sustenance, and was turning the tables on Lincoln by doing the thing he did—enjoying from a superior vantage, secretly enjoying something he did not know. (77)

Lincoln senses his mother's defection and reiterates his need to dominate her: "She'll be getting old fast now. . . . Why doesn't she have her breakfast in bed?" Although Blossom recognizes this as inappropriate for her active mother-in-law, her loyalty to Lincoln blinds her to how the Mater could "let a wretch who deserted her, hurt the son who gave her the nicest possible life" (80). Nevertheless, she is beginning to wonder whether this is indeed the "nicest possible life" for the Mater. The return of the renegade father has already left her "confused" and "troubled" about the morality of a gender hierarchy she had taken as incontrovertible (82).

Again Blossom is emboldened by her desire to shield Lincoln. She makes an appointment with her father in his office to ask him not to tell Lincoln about Ambrose Holt's return, which of course her father belittles:

"You're acting like a silly little girl. Do you want to humiliate Lincoln? He's a man, isn't he? He's a business man, and this is a thing he has to deal with" (86). Nor is her mother-in-law any help; she rejects Blossom's over-tures because her own way of survival (much like Irma's in *Fugitive's Return*) has been to "shut herself in" behind a mask of composure and authority that repels intimacy (96–97). Discouraged, Blossom leaves the Mater silently sewing, "stitching her thoughts into the void," unlike the women in "Jury of Her Peers" and *Fugitive's Return*, whose stitchery forms a semiotic bridge between them (98). Blossom feels there is no other way but to go to Ambrose Holt herself and tell him to leave.

When first spotted by Blossom's father, Ambrose had been standing "by a lumber pile," according to her mother's indignant report (59–61). Both of Blossom's parents take this as an affront, almost as outrageous as his defection: "And he's actually living down there by the lumber pile,'" Blossom's mother reiterates, "Lincoln Holt's father—the father-in-law of James Atwood's daughter—living down there by the lumber pile!" Blos-som is amused by her mother's overreaction: "Why . . . did her mother go on adding to the lumber pile?" But when she goes to find Ambrose, the lumber pile becomes the symbolic focus of her own ambivalence toward him. On the one hand she defends him, thinking, "Why shouldn't one stand by a lumber pile, if one wanted to? If she wanted to, she would get out now and stand by the lumber pile! Yes indeed she would, and they could just think what they liked!" (98). Before she has even met Ambrose, she fantasizes aligning herself with him at the lumber pile as an act of rebellion. At this point it represents a glaring accusation of the effect of her father's violation of the woods, reducing an ancient forest to a pile of milled lumber, but Glaspell also uses it to symbolize the working class— for the "father-in-law of James Atwood's daughter" to live "in a laborers' boarding house by the lumber yard" flouts the bourgeois class system (99). And while Blossom might be willing at this point to criticize her father's business practices, she is not quite ready to leap out of the bour-geoisie, for in the same moment she also thinks, "What a preposterous place for Lincoln's father to live! Perhaps the man was crazy. He must be crazy, coming back to the town where . . . he knew people, had a family, and living in a laborers' boarding house . . . Nobody she had ever heard of lived in such a place" (99).[1]

The turning point in Blossom's development occurs in chapter 12 when she converses with her infamous father-in-law for the first time. Ambrose Holt immediately begins deconstructing the dictates of masculine gender that have ruled her life: "Well, some men make money, and some make none, and who has the better time?" (101). The more Blossom attempts to scold him, the more she finds herself parried and unable to resist him. He is the first to call her "Harriette" and the first male who does not characterize her as a "fool" (103, 111). When she tries to discover why he left, he explains that the pressures upon him to conform felt "as if they were putting a pillow on my face and sitting on it," exactly the stifling of individuality she suffers(104). They instantly understand one another, but she asserts, "One must have a sense of responsibility," otherwise "How would the world get on? How would it hold together?" His reply questions the whole notion of sacrifice upon which everyone's existence in the social world of this novel is founded: "You really think that this business of everybody doing things on account of some one else is the best possible arrangement we can make about life?" (105).

While Ambrose Holt's desertion of his family might be regarded as reprehensible in our own day as it was in Glaspell's, his position is "not that which abides by the desire of the law of one's culture but that which accords with jouissance, with the drive of the other within oneself" (Mellard 406). He is another one of Glaspell's feminized males, linked with the irrational "rich, unashamed play" Glaspell so prized in Cook (*Road* 303). To Blossom, at first he seems "outrageous" and lacking "moral sense," which places him clearly beyond the bounds, "outside society" (109). However, if society is corrupt and coercive, this may be seen as positive, and Glaspell attempts to paint it so. Ambrose defends himself to Blossom by emphasizing that his abdication gave his wife "a chance to show what she could do," to work and know the pleasure of success: "She liked it, don't you think?" (109). As a feminized man, he enables Blossom to value her own pleasure, to experience jouissance, although she tries to repress it: "She was not here to enjoy herself, and she was guiltily conscious of enjoying herself" (108). In placing personal happiness above social and familial duty, he appears to be justifying his own selfish hedonism, but he is Glaspell's advocate for the primacy of the individual above any socially constructed morality, in this case a paternalism founded upon control of land, wealth, and women. "Here am I, who didn't do right, as you would say, and I have been—more or less happy. And here you are, doing right as hard as you can, and not happy at all" (110). When Blossom protests, "I am happy!" she finds herself sobbing. It is a revelation.

The following chapter opens with a reprise of the verbal duel between Lincoln and his mother from chapter 9, although now he tilts with Blossom, who has gotten "a devilish kind of courage" from meeting her father-in-law and acts "as bad as the Mater!" (114). When Lincoln enters, bantering in his usual supercilious tone, "Where are you, Blossom? A good wife should welcome her husband from his day's toil. It is a wife's duty to blossom at close of day," Blossom responds with asperity, "Please talk sensibly, for once," astounding her husband (114). In a reversal of roles and epithets, she twice tells him not to be so "silly," while he accuses her of being "superior" (115, 120). This leads to Blossom's admission that she has befriended his father. Enraged, Lincoln resorts to violence, grabbing her wrists "so it hurt," and for the first time Blossom experiences anger and fights for herself (116). When he demands to know where Blossom saw his father, she admits, "'I just met him. . . . Down by the lumber pile.' And to her horror, she laughed."

"Stop laughing," Lincoln insists, in a futile effort to repress the rebellious jouissance Ambrose inevitably arouses in women (120–21). Having abdicated the throne, that is, having let go of gender, class, and wealth, Ambrose Holt represents the exciting possibility of release from social and familial bondage for the women in his life. Unable to understand that Blossom respects his father "because he treated me like a human being and you don't," Lincoln only sees that "my father has taken my wife away from me," interpreting her defiance merely as a challenge to renew the oedipal battle with his father (116, 120). When his mother joins the fray, Glaspell deflates male competition over the possession of women by parodying old-fashioned melodrama as Lincoln shouts, "If you ever see this man again, either of you, I'll take my revolver and go down there and shoot him" (123). Oedipal melodrama continues when Lincoln yells at his mother that if she sees his father again, she "cannot go on living under my roof" (124). Glaspell wittily reveals the domineering paterfamilias as absurdly infantile, as Lincoln rants, rages, sneers, pushes, shoves, and sulks as if his toys had been taken away. Although there is an ominous tone to his violence, neither woman can help laughing at him—once again, the mocking laughter of Cixous's Medusa.

Blossom now realizes that Lincoln's "pride," the "balance between them in which he was himself," is founded upon her subordination. In declaring that she has a mind of her own and is not a fool, she "had left him nothing to stand on, no place in which to act" (126–27). She is the only one who pities him or feels responsible for his fall, however. When the Mater refuses to put her son's needs before her own and ask Ambrose to leave town, Blossom is disapproving (129–30). The Mater reveals that she married Ambrose because he "amused" her, a radical change from her previous life, trapped, much like Blossom, in her father's house. Blossom is further shocked when the Mater suggests that Blossom's father's support of his family might be considered as selfish as Ambrose's desertion of his. The question is thus raised again whether his abandonment of wife and child destroyed them or allowed them to fulfill themselves because they were not required to exist in passive subservience to his providence (132–134). With the naïveté of youth regarding age, Blossom finds it "unthinkable" that a woman of fifty-eight might put pleasure before responsibility. "There was entirely too much of this being amused! . . . Old people, she thought sternly, should act with dignity" (138). Again amusement is equated with sexually charged pleasure, but unlike male competition over the possession of women, any competitive feelings between her and the Mater over Ambrose are ultimately subsumed by their shared love for him. Blossom tries hard to be true to her tribe, to act "indignant" and feel that Ambrose is "utterly reprehensible," but she, like the Mater, is seduced by the "amusement" he offers (134). Representing the Dionysian force of disorder, the renegade father whose jouissance disrupts Apollonian patriarchal law, Ambrose enables women to place pleasure before duty, self before conformity.

Lincoln, enraged over Blossom's "betrayal," packs a suitcase and deserts his family, leaving a petulant note:

Most Helpful Wife:

Following the example of my illustrious parent, I am beating it. Your intelligence—pardon my having so long overlooked it—will tell you just how to deal with the situation. (146)

Blossom is devastated, but after reading the note, the Mater reassures her that Lincoln will soon return, since "he wasn't so desperate he couldn't think of the very things to make us feel most foolish" (148). Typically, Blossom blames herself. Unable to confide in her own parents, she realizes that "the only person who could help her understand was Ambrose Holt" (152).

Each of Blossom's two meetings with Ambrose take place in the woods, the edenic setting so important to Glaspell's portrayals of sensual love, as in Naomi and Joe's lovemaking, but also important to her portrayals of personal revelation, as in Evans's reconnection with his maternal past and Irma's healing in the forest of Kalania. Glaspell repeatedly contrasts Ambrose's association with nature against the environments of Blossom's other two men, her father's office and "Holt's Folly," the pretentious house in which Lincoln has ensconced his family. Glaspell has portrayed the male need to support women as an excuse for the accumulation of wealth and the violation of nature, represented by her father's plan to raze the woods for his cement company. Nature symbolism being consistent throughout the novels, this act represents a violation of the mother's body, just as Lincoln's study, "not unlike a cell" or a "Gothic chapel," insulates him from the same (13–15), whereas the renegade father is aligned with nature and thus with women. On her first meeting with Ambrose, Blossom had driven him in the expensive car her father gave her, in another deliberate contrast of the two fathers, "up the narrow dirt road which had followed the brook in the days when roads were for horses and long before there were cars," back temporally and spatially to a primal, edenic locus (107).

Now, on her second visit, Blossom again picks Ambrose up in the car. Angry with him, she scolds, "This is not a pleasure trip!" and tries to keep him from "enjoying" the scenery, all the while sensing him "laughing at her" (153). They end up in the very woods her father owns and has condemned for the clay underneath them (154). "She pointed to the ruined earth ahead, a wide, deep wound," and as they talk, they sit on the "edge of the unviolated woods, facing that gash, the earth despoiled" and the "wide yellow-gray scar that should have been green earth, scar of her father's greed" (154, 162, 181). These vivid images of the rape of mother earth recall Glaspell's horror at the violation of the graves in *The Road to the Temple* as well as the buried tunnels associated with the Delphic Oracle where Constantina's rape occurred and she later hides in *Fugitive's Return*. Although himself regarded as an outlaw by the community, Ambrose suggests to Blossom that it is her own father who is truly lawless. He violates a more sacred law by "vandalizing" for personal profit woods that, although he may own them temporarily, are eternal and really belong to the community (155). They talk about a number of things, but again his "difference" challenges her into new ways of thinking about God, life, death, duty, and about Lincoln, whose leaving, he suggests, might not be such a bad thing, since his "egotism" keeps Blossom from fulfilling herself. "He'll have to come back to demonstrate his superiority," Ambrose remarks caustically, "because showing it from a distance won't be nearly as satisfying" (160).

Ambrose reiterates his own reason for leaving: he felt society forcing him into a superficial role that he feared he might actually become, if he stayed (161–62). But he has paid for his iconoclasm with loneliness. Much as Blossom admires him, she realizes that "a world full of people like you" would be as "dull" as the world of social conformism that has imprisoned her. As so often, Glaspell is weighing autonomy against community, and just as in *Fidelity*, her solution evades a simplistic either/or binarism. The problem this novel proposes is whether men or women can maintain individuality within communal restraints. At the end of the chapter, Blossom has found relief in just being able to talk "freely" about Lincoln, and she reaches out to Ambrose, who has diabetes, in an attempt to include him within the familial and communal circle: "You are ill . . . and alone. I wish I could take you home with me" (171). Although grateful, he refuses.

With the help of Ambrose's somewhat cynical and certainly competitive view of his son, Blossom gives up her awe of Lincoln and begins to realize that she "knew more than she had known she knew" about him (171). First, she discovers that he has covered his tracks with his father-in-law by arranging a business trip to Pittsburgh, followed by a leave of absence in New York, and she feels she's been "made a fool of" yet again (176). She realizes that Lincoln could not afford to be "relieved of his burden," the financial responsibility of wife and children: "Perhaps he wanted a burden almost as much as he wanted her; perhaps it was very nice that she and the burden were one" (181). Ambrose Holt has taught her the meaning of the wife's role for Lincoln, as "obstacle." "A poet—a certain kind of poet—has to sing of what he hasn't," a problem for Lincoln, "for he has so much" (182). To Ambrose she complains,

> "Lincoln thinks he wants a life in which he could live simply, without obligations, without this social thing, so he could write poetry. But when I try to simplify our life he is angry with me."
>
> "Of course. That is dangerous. If he had it—how could he long for it?" (183)

So Lincoln has long hidden the two sides of his life, artist and husband, from one another, allowing Blossom "only one place in which she could dwell, as if, in a great house, one were kept in a certain room" (181).

To bolster his masculinity, Lincoln must perpetuate cultural binarisms such as art/money, New York/Illinois, mistress/wife, keeping his solitary trips to New York "a sealed book to Blossom" because as child-wife she cannot be exposed to his intellectual friends in the speakeasies. "You wouldn't like them," he tells Blossom. "They're likely to say bitch. Bitch is one of their milder words" (50). Ambrose explains the binaristic purpose of the mistress as opposed to the wife when Blossom reports having glimpsed a few words on a letter of Lincoln's to New York: "but, incomparable Margot" (184). Her father-in-law elaborates: "'You are wonderful,' he had been saying, 'but incomparable Margot, I have a wife—but, incomparable Margot . . . I am not free to go with you'" (184). When

Blossom protests that she doesn't want to be "just something in the way," Ambrose responds that she is crucial to sustaining Lincoln's myth: "You are the obstacle. The obstacle to keep him from what he wants. . . . Things not had are precious. . . . What is it the rather sentimental Nietzsche says? The pathos of distance. Don't take the unattainable from a poet" (185).[2] Ambrose scorns his son, not only for the way he confines Blossom but because "you don't have to trump up an obstacle between you and freedom. You can't have it anyway, so why blame an obstacle? Freedom is really the unattainable" for everyone. "Our limitations— there's the true obstacle, and obstacle enough, God knows," he concludes (185).

Ambrose Holt's quixotic search for freedom exemplifies, and may even parody, the American quest for self-definition through confronting the untamed wilderness discussed in chapter 1 (Baym 71–73). As Ambrose explains in a posthumous letter to Blossom, in his travels he sought the "high sky and the wideness" of the West as a "tip to the spirit, saying— There is room" (275). "I liked the sunrise, and the evening, and the nights on the prairie. I like a trail over the mountains. I like a horse, and a dog" (276). But again Glaspell has reworked this quest myth in which the constraints of society that bind the male hero are envisioned as female. From her feminist perspective, communal constructs and the exploitation of nature are both shown to be the result of the patriarchal concept of property, that is, the ownership of women, children, wealth, and land. In rejecting society and aligning himself with an unviolated natural wilderness, Ambrose Holt is thus, like Erik Helge and John Knight, a feminized male who helps the female protagonist find her own power.

However, Glaspell characteristically undermines grandiose romantic gestures with wry irony. Ambrose Holt's idealism has been tempered by reality; as he admits in the letter, his "venture" was "not a complete success." He had abandoned one role, that of the patriarch, to find himself merely "clamped upon again" in another, "the role of the buffoon." His "gesture of getting loose," of freeing his spirit, "wasn't wholly true, but it was in that direction, and what is wholly true?" Put in other terms, jouissance is an impossibility outside the unconscious, for it is a drive, a force that is unbound and unknowable. Thus this novel is, as *New York Times* critic John Chamberlain wrote in 1931, a "tragi-comedy of idealism," for Ambrose realizes that it is impossible to escape being clamped upon, yet he affirms that "the effort was not wholly a failure" for it has meaning in itself (274). Both his children, Blossom and Lincoln, need to find just such a matured vision of compromise between freedom and community, self-definition and conformity.

Blossom's growing sense of self inevitably leads to a confrontation with her father, the first patriarch who formed her and still, for her, the most intimidating (190–201). She takes a stand in declaring herself no longer willing to be characterized as a fool, defending Ambrose Holt as "wiser than you" and refusing her father's order that she write to Lincoln and ask him to come home (194). Her father attempts to force her to succumb to his will, and in the standoff that ensues, he plays his trump card as paterfamilias, using his wealth to coerce her into conformity to the all-important passing on of patrimony. If she disobeys him, he says, "I shall leave you—not one cent" in his will (200). Since this would deprive her children of their inheritance, the problem is raised again whether a parent should sacrifice self for the (material) good of children (203). Blossom must finally accept that her father, who had seemed to personify Law, is in fact "lawless" because he "made his money into a lasso, which caught, held, punished, or bribed—controlled," and because she realizes he will resort to anything, even violence, "when his power was challenged" (204, 210). Blossom evades his manipulation by realizing that her sons, already "arrogant, impertinent to the servants," would be better off not raised in wealth (210–11).

Her real concern is Ambrose. She knows her father would do anything to get rid of him and believes she must warn him, despite her father's interdiction. But Glaspell shows the ineluctable pull of money in Blossom's uneasy ambivalence. Although clearly perceiving the moral high road, she is unable to let go of the wealth that has dominated her existence, four times rationalizing ways to defy her father *and* keep the money. "She was not a person to be bought—even for a million dollars," yet she is "safeguarded by the idea that her father would never know" if she warned Ambrose, while "in the back of her head snugly rested the idea her father would leave the money in trust for the boys" (211–12). A telephone call from her mother bewailing her father's determination to get rid of Ambrose spurs her to act, and Blossom finds "it was not to her father's house she turned." She follows her heart "toward the lumber pile—away from her father, to her father-in-law," for "she would not be bullied!" (214).

Ambrose has already decamped, beating her father's "drastic measures" by his own decision to move on. Both she and the Mater are hurt, but the Mater knows she "never had him," so "why should I think I have him now?" (219). Blossom, however, feels bereft. Because of Ambrose's influence, she has "gotten loose; she was out; she couldn't go back, for it would not be the same self she took back" (203). So she proceeds forward, daring to cross into the forbidden world of Lincoln's other life, his intellectual and artistic domain. When she receives a letter from a New York literary critic, Hugh Parker, she invites him to visit, even though Lincoln is not there.[3] Anxious to understand Lincoln's poetry better and, like Blossom, mystified by the aspects of Lincoln's life he keeps hidden, the critic wants to explore the Mississippi Valley side of the poet's life. Blossom knows well that "Lincoln would be furious for he did not want to be understood," but she has the strength now to begin defying some of the false binarisms that have been imposed upon her (209).

Lincoln is contrasted with Hugh Parker, much to the former's disadvantage, as the falsity of Lincoln's attempt to sequester the two sides of himself and their loci, New York and Illinois, is revealed. Here Glaspell uses his character to comment upon the state of the arts in America, a stalemate of East versus West, city versus heartland, intellectual elite versus salt-of-the-earth folks. Her conclusion, typically, is that such divisions only hinder the artist's vision. As Hugh converses with Blossom and Lincoln's friends, Blossom discovers she is not the only one Lincoln treated with supercilious disdain and shut out of his intellectual life. Their local friends Edith and Hal reveal their resentment at being excluded from even the chance of appreciating Lincoln's art: "I may not be much, but why make me less than I am?" Hal asks (237). To his New York crowd, Lincoln gave the impression of his life in Illinois as a "prison," his family as a "handicap," and his wife as an "invalid" and a "dumbell" (227, 243). However, Lincoln's New York friends are as perplexed by him as his Illinois neighbors, as Hugh puzzles, "If it's a prison, why stay in it?" (238). Ambrose has already made Lincoln's syndrome clear. He must maintain the illusion of himself as an "alien" wherever he is to maintain his sense of superiority, as Hugh comments: "He feels he really has it on us, because he is what we aren't" (239, 256). And he believes the only way to produce meaningful poetry is to write out of an unquenchable longing for the unattainable.

Glaspell answers the question of whether perpetuating such false binarisms can in fact produce genuine art by stressing the inadequacy of Lincoln's work. Hugh wonders, "What is the matter with Lincoln's poetry? Why does one never have him in his work?" (239). Although they may sense great potential, no one, from his mother-in-law to the celebrated literary critic, really understands his work because the artist "is never all there." His is a poetry of absence, of self withheld; he writes "over an emptiness" (256). Always the poseur protecting his insecurities, Lincoln hides behind an obscurantism that prompts his mother to comment with her usual asperity that "possibly it wouldn't hurt" if he simplified (76).

Lincoln represents the modernist artist as middle-aged male, left behind as the avant-garde 1920s gave way to the socially conscious 1930s. By the time this novel was published in 1931, the heyday of the modernist experiment was drawing to a close, and, as Veronica Makowsky has commented, "through her characterization of Lincoln and his poetry, Glaspell is indicting the increasingly male entrenched modernism" with its "tendency to exclude others, and so elevate the mysterious, godlike author" (118–19). Glaspell's critique of Lincoln's inability to fuse his bohemian, artistic side with his bourgeois, familial side indicates her anger at the spurious divisions in the American literary scene between modernist/realist and experimental/regional that would soon begin prejudicing the reception of her own work.

Blossom is torn because she wants Lincoln back *and* she wants to be herself. She confesses her dilemma to Hugh Parker, the second man after her father-in-law to treat her as a "human being" (255). He befriends her and continues her education, sending her feminist books, *A Room of One's Own* and Genevieve Taggard's *Emily Dickinson*, the latter of great importance to Glaspell, for she based her Pulitzer Prize–winning play, *Alison's House*, on it. As the novel winds to its denouement, Blossom receives the letter from Ambrose in which he explains his nonconformity and the matured realization at the end of his life that his attempt to escape a role was in itself the assumption of a role, and he delivers his final caustic estimation of his son: "He wouldn't want you to understand him, for he wants to be greater than your understanding, and also he wants to suffer in not being understood" (281). Ambrose explains his plan to commit suicide, which he has already done by the time she receives the letter. One of the first people with diabetes to benefit from the new drug insulin, Ambrose feels justified in taking his life by simply halting the therapy. His suicide is thus the most extreme expression of his rejection of social constructs and his alliance with nature: "Death had me, and artifice stepped in and I think it's alright to let nature take its course" (277). Then Ambrose declares his love for Blossom in terms that fulfill the daughter's oedipal fantasy:

> I was waiting, always, for some great experience. You were it, Harriette dear . . . and for me nothing like this will come again. . . . We are two people who can understand each other, and after having long wanted it, I can say goodbye, feeling life came to something. (278)

At the end of the novel Blossom has become the daughter of two fathers. Her renegade father opens her eyes, and in parting he urges her to "see the world around you" (312). Inheriting the phallic gaze from him, she has become his eyes, for "often in the future she would be seeing for him" (289). She decides unhesitatingly that "he will be buried from my house," and her use of the first-person possessive pronoun is significant, for the house has always been considered Lincoln's. Wanting Lincoln "to join her in this," she telegraphs him to return. Blossom has finally become the active agent. Surprisingly, Lincoln backs her. Her decisive act is sanctified by his approval; nevertheless, because she insists on it as the morally right thing to do whatever the social consequences, it is also fueled by her own newfound confidence in herself. Even her father backs down, and she enjoys the irony of his attendance at the funeral of the man he excoriated, "wearing a frock coat in honor of Ambrose Holt" (312).

Blossom has taken Ambrose at last into the "home of wife, and son, and daughter-in-law," and the Mater thanks her, asserting that she is "a good woman" (297). Lincoln's return telegram had also called her "good to do this," and when he arrives he holds her, crying, "You are so good! So good!" (292, 306). Blossom's movement from "fool" to "good" can be characterized as the evolution from subservient daughter to empowered mother. Lincoln looks up to her for strength and help in understanding his father (303). He admits that he has "always been afraid," and now he needs her "not only because she was Blossom, his pretty wife, but because he needed what was herself" (305, 307). Beginning in a garden where Blossom's creativity and self-esteem were both revealed to be prohibited, the novel concludes in a graveyard where familial continuity is affirmed through Blossom's agency, as she returns Ambrose Holt to his mother and father in their graves beneath the snowberry bushes "now covered with the round white berries" (313).

In the figure of Blossom Holt, Glaspell poses the question of whether a woman who wants to remain wife and mother, who loves her husband despite his faults, can mediate the patriarchal parameters of those roles and maintain her sense of self within them. For Glaspell, marriage is a necessarily flawed patriarchal institution, but the union of man and woman also contains within it the seeds of life, and "where there has been life, it is not as a place where there has never been life," a theme she will explore more tragically in *Norma Ashe*. Blossom has no illusions regarding her husband's character. She cautions herself that "it will not always be like this" and that their marriage will inevitably "slip back, and often seem a good deal as it had been before" (314). However, Lincoln has learned to respect her, and she has gained the self-knowledge and strength to affirm her own individuality within the boundaries of their marriage: "'It is Harriette,' her heart said. 'I shall remember'" (315).

*Ambrose Holt and Family* contains some of Glaspell's most satiric dissections of gender. It is also her most comic novel, both in its humorous caricatures and in its ending in which familial and social order are maintained, the traditional mandate of comedy. Without the evocative female semiotic that elevates Glaspell's style in works such as "Jury of Her Peers" and *Fugitive's Return*, her style here can seem light and somewhat superficial. However, once her wry, parodic sense of humor is appreciated, the wit of many scenes makes enjoyable reading.

Of more serious concern is the fact that Glaspell's always meliorative vision may seem too compromising and too pat here. Previous novels have ended with protagonists poised on the brink of radical change, Ruth as she leaves to assume the life of the 1920s' New Woman in the big city, Irma as she returns with an adopted daughter to create a new life in harmony with the land, and Evans as representative of a new generation of sons who side with the mother. In this novel, community (patriarchy) is maintained through the integration of the daughter's potentially disruptive force (jouissance) into the social order. Yet even Glaspell's most meliorative endings preserve an essentially uncomfortable ambiguity. Although she always reaffirmed personal growth, Glaspell saw less and less potential for positive social change as she aged, which is reflected in this novel and even more poignantly in *Norma Ashe*. Here social integration is made possible only through the agency of a fantasized father, a Prospero whose magical love enables the Caliban-like rage of the daughter to be tamed and sublimated. However, this Prospero, a patriarch manqué, has not been restored to his throne but instead has been banished to the graveyard. The daughter has broken free of her filial bonds but only to become the "good" mother. Freedom is indeed unattainable, as Ambrose says, and that is truly where Glaspell leaves us.

Eros is the most dangerous of all these relations: while answering
most deeply to human needs of dependency, reciprocity, and
empathy, it is also perceived to threaten most seriously the
boundaries of the autonomous self and under the magnetic
pull of desire to put the self in the power of another.

—*Froma I. Zeitlin*

# 7

## *The Morning Is Near Us* (1939)
## as Euripidean Tragicomedy

Graveyards, gardens, archaeological remains, ancestral homes, edenic
loci—all reflect different aspects of the same longing for return to pre-
oedipal union for Susan Glaspell. Haunted by the imminence of death, her
novels affirm a modernist view of eternity as the natural, cyclical regeneration of human life, which is often expressed through reunion with mother
earth, for instance, when Evans reconnects with his dead grandmother by
the brook at the conclusion of *Brook Evans*. In *Fugitive's Return*, Irma
brings her newly adopted daughter to the waiting hillside, her ancestral
vineyard, to begin life anew. *Ambrose Holt and Family* opens with Blossom Holt's garden and ends with the burial of Ambrose Holt in the family
plot. *The Morning Is Near Us*, too, opens with a cemetery and an ancestral
house, this time set right up against one another in a close juxtaposition of
the abodes of the living and the dead. The Chippman family home is
deserted and the cemetery is encroaching upon it, as if to engulf the living
body into the realm of the dead. Lydia Chippman, sent away as a girl to
live and travel with a wealthy aunt, is now thirty-five years old and sum-
moned back by a letter from her brother telling her that their father has left

the house to her. However, if she does not take it within three years, the "land would go to the cemetery and the house be torn down":

> The cemetery needed it too, for the dead were moving down this slope; right against the Chippman fence they were now, and the fence breaking down, as if to let them in. Yes, the dead increased, and the Chippman land was here waiting for them. (5)

The novel begins with Lydia's telegram announcing her return, after the three-year grace period, with her two adopted children, Koula and Diego. "Let the dead go somewhere else. . . . Happy to come back and save our home" (6). Her response indicates the role she will play: the exiled child returns to forestall the doom on the ancestral home and restore fertility and continuity to the family line. With this prototypical Greek theme, Glaspell returns in *The Morning Is Near Us* to the mythic method of *Fugitive's Return*, ingeniously illuminating a modern tale with a classical subtext. Glaspell's unusual use of an epigraph taken from a somewhat obscure tragedy by Euripides, the *Rhesos* (from which the title of this novel is also derived), is another clue that myth criticism is necessary again in this chapter to explicate the classical themes and allusions at play.

Lydia brings new life to the dying house with her children, who will "climb the elm and the apple tree, play tag and hide behind the gravestones, as she and [her brother] Warren had done" (44). But in order to expiate the family curse, she must uncover the "secret" at the heart of her mother's rejection and her father's abandonment of her: "For years I've wondered what was the matter with me. Why Mother didn't love me. Why I was kept from home" (187). Believing her father to be dead, she searches for him in the graveyard:

> She went back to the space beside her mother. . . . She knelt and felt the earth. Nothing told her anyone rested beneath this earth.
>
> Her father was not buried beside her mother.
>
> A long time she just stood there. And when she began moving about it was in a panic. She went amongst the graves of other families—looking—and under her breath she was saying, "Father! Where are you?" And when she found she had called aloud, "Father!" she was terrified and she did not know how to get back home. (95–96)

This is a poignant image that seems to have haunted Glaspell. In *Fugitive's Return*, after buying a home on Cape Cod, Irma searches for evidence of her ancestors' presence there, deciphering "names she had read in her grandmother's Bible" in the "old burying-ground" (165). In *Fidelity*, Ruth wanders the "hillside where she knew she would find her mother's grave," crying out with longing for her presence. In that scene the living and dead are juxtaposed, as they are in *The Morning Is Near Us*. Ruth feels shut out "in the dwelling place of the living," but "right over there on the next hill, were the dead" where she seeks solace, as does Lydia (210). In Lydia's cry to her lost father, as in Ruth's longing for her dead mother, the theme Glaspell consistently explores throughout these novels is movingly expressed—the desire to return, to refind the lost eden of maternal/paternal love. Graveyards appear again and again in these novels because for Glaspell they reestablish familial connections, helping the protagonist rediscover an elemental parental love that can break through her existential isolation and, ironically, halt the encroachment of death upon life.

*Fidelity*, *Fugitive's Return*, and *The Morning Is Near Us* all portray exiles returning home, seeking familial and communal embrace. Yet *Fugitive's Return* ends with a mother and adopted child departing for the ancestral home, while *The Morning Is Near Us* begins with their arrival. Like *Brook Evans*, this novel explores a protagonist's pre-oedipal/oedipal oscillation between mother and father, but in a mature woman rather than in an adolescent girl. Similar to *Ambrose Holt and Family*, in *The Morning Is Near Us* Glaspell writes another disturbingly ambiguous ending made possible by a patriarchal father's sudden transformation into an idealized, loving father. Unique to this novel, however, is Glaspell's attempt to explore these themes on two levels, the familial and the national, as she delves into an issue that will increasingly occupy her in her last novels—what it means to be an American. Thus, *The Morning Is Near Us* provides a bridge between the previous three novels, constituting what I am calling Glaspell's middle period and focusing largely on psychosexual issues, and the two novels of her late period, *Norma Ashe* and *Judd Rankin's Daughter*, which focus more on sociocultural issues.

Glaspell's novels generally employ all the innovative, uniquely female narrative strategies used by the modernist women writers whose works Rachel Blau DuPlessis explicates in *Writing Beyond the Ending*, using these terms. To define the psychosocial aspects of twentieth-century women's narratives, DuPlessis turns to Nancy Chodorow's discussion of pre-oedipal and oedipal parent-child relations. Thus *Writing Beyond the Ending* extends the psychoanalytic analysis I have applied to earlier Glaspell novels to a generic analysis that is very helpful here. The aptness of DuPlessis's critical theory as a tool to explicate *The Morning Is Near*

*Us*, shows that as a novelist, no less than a playwright, Glaspell is not a throwback to the nineteenth century but ranks among modernist contemporaries such as Olive Schreiner, Virginia Woolf, Dorothy Richardson, and H.D.

According to DuPlessis, early-twentieth-century women writers inherited a romantic nineteenth-century form in which "successful quest and romance could not coexist and be integrated for the female protagonist at the resolution" (xi). They innovated narrative strategies in order to "delegitimate romance plots," such as "reparenting in invented families, fraternal-sororal ties . . . and emotional attachment to women in bisexual love plots, female bonding, and lesbianism" (5). Certainly Glaspell's novels delegitimate romance plots, as I have already shown. None of her novels ends in the subordination of the "female hero," to use DuPlessis's term, to romantic love. She may toy with the possibility of this "happy" ending, as in *Brook Evans*, but she undermines it by focusing on intergenerational themes at the conclusion. In *Fugitive's Return*, Irma clearly rejects romantic love for maternal love. In *Ambrose Holt and Family*, Blossom is already married and finds a way to coexist in that far from perfect relationship. In *The Morning Is Near Us*, a potential lover is posited in Henry, an old family friend and bachelor who helps Lydia restore her garden, but Glaspell never pursues their relationship. She believes in the power of love, certainly, and she occasionally writes about it in rhapsodic terms, but Glaspell's novels are primarily bildungsromans, quests for identity and selfhood, not for love and marriage.

Lydia's quest is to return the mother's body (life and fertility) to the ancestral home. In so doing, she will rediscover her mother for herself, which is crucial to her identity formation and her capacity to love. But she can only create a social identity in the community through her father's agency. Although she learns that her missing father is not dead, it takes her much longer to discover that the "secret" haunting the family is her mother's violated sexuality. Like *Fugitive's Return*, this is a novel about rape, but in an even more prototypically Greek theme, it is her father's incestuous rape of his adopted sister, her mother, and his continued control over her sexuality. Lydia must absolve her father of his guilt for the terrible crimes he has committed, not the least of which is his banishment of her, and then find acceptance in his love. Only with the reconnection of intergenerational love will Lydia truly be able to reclaim her home and the graveyard become a place of peace.

Another narrative strategy described by DuPlessis that Glaspell employs in this novel, and in *Fugitive's Return*, is adoption, in other words, "reparenting in invented families." The brother-to-sister bonds that Du-Plessis emphasizes are important here as well. Lydia's brother, Warren, initially expresses ambivalence about her return: "She'd look strange. Her looks had always been—well, not like the rest of them. And now she'd be stranger than ever—foreign—and act in a way nobody'd understand" (18). Warren voices the town's hostility toward difference, but as soon as she arrives, the fraternal-sororal bond is reestablished, "back in the old give-and-take" (56). Warren's wife and the townsfolk follow suit, finding Lydia "so simple and easy to know," even though "she suggested foreign things, ways they did not know" (90). Her brother's acceptance provides the first step in Lydia's reintegration into family and community. Most important of DuPlessis's strategies in Glaspell's novels, however, is female bonding, as illustrated earlier in Ruth/Annie and Irma/Stamula. In this novel, female friendship begins to restore the mother-child bond for Lydia in an emotional attachment that implies DuPlessis's "bisexual love plot."

DuPlessis identifies "the expression of two systemic elements of female identity" in twentieth-century women's writing, "a psychosexual script and a sociocultural situation," both of which are represented in *The Morning Is Near Us*, and "both structured by major oscillations" (35). DuPlessis adopts the term "oscillation" from Nancy Chodorow. As discussed in chapter 3, the intimate mother-daughter tie prolongs pre-oedipal issues into the oedipal period for women. DuPlessis quotes the following passage from *The Reproduction of Mothering*: "the asymmetrical structure of parenting generates a female oedipus complex . . . characterized by the continuation of pre-oedipal attachments and preoccupations, sexual oscillation in an oedipal triangle, and the lack of either absolute change of love object or absolute oedipal resolution" (Chodorow 133–34). For DuPlessis, twentieth-century women writers reassess gender by transcending any "oversimplified oedipal drama." Instead, they recognize the "'bisexual oscillation' in the psychic makeup of characters" and "readjust the maternal and paternal in ways that unbalance the univocal sequence of object choices," creating "an interplay between the mother, the father, and the hero, in a 'relational triangle'" (37).

In *The Morning Is Near Us*, Glaspell transcends an oversimplified oedipal drama, just as she did in *Brook Evans*, with a complex portrayal of a daughter's oscillation between pre-oedipal longing for reunion with the mother's body and oedipal longing for the father's acceptance and approval. Object choice is never univocal for Glaspell. Oedipal desire for the father is always invested with longing for the maternal body, particularly in this text where Lydia regains her mother through her father's command to return to the family home and ultimately through reunion with him. He is at once her rival and her lover. Like the other radical women writers DuPlessis explores, Glaspell consistently deconstructs binarisms and refuses to accept the conventional ending that castrates the "female hero," that is, makes her give up her first object choice (mother) and her phallic quest in order to accept her feminine destiny. Instead she writes a "female-sexed text" that attempts a constant negotiation of binary opposition (Cixous, "Laugh" 247).

The binarisms between which Lydia oscillates are beautifully symbolized by the juxtaposition of house and cemetery at the opening of the novel:

| House | Cemetery |
|---|---|
| life | death |
| mother | father |
| fluidity | rigidity |
| body | spirit |
| isolation | community |

That the hills and land are associated with maternity is expressed in this lyrical passage:

"The little hills rejoice on every side." They didn't come in too close, and they were so friendly. As a child she had loved the shadows sliding downhill and the first gleam of morning sun on the crest had always made her want to clap her hands. Sometimes they were like big patient animals. . . . You could run up and down these gentle hills and through the twisting valleys between them. The hills were fun and they were company and they were beautiful. Here were intimacies. It had a pattern—the house set amidst these waves that had paused. Yes, the hills were waves that had paused. This had always remained her idea of what home should be—a little shut away from the world, not inaccessible, but sheltered. One's own. All the years away her spirit had held it as her own, even after it was denied her. One's spirit can't be denied what is one's own. (86)

Here the recalling of a childhood hymn, the childlike tone of the whole passage, and the association of the land with bovine animals reinforce the vision of an idealized mother projected onto the land. In her memory the daughter greets the hills clapping, just as a baby might happily greet its mother's face in the morning. The child possesses the mother in total security: mother is "one's own," "a little shut away from the world" but "not inaccessible" to the child. This intimacy, however, is not overwhelmed by the narcissistic threat of the intrusive mother; she "didn't come in too close." The fluidity of the hills as "waves that had paused" recalls the soft curves of the mother's body and the flow of her milk. The daughter's pre-oedipal desire for her mother as object choice is clear: she resents that "it was denied her" and refuses to "be denied what is one's own."

That the cemetery is associated with paternity is suggested by the way Glaspell personifies the voice of the "cemetery association" as a stern, disapproving father with "plenty to say" about Lydia:

> It had been expected the Chippman land would be turned over to them that week. Now this Lydia Chippman was coming home. Anyone with a grain of sense would know she couldn't live there. It was just selfishness—spite. Most of all it was ingratitude. The town had stood by the Chippmans and it was fitting their place become the cemetery. . . . It was selfish—inconsiderate—ungrateful. The woman must be crazy. (27)

In all Glaspell novels, small-town America is portrayed ambiguously as both a nostalgic ideal of supportive communal life and a stifling enclave of bourgeois intolerance. Here "the town had stood by the Chippmans," in other words, had suffocated them with its sanctimonious cover-up of the family's secrets, so "it was fitting their place become the cemetery." As in *Fidelity*, where conservative women voice patriarchal constraints, "selfishness" is the sin of the branded woman. And as in *Brook Evans*, where the father is the voice of repressive religious morality, patriarchy again condemns women who place their needs over the community's dictates as "selfish—inconsiderate—ungrateful" and finally "crazy." The cemetery association asserts its right to possession of the house, just as Lydia later finds out her father took possession of her mother.

Lydia clings to the belief that her father's disposition of the property constitutes a "command" upon her to return. "Father wanted me to come home," she keeps saying, even though Warren repeatedly warns her that their father probably did not think she really would come home. Parental rejection had orphaned her, just like the poor peasant children whom she adopts and with whom she identifies: "What she could not stand was to see [Diego] watch others play. 'Why he's like me,' she one day said to herself. Then she took him for her own" (45). He is like her, always on the outside, excluded from community, watching others play. Since her aunt's death, she had spent her adult life wandering aimlessly across Europe and

Latin America, forming superficial friendships and then moving on, leaving others to think it "strange she didn't seem to belong to anybody" (51). Baffled as to why she was "being kept away," like any child she blamed herself. Her sense of exclusion and difference led to a fundamental disconnection between herself and others, an unbridgeable isolation:

> It was her nature to move easily and naturally among people. She was sure that was as it had been meant to be. But she would go a little way and then be stopped from within, like being afraid of being found out. When you aren't wanted by your own family you think there must be something wrong with you. What was it? If only they had told her. All her life she had been different with everyone else because they hadn't told her. (49)

Her fear of intimacy even resulted in a frigidity comparable to Marion Williams's in *Fidelity* and Irma's in the early sections of *Fugitive's Return*, as she recalls one of her lovers accusing her: "That's it—something is wrong with you. . . . You are cold—though I don't think you are really cold. But guarded—withdrawn. . . . You might live with one hundred men and you would never give yourself" (49). Without a home, without parental roots, there is no core of identity. In love she cannot "give herself because she didn't know the self she would give" (208).

"What was it?" What is the secret at the core of her banishment? She soon finds out from Warren that her father has been incarcerated in an insane asylum because he murdered a man who attempted to blackmail him with their mother's sexual infidelity. "People felt Father had been good to Mother—so they gave him this way out. They never even brought it into court—what was behind it, I mean" (104). Even after their mother's death their father was "still protecting" her (105). But Warren represses "what was behind it," presumably her adultery, and Lydia is still left very much in the dark:

> There was something more she ought to ask. If she was going to understand she ought to ask what it was they never brought into court, what it was made people kind to Father. Through that question the truth would lie—the whole truth. Why Mother had not loved her, why she had been kept away from home. Deep underneath the answer to that question lay the secret of unhappy glances, of troubled looks. Know this true answer and she would know the secret of this house. (104)

Glaspell deposits several hints that "the secret of this house" is maternal sexuality (as the word "secret" signifies in her previous texts), hidden and feared. Typically the town sympathizes with the father, protects him, and buries female sexuality with its taboos. Maddeningly, Lydia does not ask for the answer at this point. The reader is sometimes tempted to think this repeated delaying is a ploy on Glaspell's part to draw out the plot, but generally one of Glaspell's strengths is plot structure. Rather, Lydia herself feels the weight of the cultural ban of silence that, as in *Brook Evans*, restricts female expression: "She knew nothing about her mother's early years. That had been just another silence" (113). Lydia now knows "it was all about Mother," and Glaspell wants her protagonist to uncover the maternal body experientially, not verbally. As we have seen in several of her other novels, Glaspell explores the "woman-to-woman bond," to use DuPlessis's term, semiotically. The mother-daughter bond here is rediscovered first through female friendship, which as feminist psychoanalysts have shown, replicates the maternal bond (see Flax); second, through the discovery of another silenced Philomela's weaving; and finally through her mother's letters to her own lost brother.

Lydia begins to reconnect with her mother, Hertha, through another mother-daughter pair, both named Mary. The daughter Mary extends friendship to Lydia, replicating their mothers' friendship: "You and I have quite a bond, Lydia. . . . Your mother and mine were friends when they were girls" (113). Through the doubling of the Marys in the two generations, Glaspell again suggests the mirroring, so striking in *Brook Evans*, that is a sign of the daughter's identification with her mother. Without this identification, Lydia is unformed as a human being and unknown to herself, so she finds "something deeply stirring in the thought of becoming a little more acquainted with her own mother" (116). From Mary's mother, Lydia discovers that Hertha had been an orphan and was adopted by Lydia's grandparents, had lived in the Chippman house as a little girl just as she did, and had gone to the same school she did. These replications further the identification Lydia yearns to make with her mother, but they are not sufficient. From this bond of female friendship Lydia has a presentiment of the bond of intimacy that was denied her between herself and her mother:

> For why wouldn't they want her to know Mother had grown up in the house where she grew up? Such a natural, intimate thing to know. How could it be withheld, concealed, and why should it be? . . . A bond. There was not to be a bond. . . . You felt lost in the world—not knowing who your mother was or where she came from. No, it wasn't that made you lost. It was her not wanting you to know. (126)

Did "they" withhold her mother, or was it "her not wanting you to know"? There is a crucial difference. In the former, her mother has been the passive victim of silencing; in the latter, she herself coldly cuts her daughter off from the past, depriving her of origins. But Mary's mother comments that "Hertha never told who she was or where she came from. There was something about her kept you from asking questions. Those who did ask—got silence for their pains" (124). And Mary suggests that "perhaps something too hard happened to your mother when she was very young, and she couldn't speak of it. If you don't speak at first then you can't speak" (128). Thus Hertha is another mute Philomela, another rape victim, whose maternal dysfunction is related to the patriarchal domination that bound and silenced her.

This drawing of Hertha entirely from without, through the eyes of others, constitutes one of Glaspell's most intriguing versions of the absent woman, the palimpsest identified in her plays by Linda Ben-Zvi upon which male characters "inscribe their own identities, desires, and language" ("*Contributions*" 157). Hertha, whose name suggests a Teutonic goddess, is romanticized Other—nature goddess, icon, angel/whore, Beauty personified. All the male characters idealize her and lust for her. Her son, Warren, recalls her in bed, "flushed with sleep and her eyes even deeper blue because they had been long closed. Her flaxen hair was in two braids that came round her shoulders. Her full red lips would part—you could see her white even teeth; she seemed all dreamy and dewy . . . more beautiful than anyone I ever saw" (11). Older men, too, recall her as "the most beautiful woman [they] ever knew" (78). Remembering Hertha releases them as "old eyes saw beauty in which young eyes had rejoiced, and there seemed a tender gratefulness that such beauty had been in the world" (202). Lydia's father has committed murder in an effort to protect his icon, and long past her death, he still "lives with her. He doesn't want anything else to intrude" (190). It is male possession of her as object that has excluded the daughter from her love.

But Glaspell also suggests bisexual attraction, another of DuPlessis's narrative strategies, through the erotic power Hertha's beauty had for her friend Mary:

> "Your mother and I used to—What hair she had! And her eyes were as blue as bluebells. . . . Your mother was the most beautiful girl I ever saw in my life. . . . I'll never forget the first day I saw her. She was coming through the little birch thicket and when she came out of the shadows the sun was on her hair." (118)

Here Hertha emerges from the thicket like a nymph, seducing the other young woman with her beauty into a forbidden relation, as implied by the unfinished clause "Your mother and I used to—." When young Mary suggests that Hertha's great beauty must have created a rivalry between the two women, her mother responds, "'You couldn't hate Hertha. She was too beautiful. You just had to take it. Her mouth was rather heavy, except it was so luscious. Mercy!—how I'm talking—and an old woman too . . .'" (120). The elder Mary censors her bisexuality, but it is clear that Hertha is Eros, the irrational and irresistible force of erotic love: "Beauty like that shouldn't die. Well, it didn't—not in the memory of men who had seen it glorify the world" (202).

As Beauty personified, endowed with the irrational power of Eros, Hertha is identified with Helen. Like all mythic projections of woman as Other, Helen is regarded ambivalently. She is the "casus belli" whose terrible beauty reflects male ambivalence toward "the inextricable duality of glory and death that marks the heroic code" (Suzuki 19). She is the geras, the supreme prize of war that men fight over, just as John Chippman, who murders in Hertha's name, later exclaims, "Men—why, they would have given their very lives for her. Because—because there had never been such beauty in the world" (285–86). But Helen is also a "prisoner of the passions her beauty excite[s]" (Suzuki 38). Her beauty is not only the instrument of Aphrodite's power over men, but she is herself the victim of Eros, for "the power of Aphrodite is indeed irresistible" (Zeitlin 54). This has been the traditional defense of Helen, as in Book III of the *Iliad*, where Helen is unable to defy Aphrodite's will that she have sex with Paris, whom she otherwise despises (ll. 395–448), and in Euripides' *The Trojan Women*, where she defends herself against Hecuba's accusations by claiming she was forced to love through Aphrodite's action in her, a force even Zeus cannot resist. Here, too, everyone exonerates Hertha's sexual promiscuity, even her husband, because "Love sang in her and told her it was good. Her body said yes . . . she turned to their love—to the sun. She couldn't help it" (285–86).

Euripides' defense in his *Helen* is more radical, based upon a variation of the myth in which a phantom Helen, or eidolon, accompanies Paris to Troy while the real Helen was exiled to Egypt (4–6). "Eidolon" literally means "real-to-him," and Helen's prologue clearly shows Euripides' awareness of female beauty as "a construct for the warriors to justify the war" (Suzuki 15):

Hera, disgruntled in defeat, deprived
her rival's solid promise of all substance:

she gave the Trojan prince not the real me
but a living likeness conjured out of air,
so that believing he possesses me
he possesses only his belief. (22)

Hertha is just such an eidolon, eternally recreated according to the viewer's imagination, as young Mary's words illustrate:

"To me your mother seems the most romantic figure I ever knew about. Think of having such a mother! Why, you can build anything around her—and there's no fact to stop you. . . . When you don't know you can imagine. . . . maybe she was a goddess. She must have looked like one. Mother doesn't usually rave on like that. Maybe she came from somewhere beyond our world, where there is beauty such as we have never beheld." (127)

But the problem with ideals is that they are not human. Again Glaspell delegitimizes romantic love, as Lydia senses how unhealthy her father's obsession is: "It doesn't seem the right kind of love. . . . surely you can love as much and still love life and others near you" (190–91). Lydia resents her father's possessive appropriation of her mother, which excludes her. She doesn't want a phantom image, she wants an embodied mother "to tie to" (126). When she complains that her mother didn't love her, young Mary offers Lydia her own love: "The past is in the past and in this moment you have a new friend who loves you," but Lydia cannot return intimacy of any kind as long as she lacks that vital connection to her first love, her mother (129). Her unanswered longing for maternal love has, in effect, masculinized her, as Glaspell illustrates with her use of words such as "stiffness" and "rigid":

Mary was like sunshine, but this was a stiffness sunshine could not reach. To the marrow of her being it had penetrated till her spirit was rigid and she was outside the good fluid world in which one rejects and accepts—adjusts, assimilates, and is constantly renewed with life.

Yes, Mary was good, and there had been a moment of good—by the car when she could partake of that warmth; but when she went inside the house itself seemed rigid and the past was frozen country behind her—or was it that she was frozen into that past she did not know and now would never know? (130)

The past as frozen country is an apt metaphor for repression, and the image of her frozen into a static and unchanging past is an accurate portrayal of the result of repression. Again, as in *Fugitive's Return*, Glaspell shows that to repress the past is to be controlled unconsciously by it. Without self-knowledge the individual does not have freedom of choice, cannot "reject and accept—adjust, assimilate," cannot live in the fluid present. To "know" is all for Glaspell, the goal of the psychoanalytic process of uncovering the buried self that she portrays in all of her novels. But this focus on discovery or recognition of the true self also links Glaspell's work to the Greek tradition she so admired. Anagnorisis, or recognition as Aristotle defined it, is a change from ignorance to knowledge, primarily about the self. And the finest form of anagnorisis, as Aristotle says, is one accompanied by peripeteia, or reversals which, as in the *Oedipus Rex*, so often reveal the secret of the hero's birth. To discover the secret of one's origin, to have one's eyes opened and see the self plainly, unclouded by fear, desire, illusion—that is anagnorisis, and that is Lydia's psychological quest. Glaspell's use of the mythic method here is reinforced by the epigraph she provides from Euripides' *Rhesos:*

> Oh, the morning is near us, the morning!
> Even now his fore-runner approaches,
> Yon dim-shining star.

It may seem odd that Glaspell should cite this relatively obscure earliest work of Euripides, the authenticity of which was debated until recently. Such a reference provides added evidence of her deep familiarity with the classics. The *Rhesos*, as its recent translator, Richard Emil Braun, points out, "is the story of a futile quest for truth" in which knowledge and misunderstanding are portrayed in repeated metaphors of light and darkness (4). This is true also of Glaspell's metaphorical characterization of Lydia's ignorance (darkness) and her search for truth (light):

> For she could not go on trying to know. She was defeated. Her bright banner was down. It was in good faith she had sought the light, for to know would be to understand—understand, not alone the life of one house, but life itself. . . . In our untried strength we cry: "Darkness, I challenge you! Let there be light!" Had she thought she could wave a magic wand and—lo! there would be light? O bright folly and vain endeavor—life does not give up its secrets. (130)

Lydia's search for truth is not as futile as the bleak world of human blindness and folly that Euripides presents in the *Rhesos*, for she does ultimately bring the light of morning to the ancestral home. In both works, however, truth is revealed through the agency of a mythical, larger-than-life maternal figure. In the *Rhesos*, Euripides portrays the events of Book

X of the *Iliad*, where Odysseus and Diomedes go as spies into the Trojan camp at night and slaughter the sleeping allies of the Trojans, the Lykians, along with their king, Rhesos. The play takes place in the Trojan camp entirely at night, indicating the blind ignorance of all the kings and soldiers alike, as Hektor, king of the Trojans, makes one misguided decision after another. When Rhesos first arrives to offer his services to the Trojan cause, Hektor wants to reject him and send him home, but yields to cautionary advice and instead shows Rhesos and his men where they can camp, leading to their slaughter by Odysseus and Diomedes. It is at this point in the play, lines 719–20, that the chorus recites the verse Glaspell quotes in her epigraph, signifying the hope, the new light, that dawn brings. No doubt Euripides meant it ironically, for in the meaningless war he portrays, daylight does not bring revelation or liberation for anyone. The chorus of soldiers continues, describing the nightingale's song, with its tragic story of "the bed, her sister's blood, the murder of her boy, Itys" (ll. 728–34).

This reference to the rape of Philomela foreshadows the appearance at the end of the play of Rhesos's divine mother, one of the nine Muses, who comes to bear his dead body away, for Rhesos was the son of her rape by the river Strymon. The violated mother appears above the stage as a gigantic, brooding figure. She recounts the causes of her son's pointless death, predicting death for Diomedes and Odysseus, then for Helen, the cause of "tens of thousands of homes, empty." Next she curses Thamyris, the poet who arrogantly challenged the Muses, which made her "the mother of a doomed child," for on her way with her sisters to meet the challenge, she crossed the river Strymon and was raped by the river god (ll. 1148–64). She concludes and then vanishes:

> Children are the creations of accident.
> You work, you struggle, suffer and die.
> Do you see?
> Count yourselves. Add the evidence.
> If you live through the night of your lives
> childless
> you will never
> bury boys. (ll. 1252–59)

Her words are enigmatic, and of course the soldiers do not see. They again misinterpret the light, the "files of sun rays on the march," as a sign to continue warring, ignoring her message of the futility of slaughtering the seeds of continuity. Life is fragile enough, she cautions. As Braun concludes, her revelation, "which remains unspoken, hidden in the dawn of the play's new day, must surely be: to cease strife . . . and escape fear; to revere life and so save it" (16). We have already seen that the image of the raped mother was deeply resonant for Glaspell, and the Muse's revelation to revere life is one that she again and again imbues in her work: "Why did we not live more abundantly? Why did we not hold life more precious?" (*Fidelity* 212). The Muse emphasizes, as does Glaspell in *The Morning Is Near Us*, that children, as accidental as their births and parenting are, contain the future. And, like the Muse, Hertha is a larger-than-life maternal figure who is the source of revelation. But unlike Euripides' Muse, Hertha's semiotic does not take the form of a verbal pronouncement. She has been silenced, and her message is delivered in a distinctly female way of transmitting and reading signs, just as the women in "Jury of Her Peers" understand Minnie Foster through her quilting, and Irma and Stamula in *Fugitive's Return* "communicate with each other at the loom" (64).

Koula first discovers the dresser-scarf Hertha had worked in cross-stitch while she was looking in a trunk for fabric to make her doll's coat. Fittingly, it was Lydia's adopted daughter "who opened the way back into Mother's girlhood," linking the three generations. This object, with its girlish mistakes, makes Lydia's mother "real" for the first time; it was "the first thing from those years that you could hold in your hands, look upon and say: 'Yes, she had this; this is left from the years she was young in this house'" (143, 146). But the "work of her young hands had been hidden away . . . buried underneath" in "concealment." Lydia wonders, "What could the past possibly hold that was reason enough for all this hiding away?" (147). As she slowly discovers, and as Glaspell portrays in "Jury of Her Peers," *Brook Evans*, and *Fugitive's Return*, woman has been silenced, "decapitated," to refer again to Cixous, in lines that aptly summarize Hertha's position:

> Women have no choice other than to be decapitated, and in any case the moral is that if they don't actually lose their heads by the sword, they only keep them on condition that they lose them—lose them, that is, to complete silence, turned into automatons. . . . So in the end woman, in man's desire, stands in the place of not knowing, the place of mystery. . . . They always inhabit the place of silence, or at most make it echo with their singing. And neither is to their benefit, for they remain outside knowledge. ("Castration" 43, 49)

Lydia has suffered from being denied knowledge because her mother was silenced and immured as an idol in "the place of mystery," objectified into an "automaton." But like Philomela, Hertha isn't completely voiceless, for she speaks through her needlework, since, as Cixous notes, "it's the body that talks, and man doesn't hear the body," but other women can (49). The trunk is a vaginal symbol, and it is the mother's body that Lydia discovers within it. Stripping away the layers, she finds "the treasures of one girl's past," and these bodily remnants of female experience are simultaneously "eloquent and mute" (151): blocks for an unfinished quilt, a seersucker dress, a net fichu, some crocheted lace, blue hair ribbons, a white petticoat trimmed with lace, a nightgown, "some little boxes and things tied in papers. In one box a string of blue beads. In another, wrapped in tissue-paper, was a gold chain, and on it hung a delicate gold cross" (150). Almost every woman has a cache like this, of jewelry, of needlework done by grandmothers and great-grandmothers. Passed down from mother to daughter, it is the means of female inheritance and intergenerational communication. Now, as Lydia makes the doll coat for Koula, edging it with embroidery thread, she "got Koula to take a few stitches herself, so she would be part of the coat" (147). The maternal line has been reestablished through fabric, the female art, the female voice.

But there is something underneath all the layers, beneath even the heavy brown paper at the bottom of the trunk, the most precious treasure of all. These are letters Hertha wrote as a girl to her lost brother, through which Lydia discovers that her mother and uncle had lived on a barge with their poor immigrant parents and were orphaned when they drowned in a storm. The children were separated, and Hertha went to a family in which she was overworked and beaten. When she ran away to find her brother, she was sexually molested or possibly raped ("one man was bad to me"). Finally, Hertha was discovered wandering in the cemetery by John Chippman and taken into the Chippman family. What Lydia discovers through these letters is that her mother was not a cold automaton but a "loving little girl, who became not loving because something had been done to her" (156). And if she had loved a brother, then she could have loved a daughter: "Love was back of her, and it didn't matter this love hadn't been meant for a person called Lydia" (173).

Hertha's letters go on to describe her sexual maturing and her desire to "like boys and like them to like me," but she is unable to connect with others "because it makes me different—what happened—doesn't it?" (167–68). With their mutual experience of difference, Lydia's identification with her mother is complete. She has inherited her mother's status as outcast Other. She realizes with "a sudden sharp pain. It was because of her mother she understood her mother. Because of what her mother had done to her" (175), and this is the potentially tragic aspect of mother-daughter relations, as Beauvoir, Chodorow, and Flax have all discussed: whether consciously or not, mothers replicate their gender in their daughters. In Glaspell's rendering, however, the mother-daughter bond is more often strengthening, and here Lydia denies her rage toward her mother. She refuses to accept that Hertha could "let happen to another the very thing in cruelty that had been visited upon" her. No, "it must have been something farther along. Something happened. Something else," and, since her mother had secreted these evidences of her humanity, it does appear that, indeed, something outside her mother dehumanized her (176–77). Lydia oscillates now, inevitably, toward her father.

Glaspell explores in depth the painfully contradictory impulses of love and rage daughters necessarily feel toward their fathers in a patriarchal culture, again transcending an oversimplified oedipal drama. Unlike *Ambrose Holt and Family,* where this ambivalence is expressed through two fathers, one idealized and one caricatured, here the ambivalence is expressed through a strange dual ending, first one in which Lydia's father rejects her coldly and then, as if Glaspell couldn't bear that alternative, a final ending in which he changes his mind and accepts her.

Despite her brother's cautions, Lydia ventures to the asylum to see her father. She dresses carefully, shearing away signs of her difference and of her sexuality in a pathetic attempt to appear the socially acceptable "good girl" who will be acceptable to him, the beloved little girl she wants to be in relation to him, despite his abandonment of her:

> She was wearing a blue linen suit and soft hat with a brim. She thought she looked all right—clothes like everybody else's. She didn't want to startle Father. Didn't want to look like "foreign parts"—wanted, as much as she could, to look like the girl he had put on the train and sent away with Aunt Jenifer. (Sent away. Never mind that.) No lipstick. She must remember not to smoke. She wanted the people there to approve of her father's daughter. (211)

She enters the gate to the grounds and sees a man sitting on a bench who "did not seem to be seeing or hearing anything—absorbed in what he thought. That was her father." Again we see the father characterized as immobile and rigid: "There was something in his stillness made it impossible to break. . . . She wished he would cross his knees and lean back. Something. Some move—not as if fixed there. He was looking straight ahead, but she felt he did not see the waving fields his eyes could be seeing"

(214). His utter withdrawal from the outer world of phenomenal reality seems to paralyze her: "She'd wait till he moved. Then she could move. . . . He was seeing—but not what she could see. She tried to make her hands lift her up. If she sat here much longer she would become fixed too and could not move at all." Unseeing of the fields, unnoticing of a man who comes to rake near his bench, oblivious of the breeze that causes the windmill behind the house to clatter, divorced from the shared world of objective reality, the only medium through which humanity can connect, he seems to annihilate her: "For he seemed to be denying her as much as if he had said no after he knew she was there" (216). This denial of her, this seeming loss of her father's love, plunges Lydia into an oedipal regression and an existential crisis:

> She thought of how she loved him and how she believed he had loved her. "Father," voiceless words were trying to say across the gulf, "sometimes you would take me on your lap—when no one else was around. No one is around now. Can't I come to you again? You were almost crying when you put me on that train. Must I go away again?"
>
> She tried to reason with herself, tell herself this was just her own panic. But she could not persuade herself. Now she knew separateness. It was a loneliness such as she had never known could be. There he sat, and she did not know how to reach him, and she was frozen too and could not try. Never before had she really understood—We live alone. It plumbed the depth of the loneliness of the human soul. . . . There he sat, and her longing to go up and say little friendly things was a longing for the unattainable. He dwelt apart and he dwelt alone. (216–17)

These must be some of the most eloquent words expressing a daughter's longing for the unattainable father ever written. The first paragraph, with her memory of being taken on his lap, expresses her oedipal desire. Denied, she is plunged into an existential panic, as she feels to the full the unbridgeable gulf between self and the unattainable Other. Truly like God "he dwelt apart and he dwelt alone." Glaspell's biblical allusion is intended to show that what Lydia experiences here is a loss of faith, a "faith in which she had always lived," despite her abandonment by both parents (metaphoric of every child's necessary casting off from the Whole into subjectivity and fragmentation)—"that dear faith that out of the loneliness that is each one of us we can reach the loneliness of another" (217–18).

However, in this scene she never dares to approach her father. The forbidding image she sees at the asylum is a projection of her terrified fantasy (and/or memory) of paternal rejection. "She had thought him immured, inviolable, beyond wanting and beyond being reached," but soon she begins to convince herself, as we so often do with unrequited love, that her father must want what "she had wanted" (233–34). This is another basis for further identification with her mother, for her mother's letters to her brother express a transference onto her lost brother of oedipal longing for the unattainable father: "But if I see someone coming around the hill, or coming to the school—I think maybe it is you. But it isn't. It is someone else. It is never you" (154). That she identifies with her mother is clear, too, when she recalls one of Hertha's letters just before she finally convinces herself to write to her father. As her mother, she writes like a lover to the lost beloved: "All the years I was away I thought of you. . ." (238).

But her father answers her loving letter with "a ruthless blow" (254). He writes that she is her mother's love-child, that he is not her real father, and, while exonerating Hertha of all blame, admits that he didn't want Lydia "on account of your not being my child. . . . I didn't want your mother to pay attention to you, or be loving with you . . . she had to do what I said and you were sent away" (247). This is a rather shocking turn of events that is not quite believable because it contradicts the will in which he offers Lydia the house. But Glaspell may be attempting to portray, however clumsily, the intense ambivalence that characterizes the father-daughter relationship. Notice the similarity here with Caleb Evans, another distanced, adoptive father who tries to break apart the mother-daughter dyad. Here is the pre-oedipal father who, no less for daughters than for sons, is the child's rival for mother's love. Moreover, in order to preserve Hertha as his icon, he visits upon the daughter his anger at the mother's "sin." Lydia has borne the punishment for her mother's sexual transgression—paternal rejection and exile. Indeed, after receiving this letter, Lydia feels "she had no right to stay here. . . . she had been cast out" (248, 252). Despite the fraternal and communal connections she and her children have made, it is the father who determines social identity, who determines acceptance or difference within the social order, and she "was different now" (252).

Lydia, like everyone else, totally exonerates her mother's sexual transgression: "You were too beautiful. You were too much desired," she says. Also, she sympathizes with "Mother's life in this house . . . a lonely place, in a world that shut out that kind of loving" (254–56). She understands her mother's need to grasp any "opportunity" for love she could. Nevertheless, "Mother ceased to be Mother almost as much as her father was no longer Father. For how could you cherish memory of a woman who would turn from her own child at command of any man?" (254). She is angry at her mother's passivity, but on a deeper level she is angry that her mother chose her father over herself. She knows she really cannot have her mother without her father's permission, since in patriarchal family structure the father possesses the mother. She now feels she has "no right" to her mother's love letters, which meant so much to her, signifying as they did her mother's capacity to love (270). She is again truly orphaned.

It is hard to say whether the novel would have been better had Glaspell left this ending. It certainly would have had a "tragic" as opposed to a "happy" ending, which is often assumed to be more meaningful. But the futility then of all Lydia's efforts at self-discovery would be very counter to Glaspell's basically meliorative view that human struggle and suffering bring self-knowledge, which is a good. Glaspell expressed her strongest indictment of the father in Caleb Evans, her most idealized vision in Ambrose Holt. It seems that her anger toward the father mellowed over the years, moving in a steady progression to the final loving paternal portrait of *Judd Rankin's Daughter*. In *The Morning Is Near Us*, as in *Ambrose Holt and Family*, Glaspell explores the repressed incestuous longing and the hostility that characterize the father-daughter relationship, leading to her strangely ambivalent portrayal of two paternal alternatives in this novel as well, one vilified and the other idealized.

For miraculously, Lydia's father appears at her window (just as she is praying to "Our Father who art in heaven"), drenched and ill, after having taken a train from the asylum and walked from the station in the rain (272). "I have to leave one person on earth who understands," he cries, "And you're the one" (275). He explains that he spent his "whole life guarding it," that is, Hertha's sexuality, his precious possession (276). He recalls the first day he "didn't want to be her brother. The apple trees were in bloom and she was out among them," again painting Hertha as the irresistible wood nymph (277). He confesses to his daughter, "There wasn't anything else then. It filled the world—it was the world. I loved her and that was my life and my life wasn't anything else" (278).

Glaspell again portrays Eros appropriately as a kind of madness. John Chippman's obsession constitutes an indictment of romantic love, particularly in the way it sanctifies the imprisonment of woman by male desire, for "he dwelt with something he would not have the rest of them touch" (197). And Lydia fully realizes the incestuous nature of his desire (141,

205–6). Their parents having died, Hertha was terrified that she would be separated from yet another brother who was "all I have" (279). John proposed marriage as the only solution, a total violation of Hertha's feeling that they were brother and sister, as he confesses to Lydia:

> "This—it shocked her, more than I knew then, I guess. She went around so quiet. I didn't try to touch her again. And after a day or two she asked, was it the only way we could go on living together in this house. And I—God forgive me—I told her yes." (280)

This violation of Hertha's sororal feelings toward him amounts to a repeated rape of the most repugnant kind, as he now admits, "A man loves as man was meant to love. She—she tried to be good, as she put it. She said she would do anything for me. But her—I don't think it ever did anything but horrify her" (281). Like Helen, Hertha's mythic beauty arouses male desire, bringing chaos and destruction in its wake, in this case, sexual abuse and incest.

However, Glaspell tries to humanize her portrayal of John Chippman. Consumed by guilt, he spent the rest of his life trying to make up for his violation of Hertha: "I had done her a great wrong. I would make it right for her—any way I could" (285). Of course the one way to really atone would have been to let her go, but instead of giving up possession of her body, he lent it to others, exonerating and fostering her sexual liaisons with other men. He understood that for Hertha sex with him was "against nature," while "love outside—that was natural. . . . And so she blossomed and grew more lovely—with others" (285). Like the sacrificial suicide of Evan's father in *Brook Evans*, the father steps aside so that his wife's sexuality may flourish, with one huge difference here: Hertha is not a free agent as Brook was after her husband's death. As Chippman proudly claims: "Twas me made her safe—in anything she did" (287). His protection is merely another expression of his ownership of her body. But at least he understands that Eros cannot be bound: "Do you blame an apple tree for blooming?" If one constructs a sexual icon, then one cannot blame it for fulfilling its nature.

John Chippman is now portrayed as the repentant father who atones for patriarchal violation, not only of his wife but of his daughter, finally giving Lydia the paternal approval she has so hungered for: "'You were always a good girl. I always loved you. You knew that,' he asked appealingly, 'didn't you?'" (282). He explains that Hertha couldn't show her love for her daughter "because she thought she had wronged me—having you" by another man, and he had to drive Lydia away "because I wanted you—

your love, and how could I let it be you and me—... me taking what she couldn't have" (283). This contorted explanation requires a too generous suspension of disbelief on the part of the reader. But it dramatizes the kind of intense subliminal jealousies and rivalries that animate the relational triangle Glaspell is exploring. And it is important to see that Lydia has progressed from being unwanted and cast out to being denied because she was *too* much wanted by both parents. She now knows she was loved, and she has found home and identity with the knowledge of parental acceptance.

The novel thus ends with the hostile impulses of pre-oedipal and oedipal rivalry between father and daughter resolved in an image of peaceful acceptance. John Chippman dies holding Lydia's hand and speaking Hertha's name, his love for the mother no longer excluding the daughter. Lydia no longer has to oscillate between mother and father, for she now possesses both. Thus, on the psychosexual level of the novel, Glaspell has invented an "interplay between the mother, the father, and the hero" that challenges the normative "univocal sequence of object choices" (DuPlessis 37). However unsatisfactory the ending may be in literary terms, she has attempted a negotiation of binary opposition, just as she has done in every novel considered thus far, justifying their inclusion among other major twentieth-century women's narratives according to DuPlessis's definitions.

*The Morning Is Near Us* also explores sociocultural issues, expanding the movement outward in Glaspell's last novels beyond familial, psychoanalytic themes. In Lydia and her mother, Glaspell has portrayed the psychosexual plight of the orphan in two generations. With the third generation of Koula and Diego, Glaspell explores the sociocultural plight of the orphan as immigrant. She shows that these are parallel situations, both characterized by difference, abandonment, and exclusion, and she equates the orphan's longing for home/family with the immigrant's longing for home/nation. This novel is remarkably contemporary in its portrayal of a fatherless family and a childless woman's attempt to create family through adoption (themes that may be related to Glaspell's own childlessness, as well as her work with Greek refugees of Turkish genocide in Salonika during 1922). "Koula and Diego were already in the world—and no one cared for them. It seemed quite natural and right they become her children. All three of them had been alone. Now they were together, and no one of them was alone" (52).

According to DuPlessis, oscillation characterizes the sociocultural aspects of female identity as well as the psychosexual: "In the social and cultural arena, there is a constant repositioning between dominant and muted, hegemonic and oppositional, central and colonial" (38). This "debate between inheritor and critic is a movement between deep identification with dominant values and deep alienation from them" (39). *The Morning Is Near Us* exhibits just such a debate between inheritor and critic, as Glaspell, who loved the land and history of America, was also representative of the modernist generation in her rejection of nationalism, xenophobia, and provincial small-mindedness of any kind. Her love of the land is revealed in the opening of chapter 5, when Lydia and the children first arrive:

> A small house—big barn. A flat field fenced in, beyond it rolling hills. Cows in a meadow—a white horse drawing a cultivator. An apple orchard. A boy pumping water way off yonder there; colts playing. Now the straight street of a little town. . . . This was it. This the country she had known first and had not seen for many years and had never ceased to see. (42)

But what awaits her and the children as they get off the bus is the conflict between "pluribus" and "unum" that has never ceased to plague America. Warren watches the "foreigners" getting out with their "emigrant bags and baskets," thinking, "The town didn't want any more foreigners—not enough work for the Americans" (55). He finds that he cannot invite "this young Indian and the little dago girl" home to his wife for lunch as planned (58). Thus the beautiful land ("Tender green of grain beginning to come up") and the homey security of small-town life ("Three children standing behind a white fence waving at the bus. . . . Women coming to their doorways to throw out a pail of water or shake a rug") are disfigured by xenophobia and racism (42). Glaspell makes it clear that many of the townspeople are themselves German immigrants or the children of German immigrants, but they have been grudgingly accepted because of a Eurocentric racism, as Warren reveals in chiding his sister, "I should think you would have adopted Americans."

"Where would I get Americans?"

"Well, the English—or even French; or even German."

"But these were the children who needed to be adopted". . . .

"They'll seem odd here, I'm afraid."

"Oh, well, what's the difference? We can't all be Americans." (66)

However, Lydia is well aware of the pain caused by difference. She vows that never, "so far as in her power lay," will her children feel unwanted, and she worries about how they will be treated at school, where "all the children would know they were foreigners," for she knows that "children were conservative. Anyone who was different was wrong" (45, 222–23). She attempts to ease their transition by giving a party for them where the donkey she has also brought from Mexico becomes, instead of an oddity, a fun toy, as the neighborhood children all take rides on him. Informed of the donkey earlier, Warren had protested, "But, Lydia, no one has a donkey here." Like Irma, although with more irony and less "wrath," Lydia reminds him, "Christ rode a donkey" (67).

Lydia's oscillation is clear as, in DuPlessis's words, she "negotiates difference and sameness, marginality and inclusion in a constant dialogue" (43). So she tells Koula, who wants to change her name to Katie, that her name is "linked with your own past, that great past" and that her native language, Greek, was "perhaps the greatest there had ever been in the world" (46). But Koula wants to be an American "like everyone else," a longing with which Lydia deeply sympathizes (43). As in her other novels, like *Fidelity* and *Brook Evans*, Glaspell shows that female conservatism derives from the greater punishment women suffer for social difference, already being Other in their gender. In an revealing passage she describes Koula's need to conform as much greater than Diego's:

> Koula's scarf was from the market in Pueblo. Hers was from Smyrna. Koula had liked the scarf until she saw other people wearing hats for traveling. . . . They all had baskets of maguey-fiber, string bags— serapes and pottery. They had started out so gaily with their bright and unwieldy assortment of treasures, but she had seen Koula looking at other people's luggage. Diego didn't care, didn't think he was wrong. He carried his big peaked hat proudly on his lap. But Koula didn't want to be different. To be unlike other people was to be wrong. (43)

Diego does not feel the stress of cultural difference as intensely as Koula because his gender is automatically normative. By carrying his big peaked hat proudly on his lap Diego reveals that wherever he goes his phallus marks him as central, whereas Koula's scarf, a sign she shares with her mother, marks her as Other.

Alongside the Greek myths alluded to in the text, Glaspell simultaneously explores the myth of America as a land to whose shores the homeless and rootless come to create a new life in freedom. Her oscillation between hegemony and opposition is apparent in her portrayal of the children's indoctrination into treasured American myths such as the Pilgrims and the Fourth of July:

> "And the reason they came to this country," said Lydia, "was that they wanted to worship God in their own way." They were out under the apple tree, sitting on a Mexican blanket, and she was trying to tell a little girl born in Greece and a boy born in Yucatan the story of their new country. (106)

The tale proceeds happily until the Pilgrims meet the Native Americans. "'And the Indians were bad to them!' cried Koula, who had been looking at pictures in the book." Diego (himself Native American) concedes, "There are some bad Indians," but Lydia concludes: "'There are some bad people in every country . . . Everybody in America is not good.' It was a little hard to tell the whole truth in building up love of country. 'The Indians were not fairly treated,' she said firmly" (107). The prescience of Glaspell's critique, exposing historical euphemisms in children's textbooks that were not actually challenged until well over three decades later, seems uncanny. Lydia's identification with dominant values, such as the Pilgrims' search for religious freedom, and her simultaneous alienation from them are evident in this passage. But she firmly negotiates a route, a "dialogue," between love of country and truth.

Another American myth Glaspell explores is the Fourth of July: "On the Fourth of July Americans made a great noise—that was because they had a great thing to celebrate" (182). Lydia reads from the Declaration of Independence to the children, while Judge Kircher, a first-generation German immigrant, brings them firecrackers (184). Lydia contemplates the meaning of the pursuit of happiness, for her the "most courageous of all the words" (182). She asks herself, "What was this happiness they declared was our right?" In answering she connects the psychosexual and the sociocultural levels of the novel:

> Sometimes shooting off a firecracker. Often seeing others happy— seeing children happy. And sometimes a light that breaks when you have been long in the dark. . . . It's there in us—the need to understand the life we live. Perhaps that's an inalienable right—if only we knew how to claim that right. (183)

Happiness, for Glaspell, is found in the light of self-knowledge and in generational continuity, "seeing children happy." *The Morning Is Near Us* shows her sophisticated working through of these ideals both on the psychosexual and sociocultural levels. Despite the flawed ending of the psychosexual plot, this is one of Glaspell's most interesting novels, first because of her fascinating use of classical myth and drama to evaluate the effect of patriarchal constructions of female beauty on mothers and daughters, and second because of her intrepid exploration of the often hidden sexual and racist abuse of immigrant orphans in this country. These are themes that make Glaspell's novels as relevant to readers today as when they were written.

Could only youth be pure? Was it ever so: the world there
to take and change and meanly use what could have made
life more beautiful than any dream dreamed
in the days before the combat?

—*Susan Glaspell*

# 8

# The Ashes of Disillusionment in *Norma Ashe* (1942)

In *Norma Ashe*, Glaspell again presents a novel about the uncovering of a buried self. As in *Fugitive's Return*, she employs a dramatic tripartite structure, beginning late in the life of the protagonist, Norma Ashe, who has failed to achieve her goals and is consequently alienated from her inner self. This structure allows Glaspell to invert chronology and cast a poignant, ironic shadow on the idealism of Norma Ashe's youth, portrayed in the second part, because the reader is already acquainted with the sad demise of her ideals from reading the first part. In the third part, a return to the present, Norma attempts to recapture that lost self. Although she is unsuccessful, she does achieve a moment of integration and inspiration before her death in yet another of Glaspell's uneasy, ambiguous endings. Similar to *The Morning Is Near Us*, *Norma Ashe* again bridges psychosexual and sociocultural texts, although Glaspell's focus is more on the latter in this novel. She steps back from the intense psychoanalytic portraits of familial relations that characterize the novels of her middle period to portray a broader feminist analysis of the dehumanizing effects of capitalism, more historical in focus than her critique of capitalism in *Ambrose Holt and Family*.

Since Glaspell's birth in 1876, she and the nation had lived through vast changes. It is worthwhile to compare her to Virginia Woolf in this context because their lives were so contemporaneous. Although their fictional techniques were often different, many of their concerns were similar and, like Woolf in her late work, Glaspell writes here with a long backward glance from an era, the late 1930s and early 1940s, that she regarded as spiritually and morally bereft. Through Norma's attempt to answer the question "who am I?"—how did I become this external identity, so distant from my youthful ideals and so different from my better self?—Glaspell is attempting to answer the larger question: how did we, a nation and a people, come to this from all the optimism, energy, and belief in change that characterized the beginning of the twentieth century? In the second part of the novel, Glaspell shows through the disintegration of Norma's marriage how the rampant speculation of the 1920s consumed late-nineteenth-century progressivist movements and reinforced gender compliance in both women and men, resulting in a crude, amoral, "survival of the fittest" economic world. Similar to Woolf's *Three Guineas* (1938), Glaspell portrays patriarchal institutions such as capitalism as dependent upon the exploitation of women.

Glaspell also explores the conflict of the ideal versus the real by showing how the dreams of youth are inevitably buried by life's realities—poverty, money, marriage, childbearing, loneliness, moral compromise, aging. In the third part of the novel Glaspell shows Norma moving beyond rediscovery of the psychological and social origins of her fate to a more philosophical, spiritual quest for some answer to the general human fate. Is "captivity the law of life?" she asks (230). "The breast—the grave; and between the two: our chance" (345). When it seems we can make so little of our chance, what then is the purpose of life? Glaspell's answer to that question is a typically meliorative one, but it is not the simplistic idealism that critics have attributed to her. This text exposes idealism as a fraud, and, with characteristic subtlety, Glaspell undermines any easy reading of the end.

The novel opens with Norma Ashe imprisoned by her identity as Mrs. Utterbach, widowed proprietress of a declining boardinghouse, supporting a daughter and demeaned by the endless economic struggle to survive. For Mrs. Utterbach, life has become "one long mean struggle against alcohol lamps in the bedrooms and washing of underwear in the bathroom" (10). Her whole existence is focused on the need for money to keep up the house in a decaying neighborhood, as she responds when her daughter, Lorna, asks her what her one wish would be: "The money to pay my bills when they come due. . . . It would be heaven" (11).

That Norma has lost "heaven" in bending to the demands of material survival is further illustrated in chapter 2 when she goes to the room of one of her tenants to collect the overdue rent: "It was one of those times— this coming to demand money of a girl penniless and crippled—when she felt dispossessed of her birthright. What she should have been she was not let be. . . . She must be practical" (15–16). As she enters the room, one of her best, with "morning sun and afternoon sun too," the girl is sitting in the sunlight symbolic of spiritual life. "'I love the sun,' she said. 'It's almost enough in itself, isn't it?'" The girl's simple love of existence in the face of her tribulations briefly spurs a distant memory in Norma of her past life, when she could "dream of a better world, because we'd been made by the energy of the sun." Although Norma represses the memory, it leads her to ask the girl if she believes in God. When she affirms that she does, Norma asks the question typical of the unbeliever: "I'm sure I don't know why you should. What has he ever done for you?" (17).

Norma knows that "something was lost," but she keeps her thoughts "right in the groove of the days: marketing, cooking, cleaning. . . . Keeping from being cheated, or as little as possible" (20). Although Norma feels that life has not "let" her be what she might have been, Glaspell is clear that her failure is really a moral one. Under the stress of poverty and adversity she has failed to maintain her faith in either God or humanity. In her bitterness at having "come down" in the world, Norma clings to a superficial, materialistic class elitism that, in 1927, is shortly to be doomed. In the opening paragraph, an omniscient narrator, ironic in tone, posits a "mischievous sprite" to inform Norma that she is living at the height of the boom. In her poverty she would never believe it, but Glaspell's point is that, within two years, most people will be at the bottom where she is. The social standards she clings to are increasingly meaningless in the modern world. This paragraph is counterbalanced by one near the end of the novel, in which the ironic narrator describes America in 1929 as a "bedlam of prosperous people . . . sleekly unaware" of the imminent economic crash. The narrator dwarfs human catastrophe by comparing it with eternal verities: "Lives would be different, many would call it the end; yet seed planted in the earth would grow, and no star would fall" (328).

As is typical in Glaspell's work, Norma's alienation is played out through her disjunction from the women closest to her, her daughter, Lorna, and her best friend from college days, Rosie. She tries to fulfill herself by living through her daughter, which we know from *Brook Evans* is doomed to fail. Norma imposes the false, superficial values of a "genteel" bourgeoisie upon her daughter: "Time and again Lorna has been forbidden to go in any of the men's rooms. Oh, she wanted to keep her so much nicer than that, not sinking into the common life of her mother's boarding-house. . . . Always the struggle . . . to have Lorna 'keep up'— be with the nicest crowd" (25). Norma's moral degeneracy is illustrated when she hears her daughter's voice coming from a male boarder's room and eavesdrops, bent in a "posture always avid, mean" (25). Outraged at her mother's spying, Lorna tells her, "It's ridiculous to live the way we do and be a snob!" (27). She urges her mother not to "try to be what we aren't" and declares, "I don't know what my life is going to be . . . but it's not going to be any hanging on to the fringes. I am what I am and that's all there is to it" (29). Norma is more heartbroken that Lorna is "dropping out," "sinking" into what she perceives as a lower class, than she is that her daughter is ashamed of her (56). She regrets only her failure to "run a cheap boarding-house and remain a lady," even though Lorna tries to get her to see that the "riff-raff" she disdains are people like themselves: "We're right in the class with them. Then why do you have to despise them so?" (56–57).

Norma is jolted by the unexpected visit of her old college roommate, Rosie, after twenty-seven years. Rosie, who has also fallen far short of their youthful ideals, desperately needs to reconnect with her friend of the past: "You must remember—surely you remember—how much you meant to me? And what we went through together? . . . There seemed a glory about you, Norma. To me you really were—inspired'" (39). Rosie refers to their college years in the 1890s at "Pioneer College" in South Dakota, when they and three other "disciples" were taught philosophy by a Socrates-like professor, Joseph Langley, who inspired them with a love of visionary idealism and the "high resolve" to make "a better world" and "pass on the torch" of knowledge to another generation (70). Norma had been the "chosen one," receiving a scholarship to attend graduate school at the University of Chicago and become a teacher, an opportunity she abandoned to get married. In a way, what Rosie asks is unfair, that Norma be better than she, be above life's constraints, be her salvation. In fact, Norma has just endured a battle with the coal company over payment for a delivery, which has "beaten her down into a life from which she had little power to emerge," as Glaspell shows how demeaning poverty is through Norma's inability to "disentangle herself" from the "rasping" sound of the coal being delivered and "all that went with it, [to] be freed for a glory she and Rosie had once shared" (39).

Norma's envy of her friend's apparent wealth—"from the smart quill in Rosie's hat to a perfectly shod foot"—indicates again her moral inadequacy. Each bound up in her own losses, neither woman has the generosity to acknowledge the other's pain. "You've had it easy," Norma accuses Rosie, and, "It's easier to be your best when you look your best" (42, 47). Both women abdicate responsibility for their choices, as Rosie says, "With me, my life just took me, and I never really got out of it again," and Norma agrees, "It was that way with me" (48). However, it is important to realize that Glaspell is not portraying a simplistic moral universe here. As becomes clear later in the novel, the ideals Norma and Rosie aspired to are impossible to maintain in life, which is an unpredictable and powerful force. Ideals must be melded with reality and thus, perhaps, compromised, but not abandoned, for then life has no meaning beyond physical survival. Glaspell is setting up the traditional opposition of ideal versus real through Norma's conflict in order to attempt, as she always does, to find a way out of simplistic binaristic thinking.

Many of Glaspell's novels contain mirror scenes, yet each one is unique and reflects a different aspect of women's lives. "Mirror, mirror on the wall; who's the fairest of them all?" The mirror, that symbol of female vanity and narcissism in fairy tale, becomes in Glaspell's hands a portal to self-knowledge and revelation. "Know thyself," Norma recalls her professor telling her long ago (51). Alone in her bare room, she wonders how "she could be both Norma Ashe and this woman who ran Mrs. Utterbach's. . . . Did she live at all in this woman who now sat on the side of the bed taking off her stockings?" Norma looks down "from the unkindly globe to the face it lighted in the poor mirror" and suddenly feels sorry for Rosie. She realizes that despite her wealth, "Rose has *nothing*. . . . She is destitute and alone and she came to me believing I still had what we had together. How did she find me?" (53, 61). Norma's remorse over her treatment of Rosie begins her path toward redemption.

First, her more loving thoughts about Rosie evoke long-censored memories and "made real the girl Rosie remembered. Everything about her was vital, as if she grew in the sun and from roots that were rich" (54). Norma recalls her youthful self in images of light and sun, referring back to the imagery of chapter 2, and she also recalls her strength, courage, and boundless energy "to seek out the truth and the beauty" (54). She remembers that her younger self would have reaffirmed her inner identity in no uncertain terms: "But I am this, she'd have said in strong golden confidence. This is my brain and my heart; this truth is my very blood" (59). How did she come to be so "buried under living" (55)?

Ever since she'd been running this boarding-house, when she thought of the past it was her life with her husband she meant: those fifteen years they had together. What went before that was too far back now—remote, detached. She was separated from it, not only by years, but by what she herself had become. . . . Like an inaccessible country, a land one no longer knows, lost world. (59)

As this passage reveals, the fifteen years of her marriage effaced her identity and divorced her from her previous life. That time period is the subject of Part II, as again Glaspell shows a protagonist performing a kind of self-analysis by bringing the "inaccessible country" of the unconscious into consciousness. Norma has begun to speak the truth in acknowledging her failure of Rosie; now she follows the road back to that "land one no longer knows," the land of repressed memories, seeking to rediscover the truth of herself.

With symbolic irony, Part II opens with Norma at age twenty-one, on a train home after graduation from Pioneer College. As she sits primly reading Plato, the train is derailed, just as her naïve, idealistic world is derailed when she meets an attractive young German immigrant, Max Utterbach. An angry, volatile man, his life has been scarred by a poverty that the securely middle-class Norma has never known. Enraged because the train on which he is transporting his dead mother "in a box" is delayed, he represents the entrance of Dionysian "unreason" into Norma's life. Her attempt to impose Apollonian "reason" upon him is futile; she is swept away into the "impervious river," the "surge," the "torrent of words" that is the irresistible force of his narcissistic demands for her attention (78–86). "How wildly, unreasonably, he talked," she thinks, wondering what "reasonable thing" she could say to calm him (82–83). Like the train wreck, Max is an "unforeseen" force, already distancing her from the "dear familiar place that had been good to her." School had been a safe haven, a "convent," and while Norma had expected "life would be different in the world," she "hadn't known it would be different so soon, so rudely" (84). Instead of the lofty life of the mind to which Norma has seemed totally consecrated, Max will offer her the role of self-sacrificing mother in marriage to an infantile man who demands her total attention, typical of Glaspell's portrayals of heterosexual love. One might wonder how Norma could choose such a losing exchange, but Glaspell shows the gradual undermining of her plans for an intellectual life at the University of Chicago and a career as a teacher by social and familial pressures, as well as by her own sexuality (94–98).

Norma's attraction to Max is immediately and powerfully sexual. He looks at her "it seemed savagely," his gaze "still holding her" even when hers wavers (78, 85). She is attracted to "the quick way he moved, the abrupt swift changes, his concentration, fire," and she feels "something she had never felt before in her life . . . in response to his nearness" (85). However, Norma already perceives that Max's "aliveness was on the wrong side: damning the world and wishing people harm" (83). He curses his poverty and, in his guilt over abandoning his mother after she had "cooked for people and cleaned for them" to raise him alone, he lashes out at the "rotten world" (87). Norma immediately spots the flaw in his thinking: "All this damning of the world is just another way of getting out of it. . . . What have you ever done to make it a better world?" His response as she prepares to get off the train and part from him at the next station and the narrator's wry parenthetical aside indicate that she has already become, in true Victorian fashion, his moral arbiter, his angel in the house:

> "But what will I do without you?" he went on, in his tumultuous way. "Don't you see? With you—I'm all right. Without you. . ." (Through a good deal of her life that was to go: "With you—I'm all right. What would I do—without you?") (90)

Max's infantile helplessness in regard to emotion and his dynamic energy in regard to ambition mark the fulfillment of his gender. He exudes a masculinity Norma finds irresistible, even as she resents it closing in upon her: "Was it a trap? she thought angrily, when the touch of his hands, ardor of his eyes, made her think of being in his arms?" (96). "Trap" is exactly the word Glaspell uses in *Brook Evans* describe sexual intimacy, showing her portrayal, consistent throughout these novels, of young women fearing their sexuality because in patriarchal culture it is used to coerce them into conforming to their gender.

Chapters 9 and 10 chart Norma's fall from grace into sexuality and into knowledge of good and evil, as Max comes to visit her over the summer at her home in Iowa and they confront one another twice by a fallen tree in "Cutter's lane." These chapters are some of the best in Glaspell's wry, ironic style, as the lovers are at such cross-purposes in attempting to communicate. They misread one another totally, while believing they have communicated, and in the end are swept up by "the hot sharp need to meld into one" that has inevitable consequences for Norma. Her discourse dominates chapter 9, while Max's dominates chapter 10, and because their communication is largely ineffectual, it is his stronger will that prevails. Glaspell shows that life is a force that cannot be controlled and "reason" is a paltry combatant against the force of "unreason."

In chapter 9, Norma attempts to tell Max why she can't marry him. Trying to be "true" to the high ideals espoused by her teacher at college, she argues for a patriarchal logos that can transcend mortality through the written word: "I want to be closer to all the great brave men of the past. I want to know them and let them live in me and, if I'm good enough, speak through me. Great voices need not be silenced by death. Thus we conquer death—for life" (98, 100). This is a somewhat sterile version of life, however, and Max's response resonates with the sexual energy that characterizes a very different way of conquering death: "'My wonderful Norma! Beautiful Norma Ashe,' he murmured. 'I'll love you as long as I live.' His voice was low and strong. Passionate, tender and reverent. There was a long moment of no words" (101). Max's nonverbal, sexually charged semiotic has effectively overborne the logos, but Norma is not silenced yet. She naïvely assumes they have achieved "communion" and that Max "understands why they must part," so she can "love him—freely now, now that he understood" (101). Lecturing him "like a solemn little girl" in her professor, Joseph Langley's, visionary words, she goes on to use the analogy of an unborn child for the "break through," the evolutionary "leap," the "great forward thrust" that humankind "may be just on the brink of!" The childbirth analogy stirs quite different thoughts in Max, of course. He holds her close, finally remarking, "I like it . . . because it makes you so beautiful," as, once again, sexual passion "stopped everything: his words, her thoughts" (104). Ironically, Max calls himself Norma's first pupil. "Your first pupil needs you. . . . You are the light to me now. You are my life and all my hopes" (103, 108). Although both of them find the mother/child, teacher/pupil relationship erotically charged, in the long run Norma will become the disempowered pupil who adopts every Utterbach attitude. Chapter 9 foreshadows this, ending with Norma weeping and Max's "confident and joyous cry" that he will return.

Chapter 10 is a reprise and an amplification of these gender dynamics. Norma has begun to feel a "conspiracy" closing in upon her, including events such as the train wreck and a new job opportunity for Max in Texas that will enable him to marry her. She also feels family pressure: "Her father saying Max would go far, Grandmother always wanting to know if she'd heard from him, and now Aunt Nettie trying to push her right into— Well, push her" (114, 116). It is significant that Norma is motherless; as we have seen in so many Glaspell novels, the mother-daughter relationship is empowering. In *Brook Evans*, Brook's reconnection with her dead mother enables a passionate heterosexual relationship of her own choosing; in *Fugitive's Return*, the mother-daughter dyad is reestablished at the expense of heterosexual connection; and in *The Morning Is Near Us*, Lydia's rediscovery of her maternal heritage leads to self-knowledge. Motherless daughters or daughters estranged from mothers are more prey to the forces of gender conformity, as *Ambrose Holt and Family* and this novel both illustrate. The conspiracy Norma feels is the inexorable expectation that she abdicate the phallus, her intellectual idealism and career goals, for Max's and accept her gender role as selfless wife and mother.

Max returns "triumphant" as a real estate agent involved in a development scheme in the Texas Panhandle: "This visit it was Max who did most of the talking: the country down there; proposed developments; riches of the state and what the future could be." He even compares his venture to "those wonderful things that mean so much to you," a distortion Norma rationalizes in a self-abnegating pattern of thought that will become typical of her: "Selling land? Is that the wonderful thing means so much to me? Max has it all mixed up, she thought. There's no connection. Well, perhaps, in a way—a remote sort of way. New country; a chance. It had a stirring sound, and anyway she was glad for Max" (115, 116). When Max urges her to be happy for him "because, you see, my mother can't be," Norma begins to see her destiny written in her prospective mother-in-law's past: "She had to be happy for Max doubly. It was as if he couldn't be happy about it if she weren't. She must be proud of him, she alone, his mother was not there to be proud of him" (116). Norma tries to protest again that she is going to the university because "that's my life," but this time she is permanently silenced: "'No,' he said softly, before she could speak. . . . 'Your life is with me'" (117). Norma is borne along on the remorseless power of Max's egotism. While it may anger her, it is the fulfillment of his masculine gender that, at the very same time, makes him irresistible to her:

> "But darling," he smiled at her, "you don't think I'm going alone, do you? . . . Why, it wouldn't be right," he said, as if this settled it. . . .
>
> Then quickly she was angry: with him, herself, most of all with the way things seemed to be conspiring to take her. "No! I will not! I can't. Can't you see? Can't you see anything—but yourself? . . . What would there be for me in Texas?"
>
> "There'd be me," he said. "Doesn't that count—at all?"

"You know it counts. But you won't know the other things. You just won't know—anything else."

"I don't think there is much else to know," he said, with a rather wan suggestion of his smile. When he looked at her like that, as if she were hurting him and he didn't know how to bear it, she didn't know how to bear it herself, didn't know what to do. (118, 119)

Finally, in true soap-operatic fashion, their conflict enflames their sexual passion, which decides the issue for them. Norma "gives herself to Max" at the edenic locale, the fallen tree in Cutter's lane, "and she was not one to give herself without meaning. Whether it was right, or be it wrong, she was his" (120). Glaspell refers to the event of their sexual intercourse, like the train wreck and Max's new plans, as "something" that had "happened," indicating again that this is not merely a simplistic morality tale in which evil Max masters helpless Norma. Rather, sexuality and gender are forces with which idealism must come to terms and perhaps try to change, but which it cannot resist: "Life had taken her and there was no turning back. It was as simple, as devastating and wonderful, as inevitable as that" (117, 120). Glaspell shows that the optimistic nineteenth-century progressivism Norma imbibed from her teacher is not adequate to meet the demands of actual life.

These chapters also illustrate, as Chodorow, Flax, and Dinnerstein have all described in psychoanalytic terms, that female eroticism is bound up with mothering. For both sexes the mother is the first love object, and adult sexuality is determined largely by that first physical intimacy. But whereas man can rediscover the primal maternal tie in his sexual relation to woman (as Max illustrates), woman is "doomed to renounce her first love" (Dinnerstein 42–46). Nevertheless, through mothering her husband as well as her children, woman vicariously re-creates at least one half of the maternal-infantile reunion that informs human sexuality. Max's infantile narcissism seduces Norma even while it imprisons her. Their intercourse by the fallen tree in Cutter's lane, with its allusions to the fall and the tree of knowledge of good and evil, marks her castration (cutting), her loss of the phallus (autonomy and the logos), and her enforced acceptance of female passivity in marriage to him.

When they move to Texas, Norma finds that "each room of their house was like a square box," and her transformation into her mother-in-law, "shut up in a box . . . waiting for [Max] to get money," is complete (125, 80). As he did his mother, Max will use Norma up in his pursuit of money and leave her empty. During her girlhood "someone else" had always done the cooking, one of the adult women in her household, while "Norma was always busy with something else; the family had been proud of her because she was 'the brightest girl in school'" (131). As soon as she had reached womanhood, however, their expectations had changed, as her aunt said laughingly, "You wait, young lady. Your time will come. Better be silly than an old-maid" (94). Now, having been forced to assumed the gender role of her mothers, she must learn to cook and keep house, and while "she was used to being at the head of the class, now here she was in the role of the dunce" (131).

Feminist historians have shown that the 1920s, following the achievement of the vote and the demise of the suffrage movement, became a regressive backlash decade for women (see Showalter, *Modern Women*). Part II of Norma Ashe graphically portrays that historical actuality, and as in *Fugitive's Return* and *Ambrose Holt and Family*, Glaspell again shows how gender conformity undermines marriage. Riding the crest of late-nineteenth-century feminist achievements, Norma was encouraged in college to develop a career and intellectual life, only to find herself mired throughout the 1920s in a marriage that demanded her complete isolation within the home and submission to her husband, "happy with him when he had been successful" and bringing "love and sympathy to his disappointments, thus making him sure of himself and strong again," while her values, concerns, and needs "did not come into their days" (126). Norma's moral decline is inevitable as she becomes, for Max, merely her economic function of wife in the "sexual division of labor" that is bourgeois marriage (Chodorow 21–39). Max will use anything in his pursuit of economic success, and in her role as his appendage, she must conform:

> "Now here's the idea, Norma," he went on seriously. "I feel this is all up to you. I'm practically putting it in your hands. You are to sell the land. . . . I want you to make this woman like you. Mrs. Clayton's her name. Her husband is for it, but she's holding back." (132)

Mrs. Clayton, like Norma, misses the "rich earth" of her home in the Mississippi Valley and, also like Norma, finds the flat, dry landscape of Texas depressing. Norma has sublimated her homesickness to Max's entrepreneurial ambition, and now she must use it as a way to bond with Mrs. Clayton as Max instructs her, because "not for anything would she spoil his pleasure in it all, hurt that driving energy and confidence in the future" (126). But when he suggests she use her most sacred ideals, "the things you told me that first day we sat on the log" in Cutter's lane, Norma is horrified, "looking at him as if—as if she didn't know who he was," although she ought to by now (134). She objects but is once again silenced by his more forceful will and her inability to oppose the omnivorous drive of capitalist enterprise:

> "Yes; how awful of me. But you see—well, in business you use everything. You get in the habit," he went on, holding her head securely against him as she was about to raise it and speak, "Yourself—your personality—everything you've got." (134)

It is easy, now, to see how Norma Ashe becomes the Mrs. Utterbach of Part I, as she buries her beliefs more and more in order to adapt herself to Max. Although she finally adjusts to the Texas Panhandle and befriends Mrs. Clayton, sharing the early stages of her pregnancy with this friend, it is not long before she is uprooted again and they must move to Dallas, in the nomadic, disinherited lifestyle endemic to the capitalist system. Norma's need for female friendship, her ties to the land and local community, her past, her idealism, her intelligence, even her books and desk, all are sacrificed to Max's career as he uproots her again and again, moving about the country to further his business ventures and to escape punishment for deals gone bad. Max always thinks his is the initiative, that the system is working for him, but he is really never more than a drone, sent hither and thither by the company. He idolizes capital and justifies its demands and depredations in the usual ways—"'It's for you, darling,' he would say, when he made his dashing trips around the country, involved in more and more things," and "The best man wins. If I didn't do it wouldn't somebody else? It's a game, and if they aren't smart enough to play it is that my fault?" (142, 166). However, Max never really escapes the working class, as Norma discovers when he dies and she finds herself destitute. Wealth is always just around the corner, "five months" away.

Although Norma finally realizes "I can't be myself and be his wife," she also can't accept the idea of leaving him because "between her and Max was life. . . . She loved him as her lover." As in *Ambrose Holt and Family*, Glaspell portrays marriage as stifling for women; nevertheless, there is in shared sexual intimacy some seed of life, of futurity, that approaches the sacred. Against this Norma's idealism pales, "invalid, ignoble, . . . a feeling that couldn't jostle against life, but had to withdraw before it" (165). Naturally, Norma decides that "all she had given up to go with Max was to be realized through her child," displacing onto her son the phallus she has had to abdicate (155). "Nothing would be lost. He would go to the University of Chicago, she'd dream. She would be there to help him, see that he could go his true way" (144). Just as Max's values have proved more tenacious than Norma's, this baby, to be named Joseph after her teacher, dies in infancy, while her second child, named Fred after a wealthy investor Max regards as a mentor, lives. Fred grows up to become a living legacy of the moral degeneracy of their lives. Adopting his father's business practices in Texas, "snatching . . . the resources there, regardless of others who had invested of their toil and belief," the boy would "take things that belonged to the other children, bring them home and hide them" (185, 189). Like his father, too, as Norma saw in Max the first time she met him, Fred evades responsibility, "blam[ing] things on other children, things he has done himself." As a man, he abandons his mother until he needs something, again like his father, and he engages in the illegal underground liquor trade during Prohibition with excuses that echo his father's: "Had to be practical. Could he help it if the world was rotten?" (109).

Just as Norma sublimates her frustrated ambitions through mothering a son according to her gender role, Max sublimates his losses and grief after the death of their first child through an increasingly rapacious exploitation of the land, his business partners, and even his wife, to accumulate wealth. However, Glaspell portrays the patriarchal husband here, as she did with Lincoln Holt, not as a man of shallow evil but as a human being prey to forces beyond his understanding. Himself a fatherless, immigrant son, Max's grief over loss is always a "bitter resentment" of what has been done to him. He assuages pain and fantasizes getting back at the inexorable forces of life through making money, in accordance with his gender formation: "You'll see. I will take care of you. . . . I don't care who I hurt now or what I do! I'm going to make a lot of money. They can't do this to us" (154).

Again, "something" comes "crashing in" to change the course of their lives. Despite his assurances to Norma, Max has not been strictly lawful in his dealings. Either his own shady investments have been discovered or he is taking the fall for more powerful interests; however, he is paid to leave Texas immediately and given a job running a concrete business in Illinois. Once again Max "was terribly hurt; and once more she had to help him" (183–84). Once again, too, she becomes his student in playing the bourgeois game of class. When they move to Illinois, where Lorna is born, they buy a house in the "good part of town":

> "Important to live in the right neighborhood," Max said. And know
> the right people: he made a great point of this. "It's up to you,

Norma; you can make anybody like you without half trying. We're new people here, mustn't fall in with the wrong crowd. It's terribly important—for business and the kids and everything." (186)

Everything continues to be used in the service of money, as Max decides they must go to the Episcopal church instead of the Congregational, to meet the "right people." "They all believe in Christ, don't they?" he rationalizes, to which Norma grimly responds, "I wouldn't bring Christ into it," but it is remarkable that these are precisely the superficial values Norma espouses in Part I and tries to force upon her daughter. The Utterbachs become "a gay part of the best crowd" with "the right clothes, good manners, and lots of fun," playing golf, joining clubs, and attending bridge parties, "so bright, they said, and awfully attractive" (187). Norma slips into this "agreeable life . . . as if here were a biding place for the time," while Max overspends and goes into debt to keep up appearances (188). Soon Max becomes a usurer, taking on bad mortgages and hoping to profit by the war in Europe. In another futile protest Norma declares, "I do not want any gains from the sufferings of others" and "I hate your business propositions!" Max's ruthless response summarizes the crux of their relationship: "Better not, my darling. You'd have to hate me" (191, 193).

When Max dies suddenly in an accident at the factory, Norma discovers that they are deeply in debt and everything must be sold. Again there is an evasion of responsibility with the implication that he was just doing what everybody else does, except that he got caught: "There was something in the paper: a plunger, they called him, playing the market with other people's money, defrauding. She could have gone and killed the publisher. She knew him—Max knew plenty about him! His money dealings weren't as righteous as his talk. The hypocrites!" (197). Just so will Fred justify his bootlegging: "Do you think your old crowd . . . aren't getting their liquor? Is it any worse to sell it than to buy it?" (215). When society is corrupt it is hard for individuals with very little moral strength to resist the flow. Max is a casualty of the system he advocated, and his death foreshadows the impending stock market crash, also the result of rapacious, unregulated investment. In Max, Glaspell portrays the entrepreneurial capitalist typical of that decade of inflated economic boom, and just before it ends in economic depression, he dies, leaving Norma destitute. The only thing she has left is the mortgage on the hideous old Pettibone house, which she must turn into a boardinghouse to support herself and her children. "That began her life at Mrs. Utterbach's . . ." and her transformation from Norma Ashe into Mrs. Utterbach is complete. The moral failure of her life with Max, as well as the decline of the American dream into materialism and greed, is made perfectly clear, and perfectly human, in Glaspell's portrayal.

Part III returns to the present. "In Chicago things were not going smoothly for Fred Utterbach" (205). Norma must go to Chicago to bail her son out of jail for bootlegging, with wonderful irony, by pawning the diamond ring Max had given her as an "imperishable" symbol of their love (167). Drawn to the locus of her abandoned dreams, Norma stays in Chicago, bequeathing the Pettibone place to Lorna and her husband, Doc. In order to survive she becomes a cleaning woman in the boardinghouse in which she has taken a room, where she is finally divested of "Mrs. Utterbach" and called just plain "Norma" again (218). On her afternoons off she haunts the campus of the University of Chicago, "a shabby woman wrapped up in a heavy coat." Two young men, one of whom will befriend her, watch her reading an inscription, "Ye Shall Know the Truth and the Truth Shall Make Ye Free," and hear her muttering to herself, "That's not true!" (221)

Norma sees that one of the five "disciples" inspired by her teacher, Joseph Langley, at Pioneer College is going to speak at the university: "Austin Wurthen—one of them—world gone—was to speak in one of the halls at the University of Chicago. On . . . ? 'The Human Being and Industry.' [. . .] Why, didn't they know any more than that? Didn't they know Austin Wurthen betrayed the human being ages ago?" (224). As Norma has discovered, all of the disciples like herself were similarly "taken" by life and failed, to a greater or lesser degree, their teacher's expectations. Austin uses Langley's philosophy to rationalize the exploitation of workers in his father's factory; Rose, defeated by her love for a married man, married for money; Virgil became an embittered, alcoholic writer who "jeers and jibes at anything"; and Emil, the immigrant boy brutally beaten by his father, has become a vindictive labor organizer whose efforts to relieve the poor are poisoned by his sublimated rage, now directed at the "bosses." Through these vivid thumbnail sketches, as well as through Max and Norma, Glaspell portrays the dehumanizing effect of poverty, money, and class on individuals, and the disillusionments and losses that the very living of life entails. Norma attends the lecture and, appalled at Wurthen's hypocrisy, speaks out: "You can't do this, Austin! Must you cash in—on the miracle?" (232). She speaks the "truth" in the first heroic act of her life, and the truth, in a sense, sets her free: it revives her idealism whole hog. "She had affirmed her faith. Now a door long closed was swinging open" (235).

In chapter 18, the floodgates of memory swing open, and she reminisces about the founding of Pioneer College, Langley's arrival and his impact upon their lives, and the "miracle" the students witness right after his death when "something parted and they saw through" (253). Her recollections of Langley equate him with Christ. He chose his five "disciples" for an after-school discussion group; they made their weekly "pilgrimage" to his home; and under his tutelage "they were in the presence of something they felt divine" (251). Unbeknownst to Norma, however, his exhortations were more derivative of Nietzsche than of Christ: "Man does not know his own powers. We have taken the human mind too much for granted. There are not limits to what it can do. . . . Life can rise higher than man has yet had the power to dream. Grow in this power. Be the dream" (250). Most of his views smack of George Cram Cook, and there are numerous other parallels: his use of evolution as an analogy for human intellectual progress; his love of the image of the American frontier settled by hardy pioneers and immigrants and his use of it as an analogy for "the real frontier" now "opening"; his belief in a select band of people spreading the word to create a movement "that through communication from one to another man could rise to a new sense of his powers"; his brief immersion in German Romanticism at the University of Heidelberg; his devotion to Platonism and Hellenism; and his notebook of "just jottings, little things he had set down from time to time" (171, 250, 318, 325). After a decade of intimate life with Cook, no one would know more about the destructive, as well as the inspirational, aspects of idealism than Glaspell, and this portrait of Jig may be her most ironic yet.

Intrigued by Norma because of his curiosity and his desire to be a writer, a college student named Scott Neubolt befriends her. He offers her a home living with his pregnant sister and a job helping when her baby is born: "So it was the new friend—youth of today—welcomed Norma back to the world" (280). If the novel ended here, with Norma's idealism restored and her life renewed through a "spiritual son," to use Veronica Makowsky's term, Glaspell's reputation as an optimist who contrives false happy endings might be deserved, at least in this case (Makowsky 139, 146). But the young man plays a negligible role in the novel's conclusion. It is true that Norma tries to lay the burden of her "dream" on Scott, but, although very fond of her, he is skeptical of her ideals, as she urges:

"You won't be captured, will you? . . . Youth. Still there. You will . . . bring it to pass."

"I don't know what I am to bring to pass, but I'm afraid I can't do it."

"Oh, but that's the wrong idea. . . . Don't let it have that power over you. . . . how can you know what is in you?"

"I never said anything was in me!" he broke in almost angrily. (272)

While Norma tries to protect the promise of Scott's youth, the whole purpose of the novel is to show that it must inevitably confront the realities of life, and there is no evidence that his experience will be different from any of the other characters' because he fades from the narrative well before the end. As Norma will finally accept, once her childish idealization of her teacher is brought down to earth, all human beings fall short of life's potential.

The deconstruction of Norma's teacher occurs in chapter 22, in a crucial confrontation with Emil, the only one of the disciples who did not attend the college. An immigrant orphan adopted by Langley, Emil grew up to become a powerful labor leader. Because of the deprivations of his past (he is an interesting counterpart to Max), he denies himself the "luxury" of dreaming: "The game was realistic. Advance step-by-step, the thing that needed to be done. Jobs, food, plumbing, teeth fixed; children setting out to school in shoes that didn't leak" (255, 300). Norma tries to color his efforts on behalf of the working class and the poor in a rosy light, but he won't let her: "Now you can't glorify me. Don't try it! It all started with my being damn sore" (298). He repeatedly rejects Langley's visionary idealism, finally becoming so annoyed with the "exaltation" on Norma's "worn face lighted with wonder, face of one who will worship to the end," that he turns to "a terrible way—to banish an old dream that didn't fit the present pattern" (302–3). He tells her the truth about Langley, that he committed suicide by taking an overdose of drugs because he had a fatal brain tumor and, even more horrifying to Norma, "sometimes, after you were gone, he'd laugh at you" (305). According to Emil, Langley "knew the whole thing was cockeyed" (306). Norma's idealism is struck down in this confrontation with the "realist," and she calls Emil a "murderer and a thief" because he has killed and stolen her dream.

In the following chapter, Langley is recreated through Emil's memories, which present a very different picture from Norma's recollections in chapter 18. Glaspell intends us to draw our own conclusions. Emil loved the man who saved him from a life of degradation; he admired Langley and even, like Norma and the others, "worshiped" him. But there is a reason why, "all the rest of his life, he'd fought the idea of worshiping" (322). Living with Langley and taking care of him, Emil was exposed to a man the others didn't know, a fatally ill man desperate to ensure his immortality by inculcating his views in a younger generation: "It's very important to me that I give you the best I've got. You're young. I want to count on you. . . . That's very important to me; more important than anything else in this world" (246). In one sense he may have been a great inspiration for good, but in another, his megalomania blighted the lives of five young people who, no matter what they did, always believed they had failed him and that their lives were therefore a failure. "With death waiting [he] gave them the heart of his truth. Now it was a sacred obligation to them. He was to live through them," a heavy burden for each to bear (252).

Most morally suspect, however, was his use of Emil as an accomplice to his grandiose scheme. Langley told Emil "of the doom that waited" and what he wanted to do with the students in the time left to him. "'Quite easy to call it egotistical,' he had said; 'but we mustn't worry too much about that. It is my belief that I have something to leave'" (320). Langley's hints made Emil suspect his suicide plan, and, doing nothing about it, Emil felt "almost the same as if he were agreeing to it. . . . so perhaps he was little better than a murderer" (322–23). But Langley trusted him and depended on him, so the night of the suicide Emil was placed in an irresolvable moral quandary: should he go into Langley's room? All he could do was block out what he could not face, and "strange though he always thought it afterwards, he went right to sleep. To keep himself from knowing, perhaps. Keep himself out of the way" (323). Emil knew that Langley expected him to "do what must be done," so he buried the empty medicine bottle, a secret he "guarded" alone until now (324). Thus Langley burdened five young people for the rest of their lives, and in many ways Emil's burden, the guilt of a murderer, was the heaviest.

Finally, we must ask, why of all cancers did Glaspell choose a tumor of the brain? As Norma responds in disbelief, "That brain? . . . No. That couldn't be" (304). Throughout the novel, Langley is portrayed as a Socratic figure associated with Plato, the "great companion" whose thoughts reach "across the centuries" through the written word (324). Like Christ, too, Langley is a sacrificial figure who abandoned wealth, career success, even marriage to pursue his calling as a teacher of "truth" (313). He pushed himself through sickness and pain to inspire his group of handpicked disciples. Also like Christ, he served as a conduit of divine revelation for Norma and the others. But Glaspell's portrait of Langley is deeply ambivalent because, similar to Virginia Woolf, she suspects the egotism at the center of the patriarchal logos. Her portrayal of Langley corresponds with Woolf's famous lines about "the dominance of the letter

'I' and the aridity, which, like the giant beech tree, it casts with its shade. Nothing will grow there" (*Room* 104). Like a tumor of the brain, there is a rottenness at the center of such unremitting idealism. It is life-denying, sterile, rigid, an "impediment . . . which blocked the fountain of creative energy and shored it within narrow limits" (104). This has always been Norma's problem: Langley's ideals, just as much as Max's egotism, never allowed her to live her own life.

In the concluding chapters, Norma has returned to the Pettibone house to live with Lorna and Doc. Again, life has been unpredictable. "Had she been told this was where she was going to spend the last of her days she would have said no, not if the heavens fell. But she lived there now, and the heavens were as usual. One simply doesn't know" (329). Doc writes that Lorna is pregnant and longs to be reunited with her mother, but Norma doesn't return for her daughter's sake; rather, she is running away from Scott. Emil's revelations have left her spiritually and emotionally dead, unable to believe any longer in the ideals she tried to pass on to Scott. Now, "she couldn't let Scott know that none of it had ever been true at all. . . . She'd just have to walk out on him" (330, 335). Once again her impossible all-or-nothing idealism leads to a cowardly abdication.

As in so many of Glaspell's novels, Norma's inward journey, and the novel, are resolved through intergenerational reconnection, as she is re-united with her daughter, Lorna, and helps with the birth of her grand-daughter. Lorna goes into labor during a snowstorm, so there is no doctor or hospital available. Her mother must coach her through it:

> "Mother!" Lorna would cry out to her, as one trapped: "what is this?" "This is just something you have to do," she would say. "I can't," Lorna would moan. "Yes, you can. You will." Through the hours of the night, on into the morning, the pains of labor, the struggle for birth. Lorna grew weaker and whispered she wanted to die. "You can't die. This is life—not death." (343)

By helping her daughter through this trial, Norma realizes that she "shunned" her own "ordeal" because it was too painful (344). She sees in the birth of her granddaughter—"an infant who would become a woman: go to school, marry, and one day know a night like this"—an affirmation of life and humanity that allows her to forgive Langley and "grant him the right to a human weakness" (343, 348). Bathing the baby, she wants to tell her "not to grieve about what is not important" and that the "best we have [is] seeking to understand" (345).

In clearing out a back room, Doc and Lorna discover a box of Norma's notebooks and papers from college. Norma's "strength to touch them came from the little child now at her mother's breast. Denial of life must not live so close to the untouched. Hopelessness had no place under the roof of the newborn" (346). The birth of her granddaughter enables Norma to finally join life (baby) and logos (papers). She opens a notebook at random and reads a description of Langley she had written thirty years before, "looking across the field of grain to the vineyard on the hillside beyond and the grove outside the vineyard." She realizes that there was no vineyard in South Dakota where she went to college, but she had seen it that way because "in my thoughts it became one with Christ. I was writing about us—and I wrote of him. He was one of us; we one with him. Two thousand years apart—and one." This revelation convinces her that "time does not matter, does not separate and make dead" (347–48). With the birth of Norma's granddaughter, once again Glaspell portrays an intergenerational mother-child reconnection affirming the natural cycles of human existence, but here it is joined with a Christian manifestation of "the life eternally creative" (348).

Norma's redemption, spurred by the miracle of childbirth and her vision of the teacher as Christ, integrates the binarisms that have crippled her life—realism/idealism, matter/spirit. As we have seen, all of Glaspell's novels strive to negotiate and anneal patriarchal binarisms at their conclusion. In the moment before her death Norma affirms, "We have to believe in the good. . . . We ourselves may not be good, but if we feel goodness not there—why then should we live?" This presents us with another of Glaspell's uncomfortable, ambiguous endings, similar to that of *Ambrose Holt and Family*. Norma's vision of Christ in her image of the teacher reaffirms her faith in the existence of goodness, but there is little evidence in the novel that good exists, particularly since Langley is clearly not good. Norma admits, "we do not dwell with it all our days," but we need to believe in goodness because "we need something to come home to" (348). Thus Glaspell leaves open such questions as whether Norma's divine revelation is self-generated because she cannot tolerate life's meaninglessness without it; whether that even matters, since the important end, faith, is achieved; or whether we have the strength to believe in the good without divine revelation.

Similar to Woolf's *Three Guineas* and *Between the Acts*, *Norma Ashe* (written at about the same time) seems to be overshadowed by World War II, darkened by the imminence of fascism, nationalism, and rampant industrialism. These late works reveal both writers' despair that the promise of earlier twentieth-century reform movements from their youth—socialism, pacifism, and feminism—is farther than ever from being fulfilled and that perhaps the promise of justice and goodness is never to be fulfilled in any life. Woolf battles this despair in *Three Guineas* with a bitterly sarcastic indictment of patriarchy and an exhortation to women to remain separate from it even if they must work within it, offering only this as a slim hope for change. *Norma Ashe* provides an equally stringent feminist analysis of the era, and the hope Glaspell offers at the end is just as intangible.

As discussed in the introduction, Glaspell admired Woolf for making "the inner things real," but she preferred in her own fiction to attempt to balance that modernist aesthetic with more traditional realist aims, in her words, the "story, that simple downright human interest." In her best novels, particularly *Fugitive's Return*, *Brook Evans*, and *The Morning Is Near Us*, Glaspell achieves a female aesthetic with her use of a semiotic that is itself a metaphor "for sisterhood, and for a politics of feminist survival" (Showalter, *Sister's Choice* 151). In these novels she attempts to "'wrest an alphabet' from the 'speaking text' of women's bodies," creating "an aesthetics of maternal protection, an aesthetics of sisterhood" indeed comparable to Woolf's (Marcus, *"Still Practice"* 215, 219). Her late novels, however, show an increasing reliance on a straightforward realistic narrative in which verbal signs do not act in defiance of the conventions of symbolic signification. While Glaspell's portrayal of the negative effects of patriarchy and capitalism during the early decades of the twentieth century provides a daring feminist critique comparable to Woolf's expository prose, unlike Woolf's late novel *Between the Acts*, *Norma Ashe* shows a diminution of the radical evocative power of Glaspell's female aesthetic.

In her lifetime, Glaspell has witnessed the situation of women
inch forward and slide back; she has seen war and peace and then
war again. Her faith in progress is diminished, but she clings to
the hope that, though a good woman . . . cannot change the world,
she can alleviate its sufferings, elevate her own character,
and keep a spark of hope alive for the future.

— *Veronica Makowsky*

# Epilogue

## The Man's World of *Judd Rankin's Daughter* (1945)

As a writer, Glaspell believed in the power of the written word to defy the
boundaries of death. In *Fugitive's Return* and in *Norma Ashe*, she celebrates the long Western cultural heritage of the logos as itself a miracle:

> Her desire to learn Greek became a passion. All day long she would
> study. Almost with reverence she loved the letters themselves, for
> they were as keys that can unlock treasure. . . . she had a new feeling
> about language—a feeling of wonder there should be language at all
> . . . as if language had been divinely vouchsafed us. (*Fugitive's Return*
> 242)

> Words were for thoughts and words could beget thoughts: all so
> wonderfully intertwined. Books were the thoughts of others. We
> couldn't meet many great people face-to-face but we could know
> them through their books. (*Norma Ashe* 316)

But the logos is patriarchal symbolic, while female eternity and female
connection, which Glaspell also richly celebrates, are more often communicated semiotically through the actual and the metaphoric body, as
I have shown in my analyses of these novels. This issue of two different

languages runs throughout the novels as the protagonists seesaw between body and logos, mother and father. Some of her novels end with a clear swing toward the maternal (*Fugitive's Return*), others swing toward the paternal (*Ambrose Holt and Family*), and others attempt an integration (*Norma Ashe*)—but Glaspell is always exposing and negotiating the cultural binarisms that limit women in a patriarchal culture.

In her final novel, however, the mother is almost totally erased. The protagonist, Frances Mitchell, is a mother, but the title nominates her in relation to her father, and she (herself motherless) orbits in a universe dominated by men—father, husband, and son:

> Frances was a little shocked to realize how seldom she thought of her mother, whereas (she thought of [her husband] Len and was lonely) her funny father was right there in her mind all the time—somewhere near. (214)

Frances, the center of a family of men, is a Blossom Holt ten years down the road, but this novel lacks the biting gender criticism and parodic wit of the earlier work. Unlike Blossom, who deprecates her golden curly hair and the pastel dresses her husband chooses for her, Frances perms her hair and chooses a flowered dress with high heels, until admonished by her adolescent daughter to express more character by wearing navy, brushing her hair back, and donning "Grecian" sandals (146–48). Similar to Blossom's husband, Frances's husband, Len, is a writer, a literary critic who condescends to her intelligence. Characterizing her mind as "undisciplined" and distrusting her emotional "outbursts," he entraps her in the traditional female realm of the irrational, leaving her feeling "ineffectual" whenever she tries to communicate her ideas to him (19, 104). Unlike Blossom, she uncritically accepts his intellectual superiority, dismisses his faults, and idolizes his "inviolate" integrity, repeatedly insisting that "Len was so good" even though there is little overt evidence of his goodness (108, 180). "He understands so much it can be very aggravating," she admits, but in his "scrupulousness about truth" she finds security in a fractious age (108, 227).

Although Frances has a daughter, Madeleine, and her relationships with two female friends, Marianna and Julia, are briefly highlighted, these are incidental to the plot and not the focus of her deepest concern, which is "salvaging" her men (Makowsky 145). Madeleine is an immature, headstrong young woman, superficially characterized compared to her brother, Judson, a marine who returns from the Pacific with deep psychological wounds as a result of the war. While the image of her father's cousin, Adah, a nineteenth-century magna mater of warmth, sexuality, and "devilment," haunts the text, this novel lacks the dramatic "tensity" of others, in which maternal figures are more significant.

The novel opens with Adah's death. She represents Glaspell's final portrayal of the palimpsest, the absent, mythic woman upon whom male characters "inscribe their own identities, desires, and language" (Ben-Zvi, "Contributions" 157). A young soldier, Gerald, comes to her deathbed because he believes Adah has some special message about life to convey to him, but she is unconscious by the time he arrives. Memories of her delight Frances's father, the aged Judd Rankin, who recalls that her "spirit never got pinned down like a butterfly on a sheet of paper" (76). He still reveres her "gift of making you feel more than you had known you were" and her fervent belief that "it should be—our pleasure" to help one another (85, 93). Although as a girl Frances also felt Adah's warmth "as light from the sun," for her Adah "belongs to a vanished age" (11, 12). She represents a past in which society, class, and wealth had seemed so impervious, yet they had been destroyed by the Great Depression, the "sound of a hundred smashing banks," and replaced by a "far more populous and rough-shod society" (15–16).

Frances is ambivalent about the passing of this more ordered world. She feels nostalgic for the glamour of Adah's past and confused by an America of 1944 in which "the country seemed to be floating in ideas which didn't crystallize into a belief," but overall she agrees with her leftist husband and populist father that the "feudal grandeur" in which Adah lived with her wealthy capitalist husband, built upon the exploitation of workers, is wrong (14, 15). Adah had to "play the game," which she did superlatively, in order to uphold the conventions of a society she believed in and, at the same time, covertly express her forbidden sexual vitality. Frances contrasts this "hypocrisy" unfavorably with Madeleine, who, though "young and violent," is yet "more honest than Cousin Adah had ever been" (24).

Although Frances briefly connects with Adah in her moment of death and senses that in some way she is to carry on her legacy of caring for others, she believes that the elderly woman failed to pass on wisdom because she could not verbalize it. Both Gerald and Judd are content, even inspired, by Adah's nonverbal legacy to them. As Judd tries to tell his daughter, "Adah—just happened. That's the only way you can explain her." But to Frances, she "failed to speak for herself" (210). She wonders "what word of wisdom could Cousin Adah have for an age so unlike her own?" and condemns her for having "become silent a little too soon" (29, 37).

Frances seeks "words of wisdom," rational solutions and the comfort of the logos in a war-torn age that has repressed the female semiotic. She is troubled by a world in which trusted friends can suddenly be revealed as anti-Semites, in which old leftists who once got "hustled off Boston Common in the Sacco-Vanzetti rumpus" and "rushed clear down to Scottsboro about our black brothers in the boxcar" can now spout fascist rhetoric "under the guise of . . . restoring old-fashioned American democracy" (130, 145, 153). Under a pro-American nationalist banner, newspapers "used all the bad words you could print about [Hitler], and went busily ahead with a lot of the things which had built Hitler up" (145). Even though all of America has jumped on the war bandwagon, Glaspell paints the home front as a morass of conflicting ideologies, nationalism, liberalism, isolationism: "People said they believed in America. But which America?" (15).

Frances's greatest fear is that the nation is no longer worth the people's lives that are being given to protect it: "But the boys—all those boys—coming home—and to what?" (153, 163). This fear is crystallized in the figure of Gerald, who went to his death in the war with his questions unanswered because, Frances believes, Adah failed him and she herself lacked the wisdom. She "wished she knew what to say to him, wished she were wiser. Here is this boy—simple and unashamed, looking for something. We should have something to tell him" (33). She tries to explain her sense of failure to Gerald, but, similar to Blossom at the beginning of *Ambrose Holt and Family,* her confidence in her own intellect is so undermined that she feels incapable of helping him: "Heavens, what am I getting into, she thought—talking about wisdom when I haven't any" (39).

Ironically, Gerald is not at all troubled by her lack. He assures Frances he will always remember the things she said the day of Adah's death, but she insists upon her inadequacy: "I fear I didn't say anything worth remembering. How could I when I didn't know what it was all about? . . . I don't—get things." When Gerald responds that "something was close by" the day Adah died and that it was closer to Frances than himself, she denies it, and "feels very much disposed to discredit Cousin Adah" in a repudiation of the maternal semiotic that Gerald senses. "If you think I know what it's about," she says, "I should think you would try to get it out of me." Frances is floored by Gerald's response, which again points to a nonverbal relation, a "thing" that must be sensed and cannot be intellectually grasped: "Oh, no. If you know a thing is there you don't have to bother much whether you have it or not" (144). Although Frances persists in denying its validity, Gerald knows "it is there," the nonverbal semiotic of both Adah and Frances. He tells her he can go to war knowing that if he gets killed, "there'll still be you."

Gerald is comforted by his faith in an amorphous maternal presence, but Frances remains frustrated by her unanswered need to know: "What good does it do you to know a thing is there if you don't have it? If you don't even know—" (145). After Gerald's death, she recalls seeing him waiting at the door of Adah's room, "as if he must go on expectantly standing at a door," seeking answers (214). But it is not Gerald who stands expectantly at the door, desperate for knowledge; it is Frances. Logos, the realm of the father, dominates the daughter and the text. Frances rejects the semiotic wisdom of the mother and turns to her father, Judd Rankin, a writer, for answers: "You know something and I shall find out what it is or know the reason why" (209).

Judd Rankin is Glaspell's final tribute to Cook, portrayed as she imagines him had he stayed in Iowa, near the Mississippi he so loved.[1] "Very Mississippi Valley–minded" and stung by eastern condescension to the Midwest because of its lack of "culture," Judd Rankin has written a local paper for many years entitled *Out Here,* "hell bent to establish right there was the best of the world—and just let it alone, please" (15, 84). A curmudgeonly old farmer who lost his son in World War I, Judd advocates isolationism until he finally admits that Poland must be saved, even if Americans die in the process (83). Although war for Judd provides a "hell of a commentary on life" when it takes "mass killing to bring out the best in a man," he also sympathizes with the patriarchal mandate of heroic male sacrifice: "What man worth his salt didn't want to give himself to a thing bigger than he was?" (57).

Judd writes a book about the "Swamp-Neck Jenkses," celebrating the generations of pioneers who settled the Mississippi Valley and the seasonal joys of farm life—"sliding down hay piled high in the barn, and smell of the honeysuckle just outside . . . [the] earth smell of ploughed field"—that his daughter, a converted easterner but still a midwesterner at heart, also reveres (160). Here Judd briefly appears to be aligned with the maternal body in his love of nature, like Erik Helge in *Brook Evans* and Ambrose Holt. Indeed, Frances defines him as "a man whose own roots were deep-bedded like the roots of the oak, who, like the tree, was of that place and had all his years drawn life from that air and known himself for a child of this sun" (140). But his book is a grievous disappointment to her. As Len writes in his review and Frances agrees, her father's work is limited by his midwestern chauvinism: "For all its lustiness the book had the dry rot of veneration, . . . its spirit was scared to death on a tightrope, trying to prove out there superior to the rest of the earth" (156). Caught in this war of words between her two men, husband and father, Frances sides with her husband but believes her father "was meant to sing more" (209). She admits, "Father—I'm all balled up," and she needs his words to heal the pain and confusion caused by the war (225). In the novel's final section, she returns home to urge him to write again, "give it wings—be afraid no longer—let it soar" (234).

Another character who feels betrayed by the logos is Frances's son, Judson, a soldier on the Pacific front. Judson discovers the fatal disjunction between the real and the ideal in a particularly brutal way. Horrified by the killing all around them, he and a fellow soldier recite Wordsworth's "Intimations of Immortality" ode while creeping through the jungle underbrush in an attempt to comfort their fear (237). In the middle of the fifth stanza—"The Youth, who daily farther from the east / Must travel, still is Nature's Priest"—his friend is shot in the face and killed. As Judson writes to his mother, "And then there was just me. And the Ode" (239). In this deft touch by Glaspell, right in the midst of Wordsworth's angelic vision, Judson is shockingly confronted by man's brutality. Like Hamlet, he goes insane because his world is insane, and, obsessed by finishing the stanza, he flings the words defiantly into the void. "And by the vision splendid / Is on his way attended," he screams on a hill in the middle of a battle and later at home from the top of a willow tree from which a friend has just fallen. "Those horrible words," Frances recalls (207). She'll never forget them, but she still looks to words for restitution. Upon his return, Judson fittingly rejects his father, once his idol, who represents for him the failed promise of the logos. The intellectual's world of ideas and of ineffectual liberalism has failed to prevent the conflagration. "But for me Father still—lights dead faces" (241).

Frances sees in her three men a trinity. Judson, the Son, will be brought back to the Father through the agency of the Holy Ghost (Judd senior): "It was here to be found—in what was between Len and her father, alive between them, and holding something—perhaps holding salvation for Judson, right here in the room" (119). What is shared between Len and her father is of course the logos, language as symbolic signification, nomination, sign and syntax, and the vision of exalted, rational man. Judd's new manuscript, which he sends first to his grandson, brings Judson back home to his father: "'Listen,' Judson said. 'I think it's the best thing ever written. Now what do you think, Father?'" (250). His grandfather has expressed a wrath that "could strike you dead—wrath like the old prophets, maybe, and out of this wrath came the song of the earth—clear to heaven!" (251). He reaffirms transcendence, as Judson reports, and "talks about there being more in us than we know is there," a sense of enduring spirituality that Judson himself had seen on the faces of the dead (252). "'God—' Len said softly," appropriately nominating his father-in-law as deity, "I've waited a long time for somebody to say that" (252). Judson has been returned to the fold of patriarchy, to father and to war, through the word. Cleansed of his madness (revulsion at war), he now wants to "work in a war plant" (250). For Frances, it is a "miracle," her son healed, her men reunited, and she of course has played the madonna, the vessel through which the (grand)father has reproduced himself in his (grand)son, who now identifies with him thoroughly.

*Judd Rankin's Daughter*, like *Ambrose Holt and Family*, is resolved through the agency of an idealized father, not a renegade this time but a patriarch—his voice *is* the logos. However, as so often, Glaspell's seemingly pat, "happy" endings leave a strange feeling of unease. Can a magic book be written that will heal the divisiveness of a binaristic culture in which ideals are so split from reality? Can a transcendent logos answer for the bestial instinct that is its reciprocal image? Can a patriarchal voice heal a patriarchal wound? Frances imagines

> a report that might be made on planet Earth by someone observing from another planet. "Scientifically they are advanced," this report might read, "but what they want is to destroy one another. Every so often they try to kill themselves off, as if their attainment must be put to this purpose. It is a criminal instinct of which they cannot rid themselves." (163)

Glaspell's desertion of the mother, that is, of the passionate female semiotic that animates novels such as *Brook Evans*, *Fugitive's Return*, and *The Morning Is Near Us*, results in a serious weakening of her fictional power in this novel. Lacking the depth of her earlier searching psychoanalytic explorations of parent-child relations, lacking the drama of her mythological allusions and parallels, lacking even the socialist, feminist cultural critique of *Norma Ashe* and the wit of *Ambrose Holt and Family*, *Judd Rankin's Daughter* is a discursive, rambling patchwork that falls flat. It appears that the novels in which the mother-daughter relation is the most negligible are Glaspell's weakest, not because a woman's writing must contain feminist themes to be good, but because the "maternal aesthetic," to use Jane Marcus's term, is the driving force of Glaspell's creativity. It is "an aesthetics of maternal protection, an aesthetics of sisterhood, an aesthetics . . . of woman's critique of male domination" that gives imaginative fire to her style (Marcus, "Still Practice" 219).

One can only surmise what this may reflect about American culture during the war years and about Glaspell's state of mind at the end of her life. Her longing for an idealized father may have derived from her lack of intimate male companionship since the end of her relationship with Norman Matson more than ten years earlier, or from a return to Christianity as she approached her own death. However, one can say with more confidence that Glaspell's major novels reflect the trajectory of the women's movement, from the New Woman of the 1920s in *Fidelity* to the sublimation of women's issues in the war years in *Judd Rankin's Daughter*. Perhaps Frances would rather "entrust the structure of society" to her forthright daughter, Madeleine, than to the wily, seductive cousin Adah, but she herself is evidence that the possibility for an assertive womanhood has already waned (25). Familiar Glaspell images, such as Frances's love of gardening and jelly-making, "offerings of the sun" signifying an eternal "unity in things," peek through the surface of this narrative (101). But, like the hurricane that destroys Frances's garden and rips up the venerable willow tree that shadows her yard, a symbol of natural regeneration, the war seems to have "smashed" all of that (140). *Judd Rankin's Daughter* reflects Glaspell's troubled acquiescence to a war that must be won.

The war placed feminists such as Glaspell and Woolf in a terrible quandary. Against it on principle, both were quite able to see that fascism was not restricted to Hitler but flourished in the war fervor of their own self-righteous democracies; nevertheless they, like everyone else, knew Hitler was a destructive force that had to be stopped. Both realized, Woolf with far greater dismay, that the younger generation were abandoning the political views of their elders and embracing the war. Like Woolf's nephew, Julian Bell, who rejected his aunt's pacifism and volunteered for service as an ambulance driver in the Spanish Civil War, where he was killed, Judson scorns the liberal socialism of his parents' generation. Woolf was more explicit in expressing her anger at the reprise of war and her understanding of its roots in patriarchy in *Three Guineas*, while Glaspell's view here is beyond meliorative; it appears acquiescent in its idealization of patriarchal values. In this last novel, Glaspell tried to represent the panoramic sweep of generations encompassed by her own life, with its origin in the late nineteenth century and ending nearly in the second half of the twentieth, in a more roseate hue than the bleak historical review portrayed in *Norma Ashe*. Had she lived longer, one wonders how she would have portrayed a postwar America in which women were forced out of the public arena her own generation had fought so hard to attain for them and back into marriages every bit as stifling as Norma Ashe's.

Feminist critics have established that Glaspell's drama put her in the vanguard of the American theater. When her short fiction and novels are added to that achievement, the body of work that comprises Susan Glaspell's four decades of commitment to writing, particularly to the novel, is remarkable. *Fidelity*, *Brook Evans*, *Fugitive's Return*, *Ambrose Holt and Family*, *The Morning Is Near Us*, and *Norma Ashe* are distinguished by Glaspell's deep understanding of familial relations, her acute dissections of gender as it is culturally constructed and replicated within marriage and family, her integration of American narrative traditions with modernist experimentation, and her amazing evocation of a female semiotic. The integrity and craft of these novels place her among the best early twentieth-century women writers, such as Virginia Woolf and Willa Cather. It is time to enrich our literary heritage by fully acknowledging Susan Glaspell's contributions.

# Notes

### The Burial and Resurrection of a Writer

1. Chamberlain called it a masterpiece because he believed Glaspell had "distilled the essence from the most important and character revealing moments," but he determined it was "small scale" because she had "limited her canvas deliberately . . . focus[ing] on purely human values that remain eternal, irrespective of time or place." The contradiction inherent in characterizing eternal human values as small scale reveals a gender-biased standard at work, even from a critic who appreciated her writing. *Brook Evans* is primarily about a mother-daughter relationship; therefore, Glaspell's fiction must be seen as inferior to that which portrays more "universal" themes of father-son competition, masculine action, and accomplishment.

2. I intend "jouissance" throughout in a Barthesian sense as an "active pleasure . . . associated with sexuality at its most abrupt and ruthless pitch" (Howard v).

### 1. *Fidelity* as American Romance (1915)

1. Glaspell's philosophic similarities with Lawrence are remarkable. For instance, in the continuing debate of society versus the individual, Deane says, in a distinctly Lawrencian phrase: "But after all what is society. . . . A collection of individuals for mutual benefit and self-protection, I gather. Protection against what? Their own warmest selves? The real things in them?" (175, 178). This sounds exactly like Birkin's arguments in *Women in Love*: "But I should like them to like the purely individual thing in themselves, which makes them act in singleness. And they only like to do the collective thing" (27).

*Fidelity* also echoes many of the views expressed in Lawrence's World War I essays (contemporary with *Fidelity*), such as "The Study of Thomas Hardy" and "The Reality of Peace." Lawrence's discussion of Hardy's Sue as the spiritualized woman who denies sensuality, "a locked centre of self-hatred, life-hatred" (509) parallels Glaspell's portrait of Sylvia Williams, a woman bound by restraint and propriety. Divorced from their sexuality, both characters lose their capacity to love and become, in Lawrence's term, pure "will," just as Glaspell describes Marion, "There was something that displeased her in abandonment to feeling. She did not like herself when she fully gave" (356–57). Lawrence concludes, "Why are we so foul that we have no reverence for that which we are and for that which is amongst us? If we had reverence for our life, our life would take at once religious form" (510). Just as Glaspell asks in *Fidelity*, "Why did we not live more abundantly? Why did we not hold life more precious?" (212). Glaspell's rebellion against social conformity and her depiction of sexuality as a sacred life force place her securely within modernist ideology.

2. *Fidelity* fits well into Dana A. Heller's discussion of women writers' fictional quests in *The Feminization of Quest-Romance*. Unlike male heroes of romantic narratives, female questers are "marked by a conflict between an equally strong desire to take flight and the social imperative of the 'huddle' or engulfing group" (10). Heroic female protagonists must "somehow transcend the limits of an enclosed space," "let go of femininity," and finally "be able to embody the opposite impulses of separation and connection" (10–13). All of these criteria aptly describe Ruth's development.

## 2. Greece/Greek as the Mother's Body in *The Road to the Temple* (1927)

1. While it is easy to belittle Glaspell's relationship with Norman Matson, a younger man whose only enduring literary accomplishment was a novel that inspired the television show *Bewitched* and who eventually left her for a younger woman, it is necessary to see this relationship as part of the same pattern. The fact that Glaspell took up with him almost immediately following Cook's death reveals how absolutely necessary replicating the mother-child intimacy in a sexual relationship was for her psychic well-being. That she produced a trilogy of fine novels, some of her best, while with Matson (*Brook Evans*, *Fugitive's Return*, and *Ambrose Holt and Family*) also evidences how stimulating, or necessary, such a relationship was for her creativity. These moving words, written by Glaspell in a letter to Matson's young lover's mother, make this clear:

> Norman was God's gift to me. When Jig died, and I came home from Greece, I thought of myself as the observer. I thought, I will try to be brave, and I will write. Then Norman came, and loved me and instead of seeing life from death, again I saw it from life. I was again in life. That I owe Norman. And I never will forget it. (Noe 64)

2. Cook felt ambivalent about his own fatherhood, as he resented having to assume responsibility and give up the child role. However, when Glaspell proposed

bringing his daughter, Nilla, to live with them on her return to Greece in 1923, he wrote, "Now I covet for my children the cultural foundation they would have by living in this country, mastering its living language" (367). He seemed to relish the Lacanian role of père, introducing symbolic function, the logos, and patriarchal culture. Like Athene born from Zeus's brain, Nilla (as Glaspell portrays her) was truly her father's daughter: "Her table was on the balcony and hour after hour she would sit working with a Greek verb, calling through the window to Jig, who was writing a poem in ancient Greek" (376).

3. See my book, *Ritual, Myth, and the Modernist Text: The Influence of Jane Ellen Harrison on Joyce, Eliot, and Woolf.*

### 3. Mother-Daughter "Tensity" in *Brook Evans* (1928)

1. Dorothy Dinnerstein's *The Mermaid and the Minotaur: Sexual Arrangements and Human Malaise* is equally applicable. Chodorow's and Dinnerstein's theses are remarkably similar, although their emphases and styles are different: Chodorow is more clinical, Dinnerstein more philosophical. Both use a psychoanalytic approach to stress that the "asymmetric sexual privilege" embedded in Western culture derives from exclusive mothering in early childhood and that "no fundamental change in the situation of women can be achieved without full male participation in early child care" (Dinnerstein 76, 89). Both believe that "mother-dominated infancy makes the prospect of adult sexual maturity (which in her case means tearing herself away from her first love) more problematic for the girl than for the boy" (Dinnerstein 83).

Rather than burden the reader with double references throughout the text, I will note here that the chapters of Dinnerstein's work most applicable to my argument are chapter 4, in which she discusses the basis for gender asymmetry in infancy and the oedipal period; chapter 6, in which she discusses object relations; and chapter 7, in which she discusses cultural denigration of the female body. For a similar point of view, see Jane Flax, "The Conflict between Nurturance and Autonomy in Mother-Daughter Relationships and within Feminism."

2. Interesting parallels between *Brook Evans* and the Book of Ruth could be established. In general, the biblical story seems to provide a cautionary tale by contrast. The adherence of Ruth to her mother-in-law Naomi and their mutual support help each of them survive in a patriarchal culture where a woman without male kin is entirely vulnerable, whereas Brook's abandonment of her mother diminishes both of them.

3. Glaspell's satire of the now senile Caleb Evans is worthy of Evelyn Waugh and provides another example of how critics have entirely overlooked her wit. Accompanying Evans to the graveyard, Caleb, "dancing a hideous dance of gloating over the dead," shows his grandson Joe Copeland's grave (297). He who once vehemently repressed dancing is now dancing like a crazed satyr: "He has been dead thirty-nine years! And I have been alive all them years. I have been alive—all them years he's rotting the grave" (297). Ironically, Caleb is the one who repressed life, while Joe fully lived it and passed it on to another generation. The once

puritanical oppressor is now shown listening to the radio, "stupified by jazz, . . . his head and hands moving as if he were a decrepit automaton, while a Chicago cabaret told him to mix Cleopatra and Camille—add a dash of sex appeal—and what do you get? Magnolia!" (289, 303). Thus the Jazz Age banishes the late Victorians with a vengeance.

### 4. *Fugitive's Return* (1929) Part I: Flight to the Past

1. As Veronica Makowsky has ingeniously discovered, Myra is an anagram of Irma (107).

2. To quote Jane Marcus's rendition, "Pandion gave away his daughter to Tereus as part of the spoils of war. Procne wept bitterly at the separation from her sister, Philomela. Procne bore Tereus a son, Itys. Tereus then went off again, raped Philomela, cut out her tongue, and left her on an island. Philomela wove the story of that rape into a tapestry and sent it to Procne, who rescued her sister and in an awful rage at the violation of sisterhood attacked the patriarchy itself in revenge: she killed her son and served him to his father to eat. The gods turned the sisters into the swallow and the nightingale and Tereus into the hoopoe, a bird that fouls its own nest" ("Introduction" 93).

3. I would venture to suggest that the stranger who nicknamed him is Glaspell herself, a brief visitant like Joyce's man in the mackintosh to her own fiction, for he seems to derive from an actual shepherd named Elias Scarmouches whose blustering machismo frightened Glaspell and whom she described in *The Road to the Temple* as "the archaic Dorian Apollo" (339, 390).

4. See Rachel Blau DuPlessis, *Writing Beyond the Ending;* Elaine Hedges' "The Needle or the Pen"; and Elaine Showalter, "Sister's Choice."

5. The rituals of Eleusis consisted of purification by sea bathing, sacrifice of a pig, fasting, drinking of Demeter's wineless libation, and the revelation and handling of unknown sacred objects but probably including seedcakes, fruits, and flowers (Harrison, *Prolegomena*, 150–56). What Orphic and Dionysiac rites brought to Eleusis were the dramatic rituals of a sacred marriage and birth of a sacred child, according to Harrison. Dionysus, under other epithets such as Iacchos and Bromios, was celebrated as the sacred child, but sometimes he was substituted for Hades and worshiped in his adult form. In either case, as Harrison stresses, Dionysus "bears to the end, as no other god does, the stamp of his matriarchal origin" (561).

The best contemporary sources for studying the Eleusinian Mysteries are George Mylonas, *Eleusis and the Eleusinian Mysteries,* and Karoly Kerenyi, *Essays on a Science of Mythology: The Myth of the Divine Child and the Mysteries of Eleusis.*

6. The Homeric Hymn to Demeter recounts the essentials of the Demeter-Persephone myth. Persephone was carried off by Hades with the consent of Zeus. Stricken with grief at the loss of her daughter, Demeter wandered for nine days, fasting and searching with burning torches. On the tenth day Hekate told her she

had heard Persephone's cries, and together they went to the sun god, Helios, who told them what had happened. In her anger, Demeter left the gods and wandered on earth disguised as an old woman. She met the four daughters of the king of Eleusis and returned to the palace to take care of their baby brother, Demophon. As she entered, she resumed her divine form. She refused to sit until the maid Iamb gave her a stool and refused to drink wine but accepted barley water. She sat sorrowing until Iamb told her jokes and made her laugh. At night Demeter attempted to make the prince immortal by anointing him and placing him in the fire, but the queen was watching and screamed in terror. Demeter angrily condemned humanity for its folly. She revealed her divinity and ordered a temple and altar to be built in the city, promising to teach the Eleusinians her rites. Her wanderings resumed, and she caused a famine that threatened earthly existence. Zeus sent all the gods in turn to ask her to relent, but she refused. At last he sent Hermes to Hades to bring back Persephone, but Hades had given her pomegranate seeds to eat, so she must return for one-third of every year, becoming Queen of the Underworld during that time. Joyfully reunited, mother and daughter were joined by Hekate, who became an attendant of Persephone.

7. The Christian Clement of Alexandria, whose writings are a source for much information about the Mysteries, attempted to discredit them with the story of Baubo, among other things. It is amusing to see the lips of Baubo being silenced even today. George Mylonas summarizes the long scholarly debate based upon Clement, that perhaps the kteis, the female pudenda, was among the unknown sacra handled at the Mysteries, but he concludes that Clement's statements must "apply either to the mysteries of Rhea-Kybele-Attis, or to those celebrated in Alexandria," thus projecting onto eastern Other what he cannot accept in his beloved Eleusis. Not surprisingly, Mylonas prefers his mother chaste and concludes "categorically that the Eleusinian tradition has no place for Baubo at the site of Demeter" (293–304). Joseph Fontenrose just as categorically dismisses "the ancient statement that Ge and Themis spoke oracles at Delphi before it became Apollo's establishment" because "nothing but myth supports this statement" (1). The laughter of Baubo and the voice of the Oracle, however, have not been silenced in the texts of Harrison and Glaspell.

## 6. The Daughter with Two Fathers in *Ambrose Holt and Family* (1931)

1. The final epitaph on the lumber pile occurs alongside Ambrose's own. After his death, excerpts from articles he had once written for the newspaper are reprinted, "caustic, ironic, so like him" that Blossom smiles as she reads his sly attack on the society he despised:

> A lumber pile has countenance. It has more personality than is usually found in people, making one believe, if not in immortality, in the transmigration of souls. Personality lodges where it can get a hold. And why not immortality? The lumber changes. The pile remains. (296)

2. The reference to Nietzsche here suggests that Lincoln Holt may represent one of Glaspell's most scathing portraits of Cook. If so, she acutely understood all his faults, in particular why he was a failure as an artist, but she loved him (maternally) in spite of them, just as Blossom does Lincoln.

3. Hugh Parker is most likely modeled on Edmund Wilson.

### Epilogue. The Man's World of *Judd Rankin's Daughter* (1945)

1. Like Cook, Rankin writes of "the land—way back before the white man got there, land of the red man and the buffalo." Although, again like Cook, he feels guilty about "the great wrong done in getting this land" for the whites, he writes of the heroism of the pioneers coming in their covered wagons, "seeding, plowing, always hoping things were going to be better." Like Cook, too, he is mighty in his "wrath" against the exploitation of land and people by commercial interests and he relishes exposing "all the crooked deals, grafting and grabbing" in his writing (54–55). Frances even chastises a roomful of their right-wing friends by reciting an actual poem of Cook's, ending with a resounding "For the lost vision of the goal immense— / Tell us, O friends, have you found recompense?" When asked who wrote the poem she responds, "Someone my father knew—out there. Cook was the name. He's dead now." "Think so?" her husband, Len, asks (155). Despite her implication that Cook's spirit still lives (in her novel at least), one senses that Glaspell is thankful he is no longer alive "to see what we've become."

# Works Cited

Aeschylus. *Oresteia*. Trans. Richmond Lattimore. *The Complete Greek Tragedies*. Chicago: University of Chicago Press, 1953.

Baym, Nina. "Melodramas of Beset Manhood: How Theories of American Fiction Exclude Women Authors." In *The New Feminist Criticism*, edited by Elaine Showalter, 63–80. New York: Pantheon, 1985.

Beauvoir, Simone de. *The Second Sex*. Trans. H. M. Parshley. New York: Vintage, 1989.

Benstock, Shari. *Women of the Left Bank: Paris, 1900–1940*. Austin: University of Texas Press, 1986.

Ben-Zvi, Linda. *Susan Glaspell: Essays on Her Theater and Fiction*. Ann Arbor: University of Michigan Press, 1995.

———. "Susan Glaspell and Eugene O'Neill: The Imagery of Gender." *Eugene O'Neill Newsletter* 10 (Spring 1986): 22–27.

———. "Susan Glaspell's Contributions to Contemporary Women Playwrights." In *Feminine Focus: The New Women Playwrights*, edited by Enoch Brater, 147–66. New York: Oxford University Press, 1989.

Boose, Lynda E. "The Father's House and the Daughter in It: The Structures of Western Culture's Daughter-Father Relationship." In *Daughters and Fathers*, edited by Lynda E. Boose and Betty S. Flowers, 19–74. Baltimore: Johns Hopkins University Press, 1989.

Burke, Carolyn. "Rethinking the Maternal." In *The Future of Difference*, edited by Hester Eisenstein and Alice Jardine, 107–13. New Brunswick: Rutgers University Press, 1985.

Carpentier, Martha C. *Ritual, Myth, and the Modernist Text: The Influence of Jane Ellen Harrison on Joyce, Eliot, and Woolf.* Amsterdam: Gordon and Breach, 1998.

Chamberlain, John. "A Small-Scale Masterpiece in Susan Glaspell's Novel." *New York Times Book Review*, July 1, 1928.

———. "A Tragi-Comedy of Idealism in Miss Glaspell's Novel." *New York Times Book Review*, April 12, 1931.

Chodorow, Nancy. *The Reproduction of Mothering: Psychoanalysis and the Sociology of Gender.* Berkeley: University of California Press, 1978.

Cixous, Hélène. "Castration or Decapitation?" Trans. Annette Kuhn. *Signs* 7 (autumn 1981): 41–55.

———. "The Laugh of the Medusa." In *New French Feminisms*, edited by Elaine Marks and Isabelle de Courtivron, 245–64. New York: Schocken Books, 1981.

Dinnerstein, Dorothy. *The Mermaid and the Minotaur: Sexual Arrangements and Human Malaise.* New York: Harper Collins, 1976.

DuPlessis, Rachel Blau. *Writing Beyond the Ending: Narrative Strategies of Twentieth-Century Women Writers.* Bloomington: Indiana University Press, 1985.

Dymkowski, Christine. "On the Edge: The Plays of Susan Glaspell." *Modern Drama* 31 (March 1988): 91–105.

Eliot, T. S. "Ulysses, Order, and Myth." In *Selected Prose of T. S. Eliot,* edited by Frank Kermode, 175–78. New York: Harcourt Brace Jovanovich, 1975.

Euripides. *Helen.* Trans. James Michie and Colin Leach. *The Greek Tragedy in New Translations,* edited by William Arrowsmith. New York: Oxford University Press, 1981.

———. *Rhesos.* Trans. Richard Emil Braun. *The Greek Tragedy in New Translations,* edited by William Arrowsmith. New York: Oxford University Press, 1978.

Fetterley, Judith. "Introduction." In *Provisions: A Reader from 19th-Century American Women,* edited by Judith Fetterly, 1–40. Bloomington: Indiana University Press, 1985.

"Fidelity." *New York Times Book Review,* May 16, 1915.

Flax, Jane. "The Conflict between Nurturance and Autonomy in Mother-Daughter Relations and within Feminism." *Feminist Studies* 4 (June 1978): 171–91.

———. "Mother-Daughter Relationships: Psychodynamics, Politics, and Philosophy." In *The Future of Difference,* edited by Hester Eisenstein and Alice Jardine, 20–40. New Brunswick: Rutgers University Press, 1985.

Fontenrose, Joseph. *The Delphic Oracle: Its Responses and Operations with a Catalogue of Responses.* Berkeley: University of California Press, 1978.

Friedman, Susan Stanford. "Modernism of the 'Scattered Remnant': Race and Politics in H.D.'s Development." In *Feminist Issues in Literary Scholarship,* edited by Shari Benstock, 208–32. Bloomington: Indiana University Press, 1987.

Glaspell, Susan. *Ambrose Holt and Family.* New York: Frederick A. Stokes, 1931.

——. *Brook Evans.* New York: Frederick A. Stokes, 1928.

——. *Fidelity.* Boston: Small, Maynard, 1915.

——. *Fugitive's Return.* New York: Frederick A. Stokes, 1929.

——. *Judd Rankin's Daughter.* New York: J. B. Lippincott, 1945.

——. *Lifted Masks and Other Works.* Edited by Eric S. Rabkin. Ann Arbor: University of Michigan Press, 1993.

——. *The Morning Is Near Us.* New York: Frederick A. Stokes, 1939.

——. *Norma Ashe.* New York: J. B. Lippincott, 1942.

——. *The Road to the Temple.* New York: Frederick A. Stokes, 1927.

——. *Woman's Honor. Plays by Susan Glaspell.* New York: Dodd, Mead, 1931.

Harrison, Jane Ellen. *Prolegomena to the Study of Greek Religion.* Cambridge, Eng.: At the University Press, 1903.

——. *Themis.* Cleveland and New York: World Publishing, 1912, 1927.

Hedges, Elaine. "The Needle or the Pen: The Literary Rediscovery of Women's Textile Work." In *Tradition and the Talents of Women,* edited by Florence Howe, 338–64. Urbana and Chicago: University of Illinois Press, 1991.

Heller, Dana A. *The Feminization of Quest-Romance.* Austin: University of Texas Press, 1990.

Howard, Richard. "A Note on the Text." In Roland Barthes, *The Pleasure of the Text.* New York: Hill and Wang, 1975.

Hutchinson, Percy. "A Sensitive Novel by Susan Glaspell." *New York Times Book Review,* November 10, 1929.

Irigaray, Luce. "When Our Lips Speak Together." Trans. Carolyn Burke. *Signs* 6 (Autumn 1980): 69–79.

Kerenyi, Karoly. *Essays on a Science of Mythology: The Myth of the Divine Child and the Mysteries of Eleusis.* Bollingen Series 22. Princeton, N.J.: Princeton University Press, 1969.

Kolodny, Annette. "A Map for Rereading: Gender and the Interpretation of Literary Texts." In *New Literary History.* Baltimore: The Johns Hopkins University Press, 1980. Reprinted in *The New Feminist Criticism,* edited by Elaine Showalter, 46–62. New York: Pantheon Books, 1985.

Kristeva, Julia. "From One Identity to Another." In *Desire in Language: A Semiotic Approach to Literature and Art,* edited by Leon S. Roudiez, 124–45. New York: Columbia University Press, 1980.

Lauter, Paul. "Race and Gender in the Shaping of the American Literary Canon: A Case Study from the Twenties." *Feminist Studies* 9 (1983): 435–63.

Lawrence, D. H. *The Rainbow.* New York: Penguin, 1981.

——. "The Study of Thomas Hardy" and "The Reality of Peace." In *Phoenix,* edited by Edward D. McDonald, 398–516, 669–94. New York: Viking Press, 1972.

——. *Women in Love.* New York: Penguin, 1976.

Makowsky, Veronica. *Susan Glaspell's Century of American Women.* New York: Oxford University Press, 1993.

Marcus, Jane. "Introduction: A Rose for Him to Rifle." In *Virginia Woolf and the Languages of Patriarchy*. Bloomington: Indiana University Press, 1987.

———. "Still Practice, A/Wrested Alphabet: Toward a Feminist Aesthetic." In *Art and Anger*, 215–50. Athens: Ohio University Press, 1988.

McFarland, Thomas. *Shakespeare's Pastoral Comedy*. Chapel Hill: University of North Carolina Press, 1972.

Mellard, James M. "Lacanian Tragedy and the Ethics of Jouissance." *PMLA* 113 (May 1998): 395–407.

Moi, Toril. *Sexual Textual Politics*. London and New York: Routledge, 1985.

Mylonas, George E. *Eleusis and the Eleusinian Mysteries*. Princeton, N.J.: Princeton University Press, 1961.

Noe, Marcia. *Susan Glaspell: Voice from the Heartland*. Western Illinois Monograph Series, Number 1. Macomb: Western Illinois Press, 1983.

Ozieblo, Barbara. *Susan Glaspell: A Critical Biography*. Chapel Hill: The University of North Carolina Press, 2000.

Quinn, Arthur Hobson. *American Fiction: An Historical and Critical Survey*. New York: D. Appleton-Century, 1936.

Rich, Adrienne. *Of Woman Born*. New York: W. W. Norton, 1976.

Ruland, Richard, and Malcolm Bradbury. *From Puritanism to Postmodernism*. New York: Penguin, 1991.

Showalter, Elaine. *Sister's Choice: Tradition and Change in American Women's Writing*. Oxford: Oxford University Press, 1994.

———. *These Modern Women: Autobiographical Essays from the Twenties*. Old Westbury, N.Y.: Feminist Press, 1978.

Suzuki, Mihoko. *Metamorphoses of Helen*. Ithaca, N.Y., and London: Cornell University Press, 1989.

Waterman, Arthur E. *Susan Glaspell*. Twayne's United States Authors Series 101, edited by Sylvia E. Bowman. New York: Twayne Publishers, 1966.

Woolf, Virginia. *Jacob's Room*. New York: Harcourt Brace Jovanovich, 1922.

———. *Moments of Being*. 2d ed. Edited by Jeanne Schulkind. New York: Harcourt Brace Jovanovich, 1985.

———. *A Room of One's Own*. New York: Harcourt Brace Jovanovich, 1929.

———. *Three Guineas*. New York: Harcourt Brace Jovanovich, 1938.

Zeitlin, Froma. "The Power of Aphrodite: Eros and the Boundaries of the Self in the Hippolytus." In *Directions in Euripidean Criticism*, edited by Peter Burian, 52–111. Durham, N.C.: Duke University Press, 1985.

# Index

Aeschylus, 39; *Eumenides,* 34; *Seven Against Thebes,* 36

*Ambrose Holt and Family,* 2, 3, 9, 11, 41, 107, 108–30, 131, 133, 134, 147, 150, 157, 167, 168, 176, 179, 181, 184, 186; ambiguity of Glaspell's vision in, 129–30; Ambrose identified with Cook, 120; Ambrose linked with jouissance, 120–22; Ambrose's re-education of Blossom, 119–20, 123–25; Ambrose's suicide letter, 128; artist/husband dichotomy in Lincoln's life, 124; beauty a trap for women in patriarchal culture, 110–11; Blossom's real name, 111; Blossom's rebellion against class and gender symbolized by garden, 109–10; decline of modernism and rise of social realism represented by Lincoln, 128; familial and social order maintained in, 130; Hugh Parker, literary critic modeled on Edmund Wilson, 127n.3; industrialism equated with patriarchy in Blossom's father, 113; Lincoln's desertion, 122; main theme of, 109; marriage a power struggle, 116; mirror scene compared to those in *Brook Evans* and *Fugitive's Return,* 111; oedipal struggle of Lincoln and Ambrose, 113, 121, 124; opposition of paternalistic and feminized fathers, 108; patrilineal descent based on ex-change of daughters, 108, 113; problem of individualism within communal restraints, 124; razing of woods compared to rape of mother's body, 123; return of Ambrose Holt, 118; role reversal of Lincoln and Blossom, 121; sacrifice portrayed as role of men, not women, 114–16; symbolic significance of lumber pile, 118, 191n.1; unattainability of freedom illustrated by Ambrose, 125, 130; woods where Blossom and Ambrose meet compared to edenic loci in previous novels, 122

American women writers, 19th century, 3, 7, 79

Apollo, 101; Temple of, 31, 34, 36, 37, 40; the "woman-hater," 39, 74

Baym, Nina, 15, 16, 125

Beauvoir, Simone de, 53, 146–47

Benstock, Shari, 5

Ben-Zvi, Linda: *Susan Glaspell: Essays on Her Theatre and Fiction,* 6, 8, 15, 140; modernist innovations of Glaspell's drama, 14; role of women in Glaspell's drama, 13–14

Black Cat, The, 2

Boose, Lynda: *Daughters and Fathers* (ed. Boose and Flowers), 109, 113

Braun, Richard Emil, 143, 144–45

Martha C. Carpentier is associate professor and chair of the Department of English at Seton Hall University, South Orange, New Jersey. She is the author of *Ritual, Myth, and the Modernist Text: The Influence of Jane Ellen Harrison on Joyce, Eliot, and Woolf.*